The Human Body
ON TRIAL

Other books in ABC-CLIO's On Trial Series
Charles Zelden, Series Editor*

*Look for more books in this series in paperback from Hackett Publishing Company.

The Human Body
ON TRIAL

*A Sourcebook with
Cases, Laws, and Documents*

Lynne Curry

Updates to this book may be posted online at
www.hackettpublishing.com *as events require*

Hackett Publishing Company, Inc.
Indianapolis/Cambridge

For further information, please address:

> Hackett Publishing Company, Inc.
> P.O. Box 44937
> Indianapolis, IN 46244-0937
>
> www.hackettpublishing.com

Library of Congress Cataloging-in-Publication Data

Curry, Lynne.
  The human body on trial : a sourcebook with cases, laws, and documents / Lynne Curry.— 1st ed.
      p. cm. — (ABC-CLIO's on trial series)
  Includes bibliographical references and index.
  ISBN 0-87220-738-2 (pbk.)
  1. Body, Human—Law and legislation—United States. I. Title. II. On trial.

  KF390.5.H85C87 2004
  344.7304'19—dc22

                                                    2004012027

Contents

Series Foreword

The volumes in the *On Trial* series explore the many ways in which the U.S. legal and political system has approached a wide range of complex and divisive legal issues over time and, in the process, defined the current state of the law and politics on these issues. The intent is to give students and other general readers a framework for understanding how the law in all its various forms—constitutional, statutory, judicial, political, and customary—has shaped and reshaped the world we live in today.

At the core of each volume in the series is a common proposition: that in certain key areas of American public life, we as a people and a nation are "on trial" as we struggle to cope with the contradictions, conflicts, and disparities within our society, politics, and culture. Who should decide if and when a woman can have an abortion? What rights, if any, should those with a different sexual orientation be able to claim under the Constitution? Is voting a basic right of citizenship, and if so, under what rules should we organize this right—especially when the application of any organizing rules inevitably results in excluding some citizens from the polls? What about the many inconsistencies and conflicts associated with racial tensions in the country? These are just some of the complex and controversial issues that we as a people and a nation are struggling to answer—and must answer if we are to achieve an orderly and stable society. For the answers we find to these disputes shape the essence of who we are—as a people, a community, and a political system.

The concept of being on trial also has a second meaning fundamental to this series: the process of litigating important issues in a court of law. Litigation is an essential part of how we settle our differences and make choices as we struggle with the problems that confront us as a people and a nation. In 1835, Alexis De Tocqueville noted in *Democracy in America* how "there is hardly a political question in the United States which does not sooner or later turn into a judicial one" (De Tocqueville 1835, 270). This insight is as true today as it was in the 1830s. In *The Litigious Society*, Jethro K. Lieberman notes that "to express amazement at American litigiousness is akin to professing astonishment at learning that the roots of most Americans lie in other lands. We have been a litigious nation as we have been an immigrant one. Indeed, the two are related." Arriving in the United States with different backgrounds, customs, and lifestyle preferences, we inevitably clashed as our contrasting visions of life in the United States—its culture, society, and politics—collided. It was to the courts and the law that we turned as a neutral forum for peaceably working out these differences (Lieberman 1983, 13). For, in the United States at least, it is the courthouse that provides the anvil on which our personal, societal, and political problems are hammered out.

The volumes in this series therefore take as their central purpose the important task of exploring the various ways—good and bad, effective and ineffective, complex and simple—in which litigation in the courts has shaped the evolution of particular legal controversies for which we as a people are "On Trial." And, more important, the volumes do all this in a manner accessible to the general reader seeking to comprehend the topic as a whole.

These twin goals—analytical and educational—shape the structure and layout of the volumes in the series. Each book consists of two parts. The first provides an explanatory essay in four chapters. Chapter 1 introduces the issues, controversies, events, and participants associated with the legal controversy at hand. Chapter 2 explores the social, economic, political, and historical background to this topic. Chapter 3 describes in detail the various court decisions and actions that have shaped the current status of the legal controversy under examination. In some cases, that will be done through a close examination of a few representative cases, in others by a broader but less detailed narrative of the course of judicial action. Chapter 4 discusses the impact of these cases on U.S. law—their doctrinal legacy—as well as on U.S. society—their historical, sociological, and political legacy.

Part Two, in turn, provides selective supplementary materials designed to help readers to more fully comprehend the topics covered in the chapters of Part One. First included are documents aimed at helping the reader better appreciate both the issues and the process by which adjudication shaped these matters. Selected documents might include court opinions (excerpted or whole), interviews, newspaper accounts, and selected secondary essays. Next comes an alphabetically formatted glossary providing entries on the people, laws, events, terms, and concepts important to an understanding of the topic. A chronology next provides the reader an easily referenced listing of the major developments covered in the book. And last, an annotated bibliography describes the key works in the field, directing a reader seeking a more detailed examination on the topic to the appropriate sources.

In closing, as you read the books in this series, keep in mind the purposefully controversial nature of the topics covered within. The authors in the series have not chosen easy or agreeable topics to explore. Much of what you read may trouble you, and it should. Yet it is precisely these sorts of contentious topics that need the most historical analysis and scrutiny. For it is here that we are still "On Trial"—and all too often, as regards these matters, the jury is still out.

Charles L. Zelden
Ft. Lauderdale, FL

Preface

This volume explores a series of cases that came before the U.S. Supreme Court in the twentieth century. Although the actors, events, circumstances, and locations differ for each case, they are neverthe- less united by a central question: Where do we draw the line between the right to control what happens to our own bodies and the state's duty to protect us from harm to our physical beings? But if the ques- tion seems straightforward enough, the answers have not proven so simple. Arriving at them has required the Court not only to contem- plate the ways in which legal doctrine may be applied in each case but also to understand the broader context of medicine and social policy in which it was crafting its opinions. Medical understanding of the human body became dramatically transformed over the course of the twentieth century. Each new advance engendered promising ideas about how such knowledge might be put to use in the quest for a healthier society. New laws, regulations, and policies translated each medical advance into social practice.

But the process did not always go smoothly. Americans frequently disagreed, sometimes bitterly, over the causes of ill health as well as over what methods would prove to be most safe, effective, and fair in producing a healthier population. More often than not, steps that officials deemed necessary to safeguard the health of the general public required curtailing the individual's freedom to decide for himself or herself what actions to take regarding his or her own body. Although many citizens accepted this reduction of individual liberty as necessary for the advancement of the common good, many others did not agree. For each new situation, determining which health measures would be merely suggested and which would be required by law sparked public dissension and debate. Sometimes those opposed to state interference in their bodily autonomy brought their protests to the street; at other times they brought them to the courts.

Systematically examining a series of cases brought before the Supreme Court over the course of the twentieth century enables us to see the various ways in which the historical development of law, medicine, and social policy intersected at specific points in time to determine our ability to exercise control over what happens to our bodies. Such cases generate a wealth of documentary evidence. Expert testimony provided in legal briefs reveals the state of medical thought in a particular era and points us to contemporary debates within the medical community and among the public at large about the causes of and cures for ill health. Arguments brought by each party to the case highlight the tensions between perceptions of public and private rights—as well as responsibilities— in the arena of health care. The Court's opinions demonstrate the ways in which the justices sought to reformulate established legal doctrine to fit a society continually being shaped by science. To this can be added other kinds of primary source materials: official and unofficial publications by those most concerned with the issues, newspaper accounts, and illustrations or photographic images, for example, provide crucial details we can use to recreate the larger historical picture in which debates over control of the human body emerged. Taken together, the cases and their materials allow us to see how historical processes in medicine, law, and social policy developed in relation to each other and how their periodic intersections raised anew the central conflict between bodily autonomy and state control over the human body.

Nor are these debates simply relegated to history. The cases included in this volume reflect ongoing *processes* in addition to discrete events in the past; the core issues they raised remain as relevant today as they did for those whose own experiences led them to have their day in the highest court in the land. In many ways, the beginning of the twenty-first century parallels the dawn of the previous one. The rapid pace of medical discovery today, from mapping the human genome to dramatic new breakthroughs in treating diseases once thought to be untreatable, creates scenarios of both unparalleled progress in the betterment of human health and of the difficult social and personal dilemmas that such a radical transformation inevitably brings in its wake. If the precise factors creating our current dilemmas are unique to our own time, a careful investigation of the past can inform our thinking about the issues we face and suggest the questions we need to ask in order to solve them.

I came to this project through my research interests in medical and legal history. As a historian, I know well the importance of becoming fully informed about one's chosen topic, deciding what questions remain unanswered, and then carefully—sometimes even painstakingly—sorting through piles of evidence in search of clues from the past. In one respect, this volume reflects my ongoing endeavor to research the intersections of medicine and law as they have shaped our ability to determine what happens to our own bodies today.

But equally significant to this project has been my experience teaching the discipline of history to others. The rigorous research methods scholars employ are designed to ensure the quality of the narratives that eventually become part of our national story; preparing students in sound historical methodology is therefore essential. But even further, there is a particular satisfaction to be derived from engaging firsthand in the process of historical inquiry. Exploring the past illuminates our own time and place. If we are really lucky, we can come to understand something about ourselves as well.

This volume is divided into two main parts. Part One acquaints the reader with the historical narrative that demonstrates how medicine and law have shaped the rights of American citizens to determine what happens to their bodies as well as the limitations they encounter through the state's authority to regulate the human body. Chapter 1 traces the evolution of legal doctrine, including the key concepts of bodily autonomy, the "police powers" allowing the state to curtail citizens' liberties in order to protect the public health and safety, and the expansion of personal autonomy rights over the course of the twentieth century. Chapter 2 further illuminates this basic narrative by introducing the developments in medical science that altered society's perceptions of both the possibilities and the limits of the bodily autonomy. Chapter 3 examines the fascinating stories behind the most important cases challenging the boundaries between individual liberty and state authority, as well as the landmark decisions rendered by the Court that determined where the lines would be drawn. Chapter 4 explores the legacy and impact of these decisions at the beginning of the twenty-first century. Each chapter provides citations to the sources I used as well as additional readings that can serve as guides to readers' own research.

Part Two of this volume presents evidence from primary sources so that readers can evaluate for themselves how the evidence fits together to form a larger historical narrative. Examining materials left by those who made history happen will better enable readers to think about their own place in this ongoing story. Part Two concludes with reference sections that will aid in understanding the issues.

I owe a great debt of acknowledgment to numerous individuals without whose generous help and support I could not have brought this project to fruition. I am most grateful to the series editor, Charles Zelden, for introducing me to this exciting series and inviting me to contribute to it. Alicia Merritt, acquisitions editor, Melanie Stafford, senior production editor, and others at ABC-CLIO remained thoroughly professional and a delight to work with over the two years it took to produce this volume. Librarians and archivists too numerous to mention guided my inquiries at the library of the U.S. Supreme Court, the Countway Library of Medicine at Harvard University, the Historical Health Fraud Collection at the American Medical Association Library and Archives, the Boston Public Library, and the law library at the University of Illinois at Urbana-Champaign. I also benefited immensely from the efficient endeavors of my first-rate research assistant, Erik Hockenberry. A number of scholars have provided invaluable guidance at various stages as this project took shape. In this regard, I wish to thank especially Robert Johnston, Paul Lombardo, Christopher Waldrep, Michael Shirley, James Mohr, Michael Foley, and my colleagues in the history department faculty colloquium at Eastern Illinois University. A final note of deepest appreciation goes to my family, without whose flexibility and good humor none of my work would ever get done at all.

Lynne Curry

Part One

1

Introduction

Constitutionalizing the Body

Today, most Americans believe that the right to control what happens to their bodies represents one of their most basic civil liberties, a fundamental right rooted in the Constitution that they, as citizens of the United States, possess. Matters concerning the care and treatment of our bodies entail some of the most intimate details of our lives, and we therefore carry a general expectation that they will remain private, shielded from unwarranted intrusion by our neighbors, our communities, and the state. When we think about our bodies this way, we are invoking a modern version of the centuries-old notion of personal autonomy, or the freedom to govern ourselves as we see fit. But, as this volume will demonstrate, the historical path between the legal origins of individuals' right to govern themselves and current American beliefs about the rights we possess regarding our physical beings does not follow an unwavering line. Rather, it is a convoluted trail involving integrally related developments in medicine, law, and social policy.

We can think of bodily autonomy as a type of freedom in two different senses, one positive and one negative. In its positive sense, a right of bodily autonomy assumes that we have the liberty to make particular choices regarding our physical actions. We may freely choose, for example, what foods we will eat for breakfast, what regimens we will follow to keep ourselves healthy, and whether engaging

in a sexual act will result in the conception of a child. In the negative sense, bodily autonomy assumes that individuals retain freedom from undue interference by others as well as by various levels of government. We may not be coerced into undergoing open heart surgery, for instance, no matter how urgently it may be needed to prolong our lives. We cannot have our blood or organs removed without our consent, even if a neighbor or family member needs them in order to remain alive. We accept as given the premise that, as Justice Benjamin Cardozo once said, "every human being of adult years and sound mind has a right to determine what shall be done with his own body" (Dworkin 1994, 2).

And yet, if it seems obvious that we possess a certain degree of bodily autonomy as free individuals, it is also true that our bodies do not exist in a vacuum; they share physical space with numerous other people's bodies, with which we come into various degrees of contact every day. What we do with our physical beings, the behaviors we choose to engage in with them, the measures we undergo or decline to undergo in caring for our health, often carry tangible consequences for the well-being of others as well as ourselves. Society also has an expectation that it will be protected from negative consequences resulting from the choices some individuals make in governing their bodies. In other words, the community has rights, too. The state, therefore, retains the authority to regulate the human body in order to protect the health and safety of the general public.

Although the suggestion that we may not always have the legal right to control what happens to our bodies may jar our modern sensibilities, over the years the courts have determined that there exist varying degrees of bodily autonomy, ranging on a continuum from full rights to none at all, depending on the specific circumstances in which the human body is operating. One broad area in which this is especially apparent is public health. Under the laws governing public health in the United States, Americans accept certain curtailments of their ability to do as they please with their bodies as a means of protecting the health of others in the community; such measures also serve to protect us from disease spread by others. State and local governments, for example, may require schoolchildren to be immunized against certain infectious diseases and job applicants in the food industry to pass a blood screening test for tuberculosis. For the most part, modern Americans comply with such public health regulations

and regard the limitations they place on the ability to govern their own bodies as a matter of routine.

But where are we to draw the line between our right to maintain our individual autonomy and the legitimate claims that society as a whole may make upon our bodies? When do private actions involving the human body become appropriate matters for government control? How far can the state go in preventing citizens from engaging in certain physical activities? How far can it go in requiring them to undergo specific measures that affect their bodies? This volume will explore several cases addressing these questions that came before the U.S. Supreme Court in the twentieth century, a time of profound and integrally related transformations in both medicine and law. Each case serves as a sort of snapshot in which we can view these developments, as Americans revisited the problem of individual autonomy versus social claims on the human body throughout the century. Taken together, they enable us to better understand how this ongoing dilemma still plays out in the United States today. And because breaking developments in medical science continue to alter perceptions of the human body—in some ways quite radically—the questions raised by these twentieth-century legal challenges undoubtedly will remain with us well into the twenty-first century. The answers we find to these new questions will profoundly affect the choices we will make regarding our bodies, the liberties we will exercise, and our expectations that as modern Americans, we will continue to enjoy unprecedented health and longevity. Just who or what really controls our bodies remains "on trial." In order to more fully understand the contemporary context, we must first examine the origins of these issues and their historical development. This chapter discusses traditions of individual autonomy and the body as property, the rise of the regulatory state, and the emergence of a constitutional right to privacy.

The Human Body as a Form of Property

Although it may seem a commonsense notion that Americans enjoy the right to govern and control their bodies, such a right is not specifically enumerated in the U.S. Constitution. Rather, personal autonomy over one's body is an idea constructed over the centuries through differing English and American common law traditions as well as myriad judicial interpretations. One very old tradition approaches

bodily autonomy within the broad conceptual category of property rights. In its wider sense, "property" referred to a range of things individuals needed to sustain their lives and those of their dependents. Because people depended on their bodies to perform the labor necessary for subsistence, individuals retained vested rights of ownership in their physical beings. To lose control over one's body would be a threat to one's very life. In the seventeenth century, the English political philosopher John Locke explained that in a civilized society (as opposed to a state of nature, where he presumed anarchy reigned) each individual "has a Property in his own Person" and thus retains rights to keep his body free from intrusions, aggressions, or unreasonable claims by others. The flip side of enjoying these protections is the obligation to refrain from harming another's property. Thus according to Locke (1690), no one may "take away, or impair the life, or what tends to be the Preservation of the Life, Liberty, Health, Limb or Goods of another" without offending the public order (271). The seventeenth-century theoretical construction of a society governed by rules and laws incorporated notions of both a right to bodily autonomy and a duty to refrain from actions causing harm to another.

By the time Locke penned his *Second Treatise on Government,* the agricultural subsistence economies of western Europe were already being altered by market capitalism. In the new system, some people needed to sell the labor they performed with their bodies to someone else in exchange for monetary compensation. According to Locke, free people retained vested rights to do this as well, for the right to subsistence demanded personal ownership of one's own body. Over time, English common law employed Locke's metaphor of the body as property often, especially in reference to delineating the claims others may make on the products of one's labor. This common law tradition carried over into the legal discourse employed in the American colonies and subsequently in the United States, where free citizens retained the right to sell their physical labor to others and to be compensated for their labor in return. Thus a strong ideological link extending over several centuries brought together the concepts of individual liberty, private property, and bodily autonomy in Anglo-American legal culture.

Not all those living in the United States, however, enjoyed the right to govern their own bodies. Children, apprentices, and servants were all subject to legal restrictions and limitations on their personal

autonomy. Children were bound to obey the orders of their parents, and apprentices and servants could not move freely about outside the homes of their masters. In the English common law tradition known as *coverture,* a married woman possessed no legal identity of her own but rather was considered "covered" by the identity of her husband. Under this legal construct, a husband gained control over any property his wife brought to the marriage in the form of chattels (personal property) or real estate. In other words, a married woman automatically ceded ownership of her property to her husband. The laws of coverture also recognized a husband's right to exercise authority over his wife's body in much the same way he controlled other forms of property. As William Blackstone explained in his work, *Commentaries on the Laws of England* (1765–1769), the law permitted husbands to "restrain a wife of her liberty, in case of any gross misbehavior" (271). Husbands were also entitled to any monetary compensation their wives might earn by performing labor outside the home. But the law also recognized that the state of coverture disadvantaged women, rendering them dependent and vulnerable, and so it also required husbands to feed, clothe, and shelter their wives and to pay their debts. In some cases, the law even held husbands responsible for failing to control their wives' behavior in public— even to the extent of being punished for the actions of their wives. Thus for women, the act of marriage essentially entailed a transfer of bodily autonomy to their husbands, and in return they could expect certain protections for their physical well-being. This common law tradition was so deeply rooted in Anglo-American legal culture that it eroded only very slowly in the United States. Gradually, women gained increasing recognition of their autonomy as citizens in their own right, rather than as extensions of their husbands' legal identities. Yet the process remains incomplete. Many legal and feminist scholars argue that women have failed to attain bodily autonomy on an equal basis with men even today. That is especially the case with regard to issues of contraception and childbearing (see Chapter 2).

An even more extreme illustration of the law's limits concerned enslaved African Americans. Under the laws that governed the institution of slavery, those held in bondage were not individuals with rights at all but instead were considered to be chattel (i.e., personal property) themselves. Like other forms of property, they could be bought, sold, rented out, left to one's heirs, and even seized for nonpayment of debts. For the most part, slave law remained the province

of the states rather than the federal government, and slave states placed few restrictions on what a master could or could not do with his human property. He retained control over the physical work his slaves performed with their bodies as well as their reproductive work. Slave parents had no rights to their biological children, who were deemed to be solely the master's property and liable to be traded, sold, or rented out at the master's discretion. With the exception of capital crimes such as murder or rape, in which a slave would be brought before the criminal court, the master was granted considerable leeway to punish his slaves as he saw fit for most infractions of the law. Even after the Civil War, many former slave states attempted to retain a high degree of control over the bodies of the freedmen in the form of "black codes," which, among other oppressive measures, restricted African Americans' freedom to travel, marry, or move about as they pleased.

During the tumultuous period known as Reconstruction, attempts to guarantee civil rights to the freedmen ultimately led Congress to pass the Fourteenth Amendment to the Constitution, which was ratified by the states in 1868. In part, the Fourteenth Amendment reads:

> All persons born or naturalized in the United States, and subject to the jurisdiction thereof, are citizens of the United States and of the State wherein they reside. No State shall make or enforce any law which shall abridge the privileges and immunities of citizens of the United States; nor shall any State deprive any person of life, liberty, or property, without due process of law; nor deny to any person within its jurisdiction the equal protection of the laws. (U.S. Constitution, amend. 14, sec. 1)

Although the amendment's injunction against states interfering with citizens' liberties seems clear enough, the precise definition of what may or may not be considered a "liberty" is more problematic. As we will see in the cases presented in this volume, the history of attempts to apply the Fourteenth Amendment to the rights citizens retain over their own bodies has been both complex in its nature and uneven in its results.

In 1873, the U.S. Supreme Court interpreted the meaning of the Fourteenth Amendment for the first time in the *Slaughterhouse Cases.* These cases resulted from the passage of a statute by the Louisiana legislature in 1869 aimed at regulating slaughterhouses in New

Orleans for the protection of the public's health. Urban slaughter-houses were notorious for contaminating local water supplies and known to be the locus of outbreaks of infectious diseases such as yellow fever and cholera. In the mid–nineteenth century, health reformers sought to reduce the incidence of epidemics through the large-scale engineering of the urban environment. Massive sewage systems, for example, were constructed in many of the nation's rapidly industrializing cities. Under these reformers' influence, a number of states in addition to Louisiana stepped in to regulate the waste produced by slaughterhouses (Ross 1998, 655).

But not everyone was pleased with the Louisiana law. As it was written, the law granted a butchering monopoly to a single entity, the Crescent City Stock Landing and Slaughter House Company. Although ostensibly designed to eliminate health hazards posed by the numerous smaller establishments located around the city of New Orleans, the political maneuvers behind this arrangement reeked of corruption. Independent butchers thrown out of work by the statute challenged its constitutionality, claiming that it amounted to a state interfering with their liberty to profit by their labor in their chosen profession and thus should be considered a violation of the Fourteenth Amendment. In framing the argument this way, the butchers drew upon the time-honored tradition tying personal autonomy—the ability to sustain oneself by one's own labor—to private property rights. Nevertheless, the Supreme Court disagreed with the independent butchers, deeming the state's authority in safeguarding public health and safety to be the paramount interest. "The power here exercised by the legislature of Louisiana . . . is, and must be from its very nature, incapable of any very exact definition or limitation," Justice Samuel F. Miller wrote. "Upon it depends the security of the social order, the life and health of the citizen, the comfort of an existence in a thickly populated community, the enjoyment of private and social life, and the beneficial use of property" (83 U.S. 36).

Although the Fourteenth Amendment protected citizens' liberties from being infringed upon by the states, in its initial interpretation of the amendment, the Supreme Court defined individual liberty narrowly and ruled that states would retain broad authority in exercising measures regarding the protection of public health. In the *Slaughterhouse Cases,* then, we see an early example of tensions between bodily autonomy—in this case, in its ancient form of retaining rights to the labor one freely performs with one's body—and

social claims regulating the body in order to further the general welfare. This fundamental tension can be found at the core of numerous challenges brought before the courts from the late nineteenth century to the present.

The Regulatory State

But what about the Supreme Court's refusal to accept the primacy of individual autonomy in the *Slaughterhouse Cases*? Why did the butchers lose their claim that the Fourteenth Amendment protected their liberty to perform physical labor without undue interference by the state? In rendering this opinion, the Court drew from another ancient legal tradition, the state's authority to regulate individual liberty for the benefit of the general welfare. Such authority constitutes a fundamental power of the state. In fact, throughout the millennia, the protection of public health and safety has been accepted as an underlying purpose for the very existence of government. Legal measures regulating individuals' bodies to control the spread of "plagues and pestilence" are cited in the Old Testament, for instance, and elaborate sanitary codes governed the ancient civilizations of Greece and Rome (Toby 1947, 11–12).

In the fourteenth century, authorities in the Italian city-state of Venice inaugurated the *quarantine*, a mandatory isolation period of forty days for travelers arriving from areas in which the bubonic plague was known to be present (Kraut 1994, 25). In the centuries thereafter, nations adopted the practice of routinely placing newly arriving ships under quarantine, commonly for thirty days, to ensure that no contagious illnesses were brought into port along with the ships' cargoes and passengers. On land, health officials issued quarantines as an emergency measure to curtail the devastation wrought by periodic epidemics of diseases such as smallpox, cholera, and yellow fever. For the most part, the public understood the restrictions quarantines placed on individual liberties, including access to private property, freedom of trade, and the personal freedom to move about wherever and however they chose, to be necessary measures enacted for the health and safety of all. Prior to the discovery of sulfa drugs and antibiotics in the twentieth century—a very recent development in the long history of human attempts to eradicate disease—medical practitioners could do very little to cure contagious illnesses once they had been contracted. The main responsibility of the state, then,

was to control outbreaks so that they spread to as few people as possible. And, without the technological capabilities to detect pathogens inside the human body (using blood tests or throat cultures, for example), symptoms appearing on the outside of the body were the only sure means for determining the presence of contagious disease. Quarantines allowed time for symptoms of disease to appear on the bodies of new arrivals to the community. They remained the community's most effective weapon for self-protection and were sanctioned in legal systems worldwide as a legitimate exercise of governmental power.

In colonial America, the law provided for a range of public health measures in addition to quarantines, including removal of the sick— by force, if need be—to special isolation hospitals and state regulation of the "noxious trades," such as swine keeping or leather tanning, whose deleterious effects on the health of local communities were well known. Therefore, long before the Revolution, Americans were quite accustomed to local authorities exercising their powers in the service of public health, and indeed colonial citizens would have raised objections had their officials failed to fulfill such obligations to the community. In the early nineteenth century, the authority granted to local, state, or federal governments to enact laws designed to safeguard the health and safety of the people came to be known in legal discourse as *police powers.*

Prior to the late nineteenth century, police powers rested primarily in the hands of state and local governments. It was customary for state legislatures to pass the authority to local boards of health, whose members were closest to the actual sites of disease outbreaks and presumably knew best what actions should be taken. Because diseases such as smallpox, cholera, and yellow fever could devastate a population, local authorities faced with an epidemic often took measures that may appear quite harsh by present-day sensibilities. Entire towns might be placed under quarantine and schools, churches, and other public places ordered to close; individuals believed to be carrying disease might be hunted down and forcibly removed to a "pest house" or special isolation hospital; and citizens might have their property confiscated so that it could be disinfected, using procedures that commonly damaged or even destroyed it (Novak 1996, 210). Anyone refusing to cooperate could be punished with stiff fines, jail terms, or both. Although official actions taken in the name of public health were subject to review by the courts, health officials generally

retained sweeping discretionary authority to take whatever measures they saw fit, even if their actions had the effect of compromising individual liberties (Toby 1947, 144).

Understanding the potency of government police powers in relation to public health and the very deep roots underlying these powers helps to clarify why the New Orleans butchers lost their claim for individual rights in 1873. Even the four justices dissenting from the majority's opinion did not question the validity of state authority to restrict individual rights in the name of public health; instead, they questioned the legitimacy of the means by which the Louisiana state legislature went about the task—establishing a corporate monopoly. In a series of decisions following the *Slaughterhouse Cases*, the Court reiterated its position that the protection of public health and safety represented a legitimate exercise of police powers (Gillman 1993, 68–75). By the end of the nineteenth century, it seemed, the Court had drawn the boundary between public and private rights in regulating the human body decisively in the state's favor. The new century would see efforts to continue and even expand the state's reach.

Historians of the United States refer to the period from about 1890 to the end of World War I as the Progressive Era. A widespread political and social ethos sought to ameliorate the most harmful consequences of the rapid industrialization and urbanization the nation had experienced following the Civil War. Progressivism championed social reforms ranging from the prohibition of child labor to voting rights for women to the direct election of U.S. senators and increased governmental regulation of industry. Drawing from the new social sciences such as economics and sociology, progressives allied with both private and public institutions to conduct systematic studies of social conditions in the United States, identify urgent problems, and develop plans for solving them. Although their specific reform goals varied widely, at a fundamental level, progressives were united in their belief that more direct and active participation by government—at the local, state, and national levels—was essential to curing the most pressing national ills.

Progressives shared with public health advocates an optimistic vision of building a better society based on the new knowledge of disease transmission offered by recent advances in bacteriological science. With the growing acceptance of the germ theory, an energetic wave of progressive health campaigns urged governmental inspection of sanitary conditions on dairy farms, established free baby clinics

where poor mothers could obtain pasteurized milk, and educated the public to take hygienic precautions against the spread of tuberculosis. Although reformers worked for innovations employing both public and private resources, they consistently promoted an expanded role for the regulatory state in achieving a healthier populace. A hallmark of progressivism was its transformation of private health concerns into public policy issues worthy of the attention of the highest levels of government. For example, addressing the problem of infant mortality became the top mission of the U.S. Children's Bureau, an agency within the Department of Labor, when public health studies revealed that infants under two years of age continued to die in startlingly high numbers, despite an overall decline in national mortality rates. In 1906, progressives enjoyed a major victory when Congress passed the Pure Food and Drug Act. Progressives had lobbied the federal government to take a more active role in monitoring the nation's food supply, since responsibility had become difficult to fulfill now that urban Americans lived at increasingly remote distances from the original sources of agricultural production. The Pure Food and Drug Act used the federal government's constitutional authority over interstate commerce to regulate the safety and healthfulness of products that now traveled across the nation.

With a growing medical consensus that illness in the community was largely caused by the germs individuals carried, protecting the public from infected bodies seemed both more rational and more desirable as social policy. However, this rationale also enabled public health authorities to exercise even greater restrictions of the civil liberties of those who were afflicted. Although it held out the promise of a healthier society, the progressive vision also required an expanded domain of state authority over the human body. The case of Mary Mallon presents a particularly lucid example.

An Irish immigrant who made her living as a domestic cook in New York City, "Typhoid Mary" became the first person in North America to be identified as a healthy carrier of typhoid fever when epidemiologists linked her presence in several households to cases of the disease reported in the area between 1900 and 1907. Although efforts to clean up urban water supplies had lessened the incidence of typhoid fever in the early twentieth century, outbreaks continued to occur, to the considerable consternation of public health authorities. At this time, the role of vectors (intermediaries) in disease transmission was only beginning to be understood. New research revealed

that individuals who suffered no symptoms themselves nevertheless could carry the bacillus responsible for typhoid fever and transmit it to others through their excreta. After public health authorities found high concentrations of typhoid bacilli in fecal specimens obtained from Mary Mallon, she was quarantined in an isolation cottage on North Brother Island for two years. Mallon appealed her custody on the grounds that the laws allowing for the quarantine of the sick did not apply to her because she was healthy. The New York courts, however, disagreed and granted public health authorities the power to forcibly isolate individuals who were not themselves sick but who carried the potential to infect others. When Mallon was released in 1909, she agreed never to work as a cook again.

In 1915, however, New York public health authorities once again linked Mallon to a typhoid fever outbreak in the city and, because she had reneged on her agreement not to work as a cook, sent her back to North Brother Island, where she remained a "captive to the public's health" until her death in 1938 (Leavitt 1996, 14–20). Mary Mallon's story provides a vivid demonstration of the way in which protecting the liberty interests of individuals finished a clear second to the protection of the public's health in the early twentieth-century courts.

Nevertheless, the state's authority over the human body was not absolute. In determining what official actions might be allowable, the courts revisited the question of where to draw the boundary many times. One such case, *Lochner v. New York*, came before the U.S. Supreme Court in 1905. In an attempt to control the spread of tuberculosis in New York City, the legislature in Albany had enacted a law limiting the number of hours industrial bakers could work to ten per day and sixty per week. The law's sponsors had been impressed by recent medical evidence that suggested workers toiling in the "dusty trades" were occupationally susceptible to tuberculosis, an effect apparently exacerbated by physical exhaustion. City inspectors found that in many instances these debilitated workers labored in appallingly poor sanitary conditions. Placing a cap on working hours, therefore, was intended to stop the spread of tuberculosis among New York City's bakers—and, equally important, among the consumers of bakeshop goods as well. Joseph Lochner, a bakeshop owner, had been convicted of employing workers in excess of the maximum hours and ordered to pay a fine. He argued that New York's actions violated his liberty to negotiate with his employees over the terms and conditions of their employment.

The Supreme Court agreed with Joseph Lochner, refusing to accept the maximum hours law as a legitimate public health measure. "Clean and wholesome bread does not depend upon whether the baker works but ten hours per day or only sixty hours a week," Justice Samuel Peckham wrote for the majority. "The limitation of the hours of labor does not come within the police power on that ground" (198 U.S. 45). Just as they did in the *Slaughterhouse Cases,* the justices did not call into question the use of police powers to serve the ends of public health; instead, they questioned whether the means the New York law provided—placing a cap on the number of hours workers toiled in bakeshops—would effect those ends. Because the justices answered the question in the negative, individual liberty to negotiate the terms of labor (what the Court called the "freedom of contract") remained paramount, and the New York public health law fell. Although, as we have seen, governmental powers in the arena of public health were considerable, the state, too, had its boundaries.

But by what reasoning did the Court conclude that, unlike the Louisiana slaughterhouse statute, the New York bakeshop law could *not* be justified as a measure necessary to protect the public health? The answer seemingly lies in the nature of the health threat the Court perceived to be at issue in each case. In the time of the *Slaughterhouse Cases,* although the precise mechanisms by which disease was transmitted had not yet been identified, the Court could draw on ancient medical and commonsense traditions of associating bad health with bad environments. Mid–nineteenth century Americans would have been very familiar with the concept that disease was transmitted through miasmas, or foul odors polluting the atmosphere. It did not require a precise understanding of bacteriology, therefore, to associate the emissions from slaughterhouses into the surrounding air and water supply with the periodic outbreaks of diseases such as cholera and typhoid fever that plagued New Orleans. By contrast, until well into the twentieth century, tuberculosis did not constitute an epidemic disease, but rather one that was *endemic* among the urban population. Conquering tuberculosis, therefore, required a more widespread, sustained, and perhaps more intrusive program of public health actions. Since no "epidemic" of tuberculosis immediately threatened the city—the number of cases may have been high but no higher than usual in 1905—the Court may have found it much more difficult to justify the bakeshop law as a use of the state's police powers (Parmet 1996, 499).

In other instances, however, the Court did find such justifications—often for reasons that had little to do with matters of public health. As we have seen, by tradition women did not retain the same degree of bodily autonomy as did men. This difference becomes evident when we examine a case the Supreme Court decided just three years after *Lochner v. New York*. Reformers in Oregon had succeeded in passing maximum hours restrictions on female workers in industrial laundries. When Curt Muller was found guilty of employing his workers in excess of the legal limits, he, like Joseph Lochner before him, appealed his case all the way to the Supreme Court. In 1908, however, the outcome of *Muller v. Oregon* was quite different. In an extensive brief that became a landmark in twentieth-century jurisprudence, Oregon's attorney Louis Brandeis presented a wealth of information purporting to show that industrial overwork was more dangerous to women than to men because of their physiological differences. In addition to the ailments that commonly plagued male workers, such as tuberculosis and lead poisoning, female workers succumbed to pelvic diseases, miscarriages, menstrual abnormalities, and premature births and reportedly produced feeble children (Woloch 1996, 29). Thus the Court might be expected to consider the differing effects of overwork on male and female employees in deciding the validity of Oregon's protective laws.

But Brandeis's argument contained another, more novel, dimension as well. As a leading proponent of the new theory of "legal realism," Brandeis asserted that the function of the courts in a modern society such as the twentieth-century United States should not be limited to applying the law in a strictly logical or formal manner. Rather, he contended that the law must function as an organic dimension of society, growing and changing along with its political, social, economic, and cultural institutions. Brandeis argued that the freedom of contract doctrine the Court had relied on in *Lochner* did not apply in *Muller v. Oregon* because the restrictions placed on female workers furthered a larger societal interest in regulating their reproductive capacities. As "mothers of the race," women did not enjoy the same freedom as men did to negotiate the terms of their employment; society's interest in safeguarding the health of future generations represented the paramount social good, and therefore the Oregon maximum hours law was valid. Brandeis's pathbreaking brief—combining a mountain of medical evidence with a persuasive new vision of the

role of law in society—convinced the Court to uphold maximum hours for female laundry workers.

Writing for the majority, Justice David J. Brewer concluded that "continuance for a long time on [their] feet at work, repeating this from day to day, tends to injurious effects upon the body, and as healthy mothers are essential to vigorous offspring, the physical well-being of woman becomes an object of public interest and care in order to preserve the strength and vigor of the race" (208 U.S. 412). Unlike the New York bakeshop law, then, the Oregon statute represented a legitimate exercise of the state's police powers to protect public health and safety. The contrast between the *Lochner* and *Muller* decisions demonstrates the Court's attempt to delineate the boundaries between bodily autonomy and social claims on the body, a complex exercise that incorporated prevailing notions in medicine, public health, and the law.

The *Lochner* and *Muller* cases came before the Court at a time when the nation was just beginning to reap the benefits of several decades of public health reform. Deaths from well-known epidemic diseases such as typhoid fever and cholera were declining dramatically in the United States. Nevertheless, the fear of contagion remained deeply rooted in American society. The early twentieth century also represented peak years of immigration into the United States, with several million people arriving each year. The public, the press, and even misguided health authorities blamed periodic outbreaks on these new arrivals. Public health officials accused Chinese immigrants of bringing bubonic plague to California in 1900, for example, and on the East Coast authorities condemned Italians for causing a major polio epidemic in 1916 (Kraut 1994, 4). Despite a marked decline in the incidence and severity of contagious illness, the doctrine of police powers remained in force, as Americans continued to seek protection from diseases they feared would be imported to their communities by "outsiders."

Smallpox represented a particularly virulent threat. Beginning in the mid–nineteenth century, states had begun to enact laws giving local health authorities the power to mandate vaccination of all citizens when an epidemic erupted. But many people feared vaccination nearly as much as they did the disease itself, and efforts to compel people to submit to the procedure were often met with widespread resistance. In 1905, a Cambridge clergyman named Henning Jacob-

son challenged in the U.S. Supreme Court a Massachusetts statute compelling residents to be vaccinated against smallpox (see Chapter 3). Jacobson argued that the Fourteenth Amendment to the Constitution protected his right to refuse a procedure that involved injecting into his body a foreign substance—in this case, a vaccine derived from vesicles on animals infected with cowpox—which he believed to be a threat to his life and liberty. Although Reverend Jacobson lost his case, his assertion of a freedom to care for his own body in the manner he saw fit foreshadowed a different kind of bodily autonomy argument that would emerge later in the twentieth century.

The Right to Privacy

Unlike the very old tradition of regarding the body as a form of property, a right to bodily autonomy based on individual privacy is of much more recent origin. As we have seen, both the size and power of the regulatory state expanded considerably during the Progressive Era. But the 1930s marked the beginning of a far-reaching transformation of the nation's legal climate, one that would see the Court begin to shift its constitutional priorities away from regulation and toward imposing more vigorous protections for individual civil liberties by giving a liberal, or expansive, interpretation to constitutional provisions, especially the Fourteenth Amendment. In 1942, for example, the Supreme Court addressed the question of preserving the right of bodily autonomy in the modern regulatory state when it overturned an Oklahoma law that mandated sterilization of those convicted three times of offenses falling within a particular category of felony crimes. In *Skinner v. Oklahoma,* the Court established that the ability to procreate represented a fundamental right held by U.S. citizens (see Chapter 3).

Throughout the first half of the 1940s, the emergency of waging a second global war abroad instigated profound social change at home. African Americans migrated by the thousands from the rural South to the industrial cities of the North in order to fill the urgent need for workers in war industries. Additional thousands of black men served their country in the armed forces. After the war, grassroots movements to empower African Americans with their full due as citizens sprang up in cities and rural areas throughout the nation, especially in southern states, where segregation, discrimination, and lynching remained very much a fact of life for blacks. From black churches,

civic organizations, and the National Association for the Advancement of Colored People came new and urgent calls to reexamine the meaning of such basic political values as liberty, equality, and autonomy, now that the United States had emerged as the most powerful industrialized democracy on Earth. What did "equality" mean when a child was forced to attend a public school far from her home because the law designated the local school to be for white students only? What did "liberty" mean when an African American riding a public bus was required by law to give up her seat to a white passenger?

Into this rekindled debate over civil rights waded the U.S. Supreme Court. Under Chief Justice Earl Warren, the Court chose to address head-on lingering issues of racial inequality, safeguarded the rights of the accused in the criminal justice system, and set limits on the state's ability to intervene into the private lives of citizens. Through a series of far-reaching decisions—too far, the Court's critics continue to claim today—the Warren Court helped to open an unprecedented era of civil rights consciousness in the United States. A critical juncture came when Congress passed the Civil Rights Act of 1964, a comprehensive set of laws aimed at ending racial, ethnic, gender, and religious discrimination in education, public accommodations, and employment.

A vigorous revival of civil rights, then, formed the context in which the Supreme Court established a constitutional right to privacy in 1965. Since no such right is actually expressed in the Constitution, the Court based its interpretation in *Griswold v. Connecticut* on the implications for individual privacy that can be found in other constitutional protections (see Chapter 3). The First Amendment's guarantee of freedom of association, for example, implies that a citizen's lawful relationships with others will remain beyond governmental scrutiny, and the Fourth Amendment's protections against unreasonable search and seizure implies that private homes are off-limits to arbitrary intrusion by authorities. The Court reasoned that, taken together, these and other protections enumerated in the Bill of Rights had the effect of creating a "zone of privacy" around the individual that kept state authority at bay. Although the *Griswold* case originated in a challenge to a Connecticut statute that prohibited the use of contraception by married couples, the Court's establishment of a right to privacy has been extended by subsequent decisions into other areas of American life, including obtaining an abortion (see

Chapter 3), protections from unduly intrusive law enforcement techniques used by police during criminal searches, and the freedom to marry an individual of a different race.

Although the doctrine of a constitutional right of privacy has become fundamental in modern U.S. legal culture, it has not existed without qualification. As we have seen, the *Griswold* decision derived a right to privacy from the implications about personal privacy that are contained in enumerated constitutional rights. But within the structure of the Constitution, these rights are defined in terms of limits placed on government intrusion into the lives of citizens ("negative liberty") rather than a claim that people are by default free to do whatever they please ("positive liberty"). Thus, the "zone of privacy" established in *Griswold* does not preclude the state's authority to control what an individual does with his or her body—even in private—if it can demonstrate a compelling reason for doing so.

A clear demonstration of this principle may be found in the Supreme Court's 1986 decision in *Bowers v. Hardwick*. Michael Hardwick had been convicted of violating a Georgia statute that made the act of sodomy illegal. The Court rejected Michael Hardwick's claim that a law prohibiting a sexual act between consenting adults represented an invasion of his right to privacy, a right he claimed derived from the Fourteenth Amendment's guarantee of liberty against encroachment by the states. Writing for the majority, Justice Byron White noted that, at the time the Fourteenth Amendment was ratified, thirty-two of the thirty-seven states then in existence had outlawed sodomy and thus those who created the amendment could not have meant to protect a liberty to engage in the practice. The Court, White continued, was not inclined to discover new fundamental rights in the Fourteenth Amendment because "the Court is most vulnerable and comes nearest to illegitimacy when it deals with judge-made constitutional law having little or no cognizable roots in the language or design of the Constitution" (478 U.S. 186). In other words, the Court was unwilling to extend the "zone of privacy" established in *Griswold* to include a specific sexual act that had been deemed illegal by a state legislature, even if that act was performed by consenting adults in a private home. The Court's opinion in *Bowers v. Hardwick* demonstrates that extracting a right to individual bodily autonomy from a constitutional right to privacy is not axiomatic in the law but instead entails revisiting and perhaps either

redrawing or reinforcing the boundaries between public and private claims to the human body.

In the last quarter of the twentieth century, Americans entered into another debate over boundaries, this time in regard to bodily autonomy at the end of life. In 1975 the tragic case of Karen Ann Quinlan was thrust into the media spotlight. The twenty-one-year-old woman had been found unconscious by her roommates after she had attended a friend's birthday party one evening, and by the time medical personnel arrived she had fallen into a coma. Doctors at the New Jersey hospital where Karen was taken could not determine the precise cause of her comatose state, although it seemed apparent that some combination of drugs and alcohol had been involved. A month later, Quinlan sank into what physicians called a persistent vegetative state, in which the body continues to undergo cycles of waking and sleeping but remains unconscious (Filene 1998, 16–17).

Throughout the summer of 1975 she remained hospitalized, kept alive by modern machinery that provided nutrition, hydration, and respiration. By August, the young woman's body had curled into a fetal position and weighed a mere seventy pounds. Believing there to be no hope that their daughter would ever come out of her persistent vegetative state, Joseph and Julia Quinlan asked hospital personnel to remove the life support machines from Karen's body. The neurologist in charge of her case, however, refused the request. He believed that by turning off the respirator he would be causing his patient an agonizing death by asphyxiation, an act that he viewed as morally untenable, a violation of his physician's oath never to cause harm, and a breach of New Jersey law that defined the intentional causing of another's death as homicide (Filene 1998, 20–21). Legally, Karen Quinlan was an adult, but her accident had rendered her powerless to make decisions about governing her own body, leaving her parents and the physician in charge of her case at an excruciating standstill. Joseph Quinlan petitioned the Superior Court of New Jersey to be named legal guardian of his adult daughter.

When the New Jersey Superior Court denied Joseph Quinlan's request for guardianship, the family appealed to the state Supreme Court, arguing that in previous years Karen had expressed to others a wish never to be kept alive by artificial means. This time they succeeded. In *In re Quinlan*, the New Jersey Supreme Court found that by removing Karen from the respirator, her parents would be acting in accordance with her previously stated directives about how she want-

ed to govern her body, and although she was no longer an autonomous person, those directives would still be protected by Karen's constitutional right to privacy; Joseph Quinlan had won the right to render a decision his daughter could not. In a strange twist on an already agonizing story, Karen Ann Quinlan remained alive in a persistent vegetative state for ten years after being removed from the respirator, finally succumbing to pneumonia in June 1985, at the age of thirty-one. Although she was breathing on her own, medical technologies other than the respirator had continued to sustain her life for a decade.

Despite its enormous impact on the late-twentieth-century debate over what rather simplistically came to be called the "right to die," the Quinlan case ultimately did not decide the question of when a person's life ends, nor did it establish a permanent, impenetrable boundary between the individual's right to bodily autonomy and the state's interest in protecting human life. Citizens divided themselves into "right to life" "pro-choice," and "right to die" camps and state legislatures responded with myriad statutes that attempted to delineate a clear beginning and end to the human lifespan. During the decade following Karen Ann Quinlan's accident, a series of other high-profile cases involving individuals whose physical lives were being sustained by ever-advancing medical technologies demonstrated the legal, social, and medical complexities that were integrally woven into this issue. Then, in 1989 the U.S. Supreme Court entered the fray when it agreed to hear the case *Cruzan v. Director, Missouri Department of Public Health* (see Chapter 3). Nancy Cruzan had been the victim of a one-car accident and for over six years had lain in a Missouri hospital in a persistent vegetative state. As her legal guardians, her parents requested the removal of the feeding tube that was sustaining their daughter. When the hospital refused, Nancy Cruzan's fate went to probate court, where a judge ruled that their plan was allowable. The state of Missouri, however, challenged this ruling, and the case went to the Missouri Supreme Court and eventually to the highest court in the land.

The Supreme Court ruled that, in the absence of a clear directive from Nancy stating that she would not want to remain alive in a persistent vegetative state, her parents could not claim to be acting in her privacy interest, and the case was remanded back to the Missouri courts to hear more evidence of Nancy's wishes. The state attorney general, however, decided not to pursue the matter, which took the case back to the probate judge. He reissued his original authorization

that the Cruzans be allowed to suspend the artificial feeding of their daughter, who died within two weeks of the tube's removal (Filene 1998, 168–183).

In the *Cruzan* case, the very private act of feeding the body became infused with extraordinary public meaning as Americans revisited questions of individual autonomy, civil rights, and society's responsibility to protect the general welfare. And, as they had throughout the twentieth century, Americans turned to the courts for guidance, where they continue to seek answers today. In August 2001, for example, the California Supreme Court declined to allow the wife of a man hospitalized on life support for two years to have the technologies removed, citing the absence of a clear directive from the man himself as to whether he wished to remain in such a state (Nieves 2001). Today, Americans are embroiled in an impassioned debate over whether the individual retains the right to end his or her own life with the assistance of another, an issue that has been labeled the "right to die."

A Confusing Legacy

Although legal tradition does provide a solid basis for the American belief in a generalized right to bodily autonomy, the historical complexity in which the tradition has operated leaves us with considerable confusion regarding what we actually mean when we invoke such a right. One legal scholar has even characterized the current state of U.S. laws governing the body as one of "chaos" (Rao 2000, 2). In part, inconsistencies in the way the law regards bodily autonomy can be traced to the differing and at times contradictory legal doctrines identified in this chapter: private property, police powers, and a constitutional right to privacy.

Obviously, a great deal has changed since Locke's seventeenth-century assertion that the individual possesses a "property in his own person." But in many ways the law continues to conceptualize bodily autonomy—albeit rather obliquely at times—in terms of private property rights. It is lawful, for example, for people to voluntarily donate their blood for use by others. They may also receive payment for their blood, as in the case of a donor with an extremely rare and valuable blood type, and the courts have determined that any income thus derived is subject to taxation just as any other commodity would be.

However, the current legal picture is much more complex on the subject of human organs. In 1989, in the National Organ Transplant Act, Congress prohibited both the sale and purchase of human organs after a death has occurred, suggesting that an association between the human body and property would be inappropriate and perhaps even ghoulish. Yet, in enacting this law, Congress relied on its constitutional authority to regulate interstate *commerce,* thereby implying indirectly that the body is in fact a form of property. A further example may be found in the Uniform Anatomical Gift Act, enacted by all fifty states, which grants individuals the right to donate their bodies or parts of their bodies after death without monetary remuneration. Individuals may consent to the postmortem donation while they are still alive or may arrange for it after their death through a stipulation in their will or the execution of a special document. In the absence of such documentation, disposal of the body automatically passes to their heirs, much like other forms of property; the heirs may consent to donate all or part of it, as long as there is no evidence that the deceased would have objected. Current laws also afford some protections for a choice *not* to have our bodies, or parts of them, used by others in the manner of property. Researchers cannot perform experiments on our bodies without first obtaining our informed consent. Family members cannot force us to donate our bone marrow to a relative, no matter how urgent the relative's need. Thus in matters pertaining to donating, selling, or retaining particular parts or products of the human body, individuals continue to enjoy many rights and protections analogous to private property rights.

But if the operative assumption is that people are free to make choices regarding the use of their bodies because each has a "property in his person," current medical research is standing this long-held assumption on its head. For example, fertilizing human ova and sperm outside the body (in-vitro fertilization), a procedure virtually unimaginable in the 1960s, when a constitutional right to privacy was established, has become a relatively commonplace treatment for infertile couples wishing to conceive a child. For various reasons, however, not all the embryos actually become implanted in a uterus, and the question of who "owns" them—fathers, mothers, or the laboratories where they are stored—has been brought before the courts. Similarly, legal disputes over who "owns" human DNA used in bio-

engineering research have arisen between donors and researchers. Regarding the human body in terms of its constituent parts has become an exceedingly complex issue.

The power of the state to regulate the human body continues to be redefined as well. Although the saga of "Typhoid Mary" may seem a relic of a bygone era, the need to take official action for fear of stopping the spread of contagion—with or without the justification of medical science—continues to be used as a means of restricting bodily autonomy. In the 1980s, citizens of the United States became aware of the existence of a devastating but poorly understood new illness called acquired immunodeficiency syndrome (AIDS). Early researchers noted a relatively high incidence of the disease within the gay community. Initial reports, often translated incorrectly to the public by the mass media, spurred irrational fears of uncontrolled contagion among the general public. In the midst of the initial panic, a number of city governments ordered the closing of public places where homosexuals were known to congregate, despite the lack of any clear medical evidence that such measures would in fact be effective in fighting the epidemic (Mohr 1987, 36–41). The same unproven fears about the indiscriminate spread of the disease throughout the entire population led the Centers for Disease Control (CDC) to classify Haitian immigrants as a "high-risk" group in the early 1980s, resulting in thousands of Haitians in the United States losing jobs, housing, and educational opportunities (Kraut 1994, 261). Thus, even in more "enlightened" times, the very *perception* of how disease may spread to the general public continues to inform official attempts to regulate and control the human body.

The state continues to exercise its authority over bodily autonomy in other ways, many of which remain highly controversial. Despite the Supreme Court ruling in *Skinner v. Oklahoma* that procreation is a fundamental right, some states have stipulated that women on public assistance receive Norplant, a chemical form of contraceptive implanted in the arm, to prevent their becoming pregnant. The Wisconsin Supreme Court recently upheld a probation order that prohibited a man from having any more offspring. The man had been convicted of failure to provide support to his nine children (Lewin 2001). The legal boundaries between public and private control over the human body, therefore, remain elusive.

But the story becomes further nuanced when we remember Louis Brandeis's assertion that the law does not operate in a vacuum; legal doctrines concerning the human body have evolved in relation to changing views in science and medicine about the structures and functions of the human body. This is the subject we will examine in Chapter 2.

References and Further Reading

Blackstone, W. 1775. *Commentaries on the Laws of England.* Reprint, Buffalo: William S. Hein, 1993.

Burris, S. 1989. "Rationality Review and the Politics of Public Health." *Villanova Law Review* 34: 933–982.

Dworkin, Ronald. 1994. *Life's Dominion: An Argument about Abortion, Euthanasia, and Individual Freedom.* New York: Vintage Books.

Filene, Peter. 1998. *In the Arms of Others: A Cultural History of the Right-to-Die in America.* Chicago: Ivan R. Dee.

Gillman, H. 1993. *The Constitution Besieged: The Rise and Demise of Lochner Era Police Powers Jurisprudence.* Durham: Duke University Press.

Hall, Kermit L. 1989. *The Magic Mirror: Law in American History.* New York: Oxford University Press.

Hyde, Alan. 1997. *Bodies of Law.* Princeton, NJ: Princeton University Press.

Kens, P. 1998. Lochner v. New York: *Economic Regulation on Trial.* Lawrence: University Press of Kansas.

Kerber, Linda K. 1998. *No Constitutional Right to Be Ladies.* New York: Hill and Wang.

Kraut, Alan M. 1994. *Silent Travelers: Germs, Genes, and the "Immigrant Menace."* Baltimore: Johns Hopkins University Press.

Leavitt, Judith Walzer. 1996. *Typhoid Mary: Captive to the Public's Health.* Boston: Beacon Press.

Lewin, Tamar. 2001. "Father Owing Child Support Loses a Right to Procreate." *New York Times,* July 12.

Locke, John. 1690. *Second Treatise on Government.* Reprinted in Peter Laslett, ed., *Two Treatises of Government.* Cambridge Texts in the History of Political Thought. Cambridge, UK: Cambridge University Press, 1999.

Mohr, Richard D. 1987. "AIDS, Gays, and State Coercion." *Bioethics* 1, no. 1: 36–50.

Nieves, Evelyn. 2001. "California Justices Limit Families' Right to End Life Support." *New York Times,* August 10.

Novak, William J. 1996. *The People's Welfare.* Chapel Hill: University of North Carolina Press.

Parmet, Wendy E. 1996. "From *Slaughterhouse* to *Lochner:* The Rise and Fall of the Constitutionalization of Public Health." *American Journal of Legal History* 40: 476–505.

Rao, Radhika. 2000. "Property, Privacy, and the Human Body." *Boston University Law Review* 80: 360–460.

Ross, Michael A. 1998. "Justice Miller's Reconstruction: The *Slaughterhouse Cases,* Health Codes, and Civil Rights in New Orleans, 1861–1873." *Journal of Southern History* 44: 649–676.

Toby, James A. 1947. *Public Health Law.* New York: The Commonwealth Fund.

Woloch, Nancy. 1996. *Muller v. Oregon.* New York: Bedford Books.

2

Historical Background

Medicalizing the Body

The conceptual framework that surrounds the American notion of bodily autonomy has been shaped by the development of medicine and the law. The history of western medicine includes the evolution of medical theory as well as the actual practices of physicians, midwives, nurses, lay healers, and the day-to-day folk-healing methods of ordinary people (Duffy 1993, 69). But the course of medical history is not a simple story about the linear march of scientific progress. What has been accepted as prevailing medical wisdom in any one period has emerged within specific social, political, economic, and cultural contexts. Nor is the history of medicine a unidirectional story, for lay people's acceptance or rejection of particular medical theories and practices affecting the care and treatment of their bodies has also shaped the contours of the narrative; it is a story of conflict as well as consensus. Long before the U.S. Supreme Court defined a constitutional right to privacy, individuals asserted a common law right to bodily autonomy, or the ability to govern their physical beings as they saw fit. At the same time, over the course of the twentieth century, medical science exerted increasing authority in American life, an influence that extended into the areas of law and social policy as well. The legal system played an integral role in this story. Debates over theory, practice, and the growing power of medical science in American life crystallized in numerous challenges brought

before the courts. The justices' decisions sometimes privileged one medical theory over another. This chapter places the key legal issues identified in Chapter 1 within the context of the history of medicine in the United States. Specifically, it addresses sectarian medicine, the rise of the germ theory, eugenics, birth control and abortion, and end-of-life issues.

As the legal and political infrastructure for public health developed in the nineteenth century, medical paradigms regarding the structure and function of the human body also underwent change. The first half of the century saw a flowering of "sectarian medicine," a proliferation of differing schools of thought and practice regarding the workings of the human body, the etiology of disease, and the best methods for curing illness and injury. Schools such as homeopathy, osteopathy, hydropathy, Thomsonianism, eclecticism, and a variety of other sects existed alongside—and in stiff competition with—the practice of allopathic, or "regular" medicine. Alternative, or "irregular," medical sects emerged in large part because of patients' dissatisfaction with the harsh methods regular physicians employed in dramatic and, for the patient, often disastrous attempts to rid the human body of disease. Physicians employed massive bloodletting, blistering of the skin, and the use of strong purgatives such as arsenic and calomel (mercurous chloride) in their healing practices. High drama at the bedside became routine procedure for regular physicians eager to demonstrate their singular mastery of the healing arts, a practice modern scholars refer to as "heroic medicine." Although many patients and their families admired highly aggressive treatments as evidence of their physician's extraordinary knowledge and specialized skills, others sought less arduous cures. Thomsonianism, a medical sect founded by a New Hampshire farmer named Samuel Thomson, employed a battery of relatively mild botanical remedies and decried the use of harsh mineral therapies in healing. Practitioners of homeopathy administered a variety of chemical remedies in infinitesimal doses rather than the "heroic" doses commonly employed in regular medical practice. The influential New England social reformer Catharine Beecher enthusiastically advocated hydropathy, or a regimen requiring frequent bathing and drinking massive amounts of water, and discouraged others of her sex from relying on drugs and the intrusive methods of physicians to treat their ailments. With the flourishing of sectarian medicine, it became common for patients to employ several different kinds of practitioners to attend a

single illness as a kind of health care insurance policy; if one remedy appeared not to work, perhaps another one would prove effective. Although folk healing remained an important staple of nineteenth-century health care regimens in the United States, growing numbers of urban, educated, and middle-class Americans were attracted to the more organized medical sects.

Historians have linked the sectarian medical movement to the heightened spirit of democracy that marked the Jacksonian age. In an era that saw the acceptance of universal white male suffrage, the emergence of a powerful crusade to abolish slavery, and the first stirrings of the long campaign for women's rights, the proliferation of medical sects offered individuals a measure of freedom in the choices they made in governing themselves and their physical well-being. The care of one's own health, therefore, took on new meaning as an expression of individual liberty. Most of the new sects encouraged people to regulate their diets and take some form of daily exercise so they could maintain optimum health without resorting to the mysterious and risky cures offered by elite and exclusive physicians. "In my water-cure experience," hydropathy practitioner Mary Gove Nichols wrote in 1849, "I have had abundant evidence that depletion by bleeding or purgatives is never required, that counter-irritants are unnecessary tortures, and that all the indications of a rapid cure, without unnecessary weakness or poisoning can be attained by this mode of treatment" (Nichols 1849, 130). Water cure advocates like Nichols believed that ordinary people could be trusted to care for their own bodies, once they understood the basic precepts of preventive health and hygiene.

Sectarians often tied the popularization of health care to other social reform currents of the day, participating with special enthusiasm in temperance, or antialcohol, campaigns. They viewed abstention from alcohol as a logical extension of their holistic approach to maintaining physical health and well-being, a paradigm that encouraged maximum autonomy over one's own body rather than reliance on the advice and practices of elite medical experts. In their writings and speeches, sectarian practitioners revealed a decided suspicion of elite medical authority, leveling the charge that their allopathic competitors attempted to monopolize wisdom about the human body, knowledge that the sectarians believed should be shared with the common people through lay education. Thus, although nineteenth-century sectarianism reflected competing beliefs about medicine and

the most effective ways to optimize health, the movement itself was also the product of larger social and political debates about the meaning of liberty, equality, and authority in antebellum American life.

By the middle of the nineteenth century, the forces of industrialization had begun to make significant inroads into the nation. One inescapable consequence of this development was the dramatic decline of public health conditions in U.S. cities, where pollution from factories mingled with the deleterious effects of urban populations being packed together ever more densely. Reformers in the "sanitarian" school began to agitate for a more proactive, systematic, and scientific approach to protecting the public's health, especially in the rapidly expanding cities of the Northeast. Public health work, they argued, could do much more than merely attempt to control epidemics after they invaded the community. Cities undertook major public works projects such as the construction of complex sewage and drainage systems and built political and legal infrastructures for the regulation of urban life. Urban water supplies, livery stables, and the outdoor privies serving private households all came under increasingly zealous regulation. The new efforts sanitarians embarked upon required not only widespread cooperation from the urban population but also more direct and expansive involvement on the part of state and local governments. As we saw in Chapter 1, the growth of new public health policies and programs inspired by sanitarian reform also enjoyed the backing of the courts, as in the U.S. Supreme Court's support of a statute regulating the butchering trade in its 1873 *Slaughterhouse Cases* opinion. Health authorities and judges alike agreed that the state's police powers may and should be employed extensively in order to keep the U.S. population free from contagious disease.

Mid–nineteenth century public health was predicated on the *zymotic theory* of contagion, which held that disease could be generated spontaneously by decaying matter in the environment and spread through foul odors, or "miasmas," floating in the atmosphere. Although many of the proposed remedies, such as the construction of massive "stench traps" to contain the noxious miasmas, proved to be ineffective in fighting ill health, sanitarians' attentions to cleaning up the urban landscape did make recognizable inroads into keeping epidemics under control. A major turning point in public health reform came during the Civil War, when the U.S. Sanitary Commission demonstrated irrefutably the effectiveness of prophylactic mea-

sures such as ensuring proper drainage in military encampments and systematically applying domestic and personal hygiene techniques in hospitals. Although contagious diseases like measles and typhoid fever visited military installations with distressing regularity throughout the Civil War, northern sanitarian reforms noticeably reduced the rate of mortality from the outbreaks.

The momentum for sanitarian reform carried over into the postwar decades as increasing numbers of public health officials rallied around the cause of promoting urban sanitation and encouraging individual and domestic hygiene. Significantly, the Civil War experience had also convinced both health care practitioners and the general public that by applying the rules of sanitary science efficiently and comprehensively, many diseases could be *prevented* from occurring in the first place (Hoy 1995, 60). The new promise of sanitarian public health reform inspired a proliferation of regulatory laws and administering agencies in states and cities throughout the nation. Sanitarian public health reform thus played a significant role in enlarging the bureaucratic infrastructure of state and local governments in the last decades of the nineteenth century as the regulatory state expanded.

The Germ Theory

In the last quarter of the nineteenth century, a new understanding of how diseases were contracted and spread began to take hold among medical researchers. Advocates of the new theory relied not on the traditional method of observing the outward signs of illness exhibited by patients but rather on identifying disease-causing organisms under the lens of a microscope. In the 1870s and 1880s, the experimental work of European bacteriologists Robert Koch and Louis Pasteur initiated a flurry of laboratory research into the environmental causes of contagious illness, and within years medical researchers could link several specific germs to particular diseases. Unlike the zymotic theory, the new germ theory offered a much more precise and, its promoters argued, useful way to protect the health and safety of the public. Enthusiasm for the new science of bacteriology quickly spread to the United States, but its acceptance was not universal at first. Many public health practitioners believed that the zymotic theory already offered a perfectly adequate explanation for contagion, and thus they remained rather cool toward the new paradigm. Nor was the general public universally agreeable to being told that organisms they could not see, touch, feel, or smell were making them sick. After many years of debate in U.S. medical circles as well as the popular press, at the close of the nineteenth century the germ theory finally became established as a central tenet of medical orthodoxy (Tomes 1998, 28).

With its stress on manipulating the environment to control the spread of disease, the germ theory actually confirmed rather than contradicted long-held precepts of sanitation and hygiene among public health reformers. In one important way, though, the germ theory did shift the direction of public health work in a decidedly new direction. Because disease-causing germs could be found lurking virtually everywhere and at all times in the human habitat, advocates of the new public health expended fewer efforts toward keeping the community safe from diseases attacking from the outside and paid more attention to altering the domestic rituals and personal hygiene habits of people within the community. Reformers of the Progressive Era linked the new germ-theory-driven public health movement to their wider vision of promoting society's overall advancement. Popular educational activities disseminated the germ theory to the general public by stressing the importance of washing one's hands frequently, boiling well water before drinking it, and feeding babies pasteurized milk in sterilized bottles (Curry 1999, 4). Laboratory research into new vaccines offered hope that a host of diseases once endemic to the community could one day be prevented entirely—if whole populations were willing to submit their bodies to vaccination procedures. With the effort to disseminate the new "gospel of germs" as widely as possible, the reach of public health work now stretched well beyond the public streets and sewer lines of the urban landscape. It had moved behind the front door of the private family home.

Eugenics

Progressive reformers did not limit their faith in science to bacteriology and the unprecedented possibilities of the germ theory for preventing disease. Many activists of the era found themselves attracted to *eugenics*, an amalgam of biological and social theory that urged the improvement of the human condition through controlling human reproduction. The term itself had been coined in 1869 by Francis Galton, a British scientist and cousin of Charles Darwin, who became interested in the possibility of using direct human intervention to create a society of "well-born" individuals. Although the precise mechanisms by which human characteristics were transmitted between generations had not yet been identified, Galton used his training in both medicine and mathematics to develop a theory that promised the eventual eradication of a range of social ills plaguing mankind, from chronic poverty to congenital physical defects to low levels of intelligence. Eugenics quickly caught on among reformers in Europe and the United States, and by the Progressive Era it had been transformed into a rather amorphous endeavor combining tenets from both biological and social sciences. For example, eugenicists' notion of "inherited traits" was quite broad when measured by the twenty-first-century understanding of the term, encompassing virtually everything one acquired from one's parents, from social and economic standing to eye color and physical height. One could "inherit" tuberculosis, for example, from a family predisposition for the disease. Conversely, one could squander one's good breeding by engaging in unhealthy personal habits (Pernick 1996, 42–43). Under the banner of eugenics, public health reformers staged "better baby" contests that in reality rewarded parents for the proper care and feeding of their children rather than the transmission of their biological traits to their offspring. Advocates of achieving the well-born society distinguished between "positive" eugenics, which encouraged the propagation of those human traits they deemed most desirable, and "negative" eugenics, which prevented traits deemed undesirable from passing on to succeeding generations. Eugenicists believed both approaches to be necessary to achieve the desired social ends.

Defining what is and is not biologically "normal" within any given population was (and remains) an exceedingly complex exercise, and eugenicists' enthusiasm for perfecting human society frequently overrode both scientific accuracy and individual rights. The majority of the movement's adherents were white and of Anglo-Saxon descent and generally took the characteristics of their own group as the normative standard by which all humans were to be judged; many went further and held up their own traits as indicators of superior human breeding (Kevles 1985, 64). Eugenicists posited that through the careful control of human reproduction using various positive and negative tactics, the well-born American society of the future would look and act increasingly white, Anglo-Saxon, and middle class. President Theodore Roosevelt, an ardent champion of a more vigorous and physically fit America, once famously proclaimed to the press that it was the duty of every white, Anglo-Saxon female in the United States to produce at least four children.

But many within the movement were impatient with the notion of a slow and steady march toward human perfection. For these reformers, the nation faced a much more immediate threat of rapid genetic deterioration. In scientific and popular publications, this group of eugenicists claimed that the United States stood in danger of committing nothing less than "race suicide" because its "best" citizens were reproducing at lower rates than other, less socially desirable groups, among whom they included African Americans, recently arrived immigrants from southern and eastern Europe, and poor whites. Although scientific documentation that Americans were in a state of rapid genetic decline was in fact nonexistent, those sounding the alarm managed to catch the attention of a public dismayed by the rapid social and cultural changes brought by the forces of industrialization, urbanization, and immigration. Eugenic arguments about the urgency of maintaining the vigor and quality of the American population figured prominently in the debates that led to Congress's passage of the Immigration Act in 1924, legislation that placed new and much tighter restrictions on the numbers of specific national and ethnic groups that would be allowed to enter the country. Two years earlier, eugenicist Harry Laughlin had testified before the House of Representatives Committee on Immigration and Naturalization that the high numbers of recent immigrants from southern and eastern Europe represented a threat to the country's future well-being. "Making all logical allowances for local conditions," Laughlin asserted, "the recent immigrants, as a whole, present a higher percentage of inborn socially inadequate qualities than do the older stocks" (Shapiro 1985, 37). Although the eugenicists' warnings of race suicide may have grabbed headlines in the early twentieth century, progressive reformers differed widely in their positions regarding the extent to which individuals could be ethically and legally compelled to place saving the nation over their own bodily autonomy. At a minimum, most progressives supported various educational activities such as public lectures and the distribution of literature promoting eugenic awareness and encouraging individuals to make sound judgments about whom they would marry, how many children they would bear, and the precautions they might take to prevent contracting sexually transmitted diseases. These reformers preferred intellectual suasion over legal compulsion, relying on widespread public education and peoples' voluntary responses as the primary means to ensure the optimal fitness of future generations.

But for other, more ardent, supporters of the eugenics cause, the imminent social dangers of uncontrolled human breeding were much too urgent to be left to such haphazard approaches, and they lobbied their state legislatures for more decisive and direct action. A very few went so far as to advocate euthanasia for severely deformed newborns (Pernick 1996, 19–39). A somewhat larger number urged sterilization of those who, by one set of criteria or another, must not be allowed to procreate for the future well-being of society. Their social goals were supported by recent advances in medical science that made safer surgical operations for preventing human reproduction possible. The technique of vasectomy had been developed in the 1890s, originally as a less dangerous and devastating alternative to castration in treating men for prostate disease. In addition, the German surgeon M. Madlener had developed the procedure known as salpingectomy, or the tying of the fallopian tubes, as a means of sterilizing female patients. To the most enthusiastic advocates of negative eugenics, these surgical innovations provided safe and effective means by which to regulate human reproduction. They sought governmental support for mandating sterilization to ensure the well-being of society.

In the first decade of the twentieth century, a number of states began passing measures to regulate the sexual reproduction of their populations by law. Some states prohibited marriage among those judged to be mentally defective, for example, or to anyone diagnosed with a communicable disease such as tuberculosis or syphilis. In 1907, Indiana became the first state to enact legislation mandating the sterilization of people convicted of specified crimes. Within ten years, sixteen states had laws on the books compelling sterilization of particular populations, most often criminals and those committed to institutions for the "feebleminded" or the insane (Kevles 1985, 100).

Although the oppressive implications of such laws for individual civil rights alarmed some Americans, compulsory sterilization statutes enjoyed the solid backing of the courts in the early twentieth century. Drawing upon the well-established legal tradition of allowing states to exercise broad authority in the name of public health and safety, supporters of eugenics laws argued that the genetic deterioration of the U.S. population represented an imminent threat justifying states in exercising their police powers, even if the infringements on individual liberty that resulted would be severe. To continue human breeding unmanaged, they claimed, meant the certain destruction of American society within the space of a few generations. Although eugenicists faced numerous critics in contemporary scientific, social, and political circles, their arguments favoring compulsory sterilization of targeted populations generally fell upon sympathetic ears in the legal system throughout the 1920s and 1930s (Kevles 1985, 116). Key among these cases was the 1927 Supreme Court opinion *Buck v. Bell.* Seventeen-year-old Carrie Buck had been committed to the Virginia Colony for the Epileptic and Feeble-Minded, after a court hearing purporting to demonstrate that a genetic disposition for imbecility ran in her family. According to the court, allowing her to procreate would endanger the nation's gene pool, and so she was ordered to be sterilized by the colony's physician using the procedure of salpingectomy. The opinion by Justice Oliver Wendell Holmes, Jr., an enthusiastic supporter of eugenic laws, upheld the Virginia law that prescribed sterilization of "feebleminded" inmates of state institutions before they could be released into the general population (see Chapter 3).

The Crusade for Birth Control

The Progressive Era saw another major—and equally controversial—movement for social reform, that of legalizing and promoting the use of contraceptives to control human reproduction. Strategies for preventing pregnancy, of course, have been practiced throughout human history. In addition to the time-honored methods of abstinence and male withdrawal before ejaculation, an intricate knowledge of botanical and mechanical ways to induce abortion made up part of the folk-healing tradition shared privately among women over countless generations. In the United States, demographic evidence clearly illustrates that white, middle-class families living in northern states had begun to limit the number of their children as early as the Jacksonian era, taking advantage of the new chemical douches and rubber condoms that became available at the time, as well as more traditional methods (Reagan 1997, 41). Nevertheless, although birth control was widely practiced, it still was not a subject for open discussion in polite society or the popular press. By the early twentieth century, however, progressive advocates of birth control worked to redefine the issues and alternatives surrounding family planning as not solely private matters but rather important social concerns that deserved to be addressed in the public arena. For progressives in the birth control movement, enhancing people's understanding of the physiology of sex and reproduction was essential in order for individuals to make sound decisions regarding their own health care.

But birth control advocates faced a major obstacle in the form of the federal Comstock laws. Passed by Congress in 1873, these regulations prohibited importing, transporting, or mailing any article of an "indecent or immoral nature," a designation that was cast broadly enough to include information pertaining to birth control as well as any device or drug that would cause abortion. Individual states supplemented the federal law with their own statutes along similar lines, creating a solid legal barrier to reformers' goal of educating the public about contraception. Progressives therefore worked to move the discussion of sex and birth control out of the shadowy world of brothels and the vice trades where the Comstock laws had put it and into a more respectable public discourse about advancing public health and social progress. In doing so, they also challenged the existing boundaries between private and public prerogatives concerning the human body.

But although the movement's adherents could agree upon the wider pragmatic goal of disseminating birth control information, their specific ideological reasons for promoting contraception varied. For some, the central issue was "voluntary motherhood," or a greater degree of control for married women over their own physical and reproductive health. The hazards of childbirth remained very real in the early twentieth century, and reformers despaired at the high rates of maternal mortality reported throughout the nation. Before the advent of sulfa drugs and antibiotic remedies, infection following childbirth remained second only to tuberculosis as the most common cause of death for adult women. Further, the absence of prenatal care meant that complications during pregnancy often went undiagnosed until it was too late to save the health or life of the mother. For this group of reformers, the issue of birth control represented a fundamental tenet within a larger project to advance the health, safety, and status of women. Women could never exercise true autonomy as equal citizens with men, they argued, without the ability to control their own reproductive health.

For other, more socially radical advocates, the aim was greater acceptance of the idea of separating sex from reproduction. This group promoted the right of bodily autonomy as the liberty to enjoy the perfectly natural act of sex free from the burdens of unwanted pregnancy. Sigmund Freud's explorations of the human psyche were taking the western world by storm, and the work of other early psychologists such as Havelock Ellis brought discussion of human sexuality outside of its traditional context of morality and religion. The radical publication, *The Masses,* for example, addressed contraception and "free love" alongside the most important political and economic topics of the day. New York City's bohemian Greenwich Village attracted artists, writers, and intellectuals who advocated freedom of sexual expression as an inherent aspect of individual liberty. For this group, greater access to birth control was not an end in itself but rather a vital means for bringing about their ultimate vision of enabling people to realize their fullest potential as human beings.

Still other Progressive Era reformers saw legalized birth control as an essential mechanism for advancing eugenic goals. In the "well-born" society, they claimed, informed and responsible persons who chose not to pass on their genetic legacy to future generations should be able to do so without risking arrest or imprisonment. Although mandatory sterilization laws applied to a narrow range of the genetically "unfit," those who for genetic reasons chose not to bear children, but were neither convicted criminals nor diagnosed as feeble-minded, needed a safe and reliable way to prevent procreation. Eugenicists had faith that their educational activities would eventually convince individuals with a variety of genetic "defects" not to bear offspring, and to this end the widespread availability of birth control information and technologies was essential.

Finally, an increasing number of physicians joined the movement to reform the Comstock laws and legalize contraception because they viewed such restrictions as an unwarranted imposition on their professional prerogatives as health care professionals. For this wing of the birth control movement, the key issue was that, as an aspect of physical well-being, contraception represented a legitimate concern of medical science, and certified professionals ought to be able to discuss it with patients and among themselves without fear of arrest or imprisonment. They cited clinical evidence that women's health was compromised by stressful pregnancies and frequent childbearing. Although by cultural tradition birth control had remained within the sphere of women's control, physicians began to advance the position that in a modern and enlightened society such as the twentieth-century United States, contraceptive information and technologies should be managed by medical experts. Arriving relatively late on the reform scene, over the next several decades physicians gathered considerable momentum for the repeal of birth control prohibitions and by the 1950s they had emerged as one of the dominant forces behind the legalization of contraception.

The diversity of perspectives concerning the desirability of promoting contraception meant that the birth control movement enjoyed substantial grassroots support in the first decades of the twentieth century, with overall ideological and political leadership shared among a number of individuals and organizations. Today, however, perhaps no other single figure is as indelibly linked with the fight to legalize birth control as Margaret Sanger. A public health nurse who worked among poor and working-class families in New York City, Sanger became involved in campaigns for workers' rights and soon came to identify the inability to control the number and spacing of their children as a central cause of workers' continued impoverishment. In 1914, Sanger attempted to publish a column discussing birth control in a socialist magazine, only to have it banned by the post office under the Comstock law, a sanction that garnered her widespread support among U.S. radicals. Later, Sanger herself coined the term *birth control* in her publication, *The Woman Rebel.* She opened the nation's first birth control clinic in a working-class immigrant neighborhood in Brooklyn, New York, for which she was again arrested for violating the Comstock laws. Although her early associations were with socialists, radical labor organizers, and the bohemian wing of the birth control movement, Sanger eventually took a more politically pragmatic course and allied her efforts more closely with socially conservative physicians. Although by adopting this approach Sanger seemed to take a decided step back from her earlier, more radical vision of a society that valued and protected individual sexual liberation, the new strategy proved highly successful in attaining the concrete end of getting birth control information and technology to people who wanted it. Over the course of a career that spanned several decades, Sanger opened numerous birth control clinics and in 1921 founded the American Birth Control League, eventually taking the movement overseas in what became the International Planned Parenthood Federation in 1953. Sanger was by no means alone in her struggle to promote birth control in the United States, but the trajectory of her long public career links the early social radicalism of the movement to its eventual establishment within the social and political mainstream—and the control of the medical profession—after World War II.

With the onset of the Great Depression in 1929, the subject of birth control moved more decidedly into the realm of social respectability. A series of court rulings diminished the effectiveness of using the Comstock laws to suppress information about preventing unwanted pregnancies. Condoms became widely available in drugstores and gas stations, and by the late 1930s the American Birth Control League was operating over 500 private clinics throughout the United States. Although for years many individual physicians had argued that prescribing contraception should remain the business of medical professionals rather than the state legislatures, in 1938 the American Medical Association (AMA) took the important symbolic step of officially abandoning its formal opposition to birth control (Reagan 1997, 134).

But in this era of large-scale unemployment, hunger, and homelessness, public discourse concerning birth control seemed to be more about social responsibility at a time of national economic crisis than about the individual's rights concerning his or her body. The liberalization of contraception laws in the 1930s was closely tied to governmental efforts to reduce public dependence on relief. Throughout the decade, public health authorities discussed the need to make contraception widely available to contain the growth of nonwhite populations, including African Americans and Puerto Ricans, who had been disproportionately affected by the Depression. The Roosevelt administration established a birth control program under the Puerto Rican Emergency Relief Administration. Although the administration dropped the program in 1936 because of conservative political pressures at home, contraceptive services continued through the island's public health department. In the late 1930s, patients at these clinics acted as human guinea pigs for U.S. pharmaceutical companies eager to test new birth control products. Puerto Rican hospitals enjoyed wide latitude in performing salpingectomies on women admitted to deliver a third or subsequent child (Shapiro 1985, 53). Although leadership of the U.S. birth control movement had become dominated by health care practitioners rather than social reformers, the movement never completely lost its association with eugenic goals (Rowbotham 1997, 217). In contrast to the movement's Progressive Era origins, contraception as an issue of individual liberty had become a secondary concern. In fact, in many states, prescribing birth control was still against the law, and in others even its use among married couples remained illegal.

A Revival of Rights

After decades in which medicine, law, and social policy underwent extensive and simultaneous change, the middle of the twentieth century once again witnessed a major reexamination of public and private claims on the human body. Despite its popularity in the first half of the twentieth century, by the 1940s eugenics fell from grace in both the United States and Europe. In Germany, the atrocities committed by the Third Reich, in which millions of Jews and other "non-Aryan" peoples had been exterminated in the name of racial purity, left a legacy of revulsion and fear regarding large-scale, systematic, and forced attempts to "perfect" humankind. Further, the work of legitimate geneticists had begun to demonstrate the myriad complexities surrounding biological inheritance, exposing the theoretical mistakes as well as the scientific naiveté of the previous generation of eugenicists. A more sophisticated understanding of dominant and recessive traits in human genetics, for example, brought to light the inherent fruitlessness of schemes aimed at wiping out a particular undesired characteristic within a few generations. Although eugenicists had come under fire from many in the scientific community before the 1940s, in the wake of the horrors exposed in Nazi Germany these critiques found a new resonance among a somewhat wiser and more circumspect public audience.

When it handed down its 1942 opinion in *Skinner v. Oklahoma* (see Chapter 1), the U.S. Supreme Court decried the naive and unscientific assumptions that had informed state laws mandating the sterilization of penitentiary inmates in order to breed criminal traits out of the population. In a concurring opinion, Chief Justice Harlan F. Stone even chided Oklahoma lawmakers for presuming to know more about human genetics than scientists did. "[I]f we must presume that the legislature knows—what science has been unable to ascertain—that the criminal tendencies of any class of habitual offenders are transmissible regardless of the varying mental characteristics of its individuals," he asserted, "I should suppose that we must likewise presume that the legislature, in its wisdom, knows that the criminal tendencies of some classes of offenders are more likely to be transmitted than those of others" (316 U.S. 535). The Court's decision to rein in states' efforts to control the reproduction of their populations privileged the authority of medical scientists over the political judgment of legislators.

With the rekindled discourse about liberty and equality that followed World War II, the subject of birth control reemerged as a civil rights rather than a eugenic issue. But new and improved contraceptive technologies continued to come up against laws, now many decades old, proscribing their use. In the 1950s, doctor-prescribed diaphragms for women joined condoms as a popular choice among couples wishing to prevent pregnancy. The introduction of a relatively safe and effective birth control pill in 1960 represented a major milestone, virtually revolutionizing the issue of contraception. Public discussions of birth control—now freed by the courts from criminal prosecution under the Comstock laws—focused more on marriage, family, and the individual's freedom of choice and less on society's supposed interest in breeding future generations of the "well-born." Then, in 1965 the Supreme Court issued the landmark ruling in *Griswold v. Connecticut* striking down a Connecticut statute prohibiting married couples from using contraceptives because it violated a married couple's fundamental right to privacy.

But although the use of contraceptive methods to prevent unwanted pregnancies had become legal by the early 1970s, public discussion of abortion—a traditional method of controlling family size—remained outside the pale of social respectability. Although abortion was quite commonly practiced in the early twentieth century, calls to legalize the operation had not been a central tenet of the Progressive Era birth control movement. In fact, as the AMA sought to enhance doctors' control over contraceptive information and prescription, it simultaneously supported vigorous efforts to prosecute abortionists. Midwives, who remained an important part of health care systems in many urban immigrant communities until the 1940s, became the AMA's primary targets because they offered abortion services. Abortion, unlike birth control, retained its association with the darker and unseemly side of life, and a woman's death from a botched procedure made sensational newspaper headlines. By the 1970s, however, advances in medical procedures, especially the systematic use of more effective antiseptic measures in surgery, had made abortion statistically as safe as childbirth and even safer for women who were very young. However, mortality rates from abortion remained high and serious injuries common because so many operations were being performed outside sterile hospital and clinical settings.

In essence, a two-tiered, highly discriminatory system of abortion provision had developed by the 1950s. Many state laws that allowed abortions for therapeutic purposes (to save the health or life of the mother) primarily benefited white, middle-class women, who could afford both the services of physicians to diagnose their need for the procedure and access to modern clinics and hospitals to have the operation performed. Lacking the resources of their middle-class sisters, poor and minority women were forced to face the dangers associated with illegal, "back alley" abortions. Many doctors encountered the tragic result of this dual system firsthand, when poor women who had been injured in illegal operations arrived seeking help in hospital emergency rooms. These physicians came to view antiabortion laws as contributing to deaths and injuries that were completely preventable when the procedure was performed by trained professionals in a sterile setting. They argued that, like the prescribing of contraceptives, providing abortion services should be the prerogative of licensed medical professionals. Beginning in the mid-1950s, an alliance of physicians, public health workers, and lawyers began organizing to overturn state abortion laws; by 1969 a majority of physicians polled favored repeal of such laws (Reagan 1997, 214–218; 234).

The members of this early alliance were soon joined by a groundswell of new supporters of the cause, who shifted the focus of the movement away from the professional concerns of health care practitioners and toward the repeal of abortion restrictions as a matter of individual bodily autonomy. The civil rights and student protest movements of the 1960s had produced a "second wave" of feminists who, like their counterparts in the earlier voluntary motherhood campaigns, saw a woman's ability to control her body as fundamental to the full exercise of her citizenship rights. In 1971 the Boston Women's Health Collective published the first edition of *Our Bodies, Ourselves,* a health care manual designed to both educate women about the structure and functions of their bodies and to empower them as fully autonomous individuals who could make their own health care decisions. Feminists, especially younger women who came into political consciousness in the radicalized atmosphere of college campuses in the 1960s, injected a heightened sense of urgency in the effort to appeal prohibitions on abortions. They introduced more militant tactics for publicizing the dangers of illegal operations, including organizing large public protests and staging guerrilla theater events. Some women also organized underground networks of feminist health care providers who were willing to perform abortion services. By 1970, the repeal of abortion laws became a topic of open, and often heated, public debate.

The differing strands of the movement—medical and feminist—came together in a series of legal challenges to state laws prohibiting abortion (Reagan 1997, 235). The right to privacy established by the Supreme Court in *Griswold v. Connecticut* served as a vital precedent for overturning antiabortion laws. Supporters of decriminalizing abortion argued that the individual's constitutional privacy interest in deciding whether or not to conceive a child must be extended to include a woman's right to choose whether or not to carry a pregnancy to full term. In 1972, a case from Texas came before the Supreme Court and resulted in a landmark ruling the following year. In *Roe v. Wade,* the Court determined that the decision of whether to continue a pregnancy to term was first and foremost a medical matter; state laws that criminalized abortion in the first three months of pregnancy represented an unconstitutional violation of the privacy interest that exists between physicians and their patients. Justice Harry Blackmun's opinion, in fact, used a medical model of human pregnancy in which the fetus's development toward viability (the ability to live independently outside the mother's body) occurred in stages over the course of three twelve-week terms, or trimesters. This scheme served the justices as a sort of legal compass for navigating the line between a woman's right to bodily autonomy and the legitimate interest of the state in protecting human life (see Chapter 3). The underlying assumption was that the fetus moved further toward viability as it entered each successive stage. The new framework replaced the traditional common law standard that recognized the "quickening"—the first fetal movement detected by the mother—as the point at which the fetus was recognized as a potential human life. Thus the Court's decision in *Roe,* like the one it rendered in *Griswold,* is more fully understood as both a continuation of an era of expansive interpretations of individual civil rights that had begun with the Warren Court and a reflection of the growing authority of medical science in matters relating to the regulation of the human body.

In *Roe v. Wade,* the Supreme Court wrestled with the exceedingly difficult question of determining precisely when a developing fetus becomes a person entitled to the protections afforded by the Constitution. Biologically speaking, fetal development is a process rather than an event, and yet the legal and social policy issues surrounding the case required the Court to reason its opinion with a degree of precision to ensure that the constitutional guarantees of liberty and the equal protection of the law are granted to all citizens. In attempting to navigate these troubled waters, the Court anchored its opinion in the medical paradigm of trimesters, but conceivably there exist other ways—cultural, religious, and philosophical, for example—of defining what it means to be a person. If medical authority in American life had expanded significantly over the course of the twentieth century, not everyone was willing to concede to doctors the power to define when life begins. The decision handed down in *Roe v. Wade* was met with both approval and scorn, and it remains one of the most controversial decisions in the Court's history.

In 1992, the justices turned back a challenge to legalized abortion in *Planned Parenthood v. Casey,* reaffirming that women's reproductive choices were civil rights that enjoyed constitutional protection. Further, the plurality opinion (jointly written by Justices Sandra Day O'Connor, Anthony M. Kennedy, and David Souter) recognized limits on state power over rights of personal autonomy and bodily integrity, based on the protection of liberty found in the Fourteenth Amendment.

The End of Life

This renewed validation of individual rights did not mean that the role of medical authority in American life would be diminished, however. In the wake of the *Quinlan* and *Cruzan* cases (see Chapter 1), a new debate ensued over the appropriate role of physicians at the end of life.

By the 1990s, modern medicine had prolonged the average lifespan by dramatically reducing the incidence of contagious disease that had plagued the U.S. population for generations. But medical science had also prolonged the process of dying, for if people were safeguarded from epidemics, they were now much more likely to succumb to a chronic illness such as congestive heart failure or cancer. Americans spent an average of eighty days during their last year of life in hospitals or nursing homes. Technology had even blurred the definition of death itself, enabling some parts of the body to continue functioning after others had ceased (Filene 1998, 51–55). Despite the ostensibly objective measures produced by new instruments such as the electroencephalogram, which is used to register brain activity, determining the precise moment of death seemed to become more, not less, subjective. Which organs must stop functioning for a person to be considered dead? Was an individual in a persistent vegetative state alive in any sense beyond a purely medical one? Even further, who would have the authority to determine when a life had ended? Physicians, lawyers, legislators, religious leaders, family members, and patients themselves all claimed decisionmaking authority in the process of dying.

With the Court's affirmation of a right to govern one's body in *Planned Parenthood v. Casey,* new calls for personal autonomy at the end of life began to coalesce in a campaign for what came to be known as the "right to die." Medicine had lengthened the end stages of life without assuaging the physical, psychological, and emotional pain of dying, and many people anticipated their own deaths with a new sense of dread. Many believed that the decision whether to prolong life under unbearable circumstances should remain with patients themselves. Common law tradition held that a patient could not be forced to undergo treatment against his or her will, and as illustrated by the flowering of sectarian medicine in the Jacksonian era, Americans had long believed themselves empowered to refuse the dictates of medical science. Therefore, many people believed that patients retained the right to have treatment stopped, even if it meant their certain death. For others, the right to bodily autonomy extended further to actively taking steps to cause one's own death. Organizations such as the Hemlock Society pursued this claim, and in 1991 the society's founder, Derek Humphrey, published *Final Exit,* which became a national best-seller. But because the modern way of dying often took place in hospitals rather than homes, ending one's life often required the collaboration of medical personnel. Euthanasia remained illegal, however, and physicians and nurses who actively hastened their patients' deaths were prosecuted. Calls for individual self-determination clashed with the state's interest in protecting life, and Americans engaged in a new debate over whether to legalize suicide when performed with the aid of a physician.

California, Oregon, and Washington put the issue to voters in statewide referenda. In 1994 Oregon's referendum passed, making it the first state to legalize physician-assisted suicide, albeit under a narrow set of clearly specified conditions. For example, a doctor could write a prescription for a lethal dose of a drug only if his or her patient was likely to die within six months; also, after receiving such a prescription, a patient must wait fifteen days before having it filled. Then, in 1997 the U.S. Supreme Court ruled that assisted suicide was not a right protected by the Constitution. Chief Justice William Rehnquist's opinion noted that such a claim was contradicted by centuries of common law tradition that banned the taking of one's own life. Further, Rehnquist found ample state interest in protecting the lives of those who might be vulnerable, such as the poor, elderly, and disabled, if the law permitted physicians to hasten their patients' deaths. The chief justice placed doctors among the potentially vulnerable groups, for conceivably they might be put under undue pressure to assist in a suicide in violation of their Hippocratic oath never to do harm.

Legal scholars have pointed out, however, that the concurring opinions in *Washington v. Glucksberg* and *Quill v. Vacco* left considerable room for future challenges, especially if state regulation of medical treatment at the end of life were to become so restrictive as to deny patients their liberty under the Fourteenth Amendment (Urofsky 2000, 901–906). However, some scholars have argued that patients' desires should not be the sole consideration in determining whether the Constitution protects assisted suicide. Despite the image of self-sufficiency conjured up by the phrase "bodily autonomy," the vast majority of people are not truly alone at the time of their deaths; family, friends, dependents, and medical practitioners all may be integral to the process of dying, and proponents of this view argue that these people also have rights. Opponents of assisted suicide note that suicide constituted a felony in Anglo-American law for 700 years and also mention the numerous incursions on bodily autonomy, such as mandatory vaccination of schoolchildren and the giving of blood samples by persons arrested for drunk driving, that the law still permits today (Bleich 1997, 804).

Americans entered the twenty-first century much as they had the twentieth, debating the appropriate boundary between the right to bodily autonomy and society's claims on the human body. As we have seen, it is an ongoing discourse shaped by the history of medicine as well as by the evolution of legal doctrine. Chapter 3 examines in depth cases brought before the U.S. Supreme Court that shaped this story in important ways.

References and Further Reading

Bleich, J. D. 1997. "Physician-Assisted Suicide: Rights and Risks to Vulnerable Communities: Is There a Right to Physician-Assisted Suicide?" *Fordham Urban Law Journal* 24: 795–814.

Curry, Lynne. 1999. *Modern Mothers in the Heartland: Gender, Health, and Progress in Illinois, 1900–1930.* Columbus: Ohio State University Press.

Duffy, John. 1993. *From Humors to Medical Science: A History of American Medicine.* 2d ed. Urbana: University of Illinois Press.

Filene, Peter G. 1998. *In the Arms of Others: A Cultural History of the Right to Die in America.* Chicago: Ivan R. Dee.

Garrow, David J. 1994. *Liberty and Sexuality: The Right to Privacy and the Making of* Roe v. Wade. New York: Maxwell Macmillan International.

Gordon, Linda. 1990. *Woman's Body, Woman's Right: Birth Control in America.* Rev. ed. New York: Penguin Books.

Haller, J. S., Jr. 1981. *American Medicine in Transition, 1840–1910.* Urbana: University of Illinois Press.

Hoy, Suellen. 1995. *Chasing Dirt: The American Pursuit of Cleanliness.* New York: Oxford University Press.

Kevles, Daniel J. 1985. *In the Name of Eugenics: Genetics and the Uses of Human Heredity.* New York: Alfred A. Knopf.

Lombardo, Paul. 1982. "Eugenic Sterilization in Virginia: Aubrey Strode and the Case of *Buck v. Bell.*" Ph.D. diss., University of Virginia.

Nichols, M. G. 1849. "Mrs. Gove's Experience in Water-Cure." *Water-Cure Journal* 7: 40–41, 68–70, 135. Reprinted in J. H. Warner and J. A. Tighe, eds., *Major Problems in the History of American Medicine and Public Health.* Boston: Houghton Mifflin, 2001: 129–130.

Pernick, M. S. 1996. *The Black Stork: Eugenics and the Death of "Defective" Babies in American Medicine and Motion Pictures since 1915.* New York: Oxford University Press.

Reagan, Leslie J. 1997. *When Abortion Was a Crime.* Berkeley: University of California Press.

Rowbotham, S. 1997. *A Century of Women.* New York: Penguin Books.

Shapiro, T. M. 1985. *Population Control Politics: Women, Sterilization, and Reproductive Choice.* Philadelphia: Temple University Press.

Tomes, Nancy. 1998. *The Gospel of Germs.* Cambridge, MA: Harvard University Press.

Urofsky, Melvin I. 2000. "Justifying Assisted Suicide: Comments on the Ongoing Debate." *Notre Dame Journal of Law, Ethics, and Public Policy* 14: 893–936.

Weddington, Sarah. 1992. *A Question of Choice.* New York: Putnam's.

3

Cases

We have already seen how, during the twentieth century, issues in medicine and law developed in tandem. In this chapter, we will explore particular points in this history in more depth, using a series of cases that came before the U.S. Supreme Court as "snapshots" for understanding these developments. Although each case arose from a specific set of circumstances and affected the lives of unique individuals, the cases also reflect larger questions about the individual's right to control his or her own body and the state's authority to place restrictions on that right. Although expressed in differing modes, the key questions underlying each case are: What is the individual's liberty interest? What is the state's interest in curtailing that liberty? Where did the Court draw the line between the two?

Compulsory Vaccination:
Private Rights versus Police Powers

Jacobson v. Massachusetts (1905)

In the summer of 1902, local health authorities in Cambridge, Massachusetts, arrested the Reverend Henning Jacobson, pastor of the Swedish Lutheran Church, because he refused to be vaccinated against smallpox. Earlier that year, the Cambridge Board of Health had ordered the procedure for all the city's residents over the age of twenty-one who had not been vaccinated or revaccinated in the previous five years. Massachusetts law allowed local authorities to compel vaccination when the health and safety of the public was at risk from the presence of contagious disease. The Cambridge controversy arose at a time when a major smallpox epidemic had been ravaging the Boston and Cambridge areas for over six months. The local criminal court found Reverend Jacobson, along with two other Cambridge citizens who refused to be vaccinated, guilty of violating the ordinance and ordered them to pay a fine of five dollars each (197 U.S. 11 1905).

Reverend Jacobson appealed to the Supreme Judicial Court of Massachusetts the following year, but the higher court upheld his criminal conviction, saying that the Massachusetts statute allowing local authorities to compel residents to be vaccinated fell within the reasonable exercise of the state's "police powers" (see Chapter 1). But, the court went on to say, statutes relying on police powers may not unduly invade personal rights to liberty or property without a clear benefit to the general welfare. Further, the court affirmed that any statute infringing on personal rights must confer a demonstrable benefit to the public. Although they lost their case, attorneys representing Reverend Jacobson saw an opening here: A stronger case must be made that the Massachusetts compulsory vaccination statute did, indeed, unduly infringe on personal liberty without clearly benefiting the people of Cambridge. In June 1903, Reverend Jacobson's attorneys filed another appeal, this time to the U.S. Supreme Court (*Transcripts* 1903, 15–19).

Jacobson v. Massachusetts was argued before the nation's highest court in the October term of 1904. Counsel for Jacobson claimed that the Massachusetts statute enabling local authorities in Cambridge to compel their client to be vaccinated or to face fine or imprisonment violated the Fourteenth Amendment's guarantee that no state may deprive any person of life, liberty, or property without due process of law. They did not deny the well-established legal principle that police powers allowed the state to take action when measures were necessary to protect public health and safety, asserting that if Jacobson's body or his property were diseased, or if their client were to commit any "noxious act" that threatened the community's physical well-being, then such action certainly would be permissible. But neither the Reverend Jacobson's person nor his property had been infected with any contagious disease, they argued, and therefore the state's police powers could not be brought to bear on their client without violating his constitutionally protected liberty. He had gone about the community "healthy and law-abiding" and thus had been doing no injury to the community or the state at the time of his arrest. "This court has not yet decided," they declared, "that the police power can be imposed upon healthy citizens, merely because they have the potentiality of contracting contagious disease. . . . There is no such offense known to the law as neglect or refusal to protect one's self from disease. It is not a nuisance for the plaintiff to remain healthy." To force him to undergo a risky medical procedure without establishing that he posed a discernible threat to the community amounted to a violation of Jacobson's bodily integrity (197 U.S. 11).

Jacobson's counsel also argued that the Massachusetts statute violated the Fourteenth Amendment's guarantee of the equal protection of the law to all citizens because it excepted children, who were deemed unfit subjects for vaccination by a physician. Although an adult, Jacobson believed that he also should be considered an unfit subject because he had previously undergone the vaccination and it had made him sick. Although he had no physician's certification to this effect, nevertheless he had been improperly prevented from providing evidence that would have supported the plausibility of his claim in the lower courts. Finally, lawyers for Jacobson presented a more general charge that a government founded for the purpose of promoting the general welfare and securing the blessings of liberty should not force its citizens to be injected with a virus against their will. Compulsory vaccination was, they claimed, "unreasonable, arbitrary, and oppressive, and therefore, hostile to the inherent right of every freeman to care for his own body and health in such a way as to him seems best." Indeed, the execution of a law that subjected Reverend Jacobson to fine and imprisonment for refusing to submit to vaccination represented "nothing short of an assault upon his person" (197 U.S. 11). To permit such a law, they insisted, violated the very spirit of the U.S. Constitution.

In a seven-to-two decision, the Supreme Court disagreed with Reverend Jacobson and allowed the Massachusetts compulsory vaccination statute to stand. A state's police powers, Justice John Marshall Harlan reasoned, embrace "reasonable regulations established by legislative enactment as will protect the public health and the public safety." He acknowledged that these regulations may not expressly invade individual rights secured in the U.S. Constitution. Jacobson, however, had not demonstrated that the Massachusetts compulsory vaccination statute stood in violation of any recognized constitutional right. The liberty he claimed to be invaded by the state—that of an individual to care for his body in the way he believed to be best—was not a liberty recognized by the Constitution at all, the Court maintained. "Real liberty for all could not exist under the operation of a principle which recognizes the right of each individual person to use his own [liberty], whether in respect to his person or his property, regardless of the injury that may be done to others. This court has more than once recognized it as a fundamental principle," Harlan continued, "that 'persons and property are subjected to all kinds of restraints and burdens in order to secure the general comfort, health, and prosperity of the state'" (197 U.S. 11). The "restraint and burden" in Jacobson's case was the obligation to submit to vaccination or, alternatively, to pay a fine or go to jail. In the Court's view, this demand was not unreasonable when the health and safety of the wider community were at stake. An epidemic of a life-threatening disease had been raging in the area at the time the statute was enforced, and thus the state not only had the power but even the duty to employ any available medical weapons against its further spread. Thus the Court affirmed the state's power to protect the public during an obvious public health emergency, even if it meant the curtailing of some civil liberties.

Zucht v. King (1922)

Seemingly, then, the Court had put to rest the question of how to determine the boundary between individual bodily autonomy and state authority to regulate the body. But, as we saw in Chapters 1 and 2, the law does not function in a vacuum, and from this point early in the twentieth century, both medical science and legal doctrine continued to evolve. A second challenge to compulsory vaccination laws came before the U.S. Supreme Court in 1922.

In this case, a citizen of San Antonio, Texas, challenged a city ordinance mandating smallpox vaccination for all public schoolchildren. Fifteen-year-old Rosalyn Zucht had been expelled from Breckinridge High School for remaining unvaccinated. Rosalyn did not wish to be vaccinated, nor were her parents willing to allow her to undergo the procedure because they feared it would endanger her health and life. Her father filed suit for $10,000 in damages against the school board, high school principal, city sanitary commissioner, and city physician, charging that these authorities' actions amounted to "wrongful, willful, and malicious conduct" resulting in an injury to Rosalyn's standing in the community. After losing his case, A. D. Zucht petitioned the Texas Supreme Court, claiming that since its enactment thirteen years previously, the San Antonio ordinance had never been enforced until his daughter's recent expulsion; thus his daughter's right to a public education in Texas had been violated, and she had been the victim of discriminatory enforcement of the ordinance. Zucht contended that the authorities' actions in expelling Rosalyn from school had been taken without justifiable reason since smallpox had not been present in San Antonio for ten years, nor had a single case of the disease ever been recorded in the district where the Zuchts resided. The city's public school buildings and grounds were continuously maintained in a "thoroughly sanitary manner," and therefore, the petitioner claimed, his daughter's unvaccinated body could pose no discernible threat to the community's well-being. Indeed, he continued, there was much more danger of disease contagion in locations other than the city's public schools, such as streetcars, theaters, and churches, especially in the city's Mexican Quarter, an area of approximately 20,000 inhabitants where people crowded the sidewalks, public parks, and swimming pools "daily and nightly in close personal contact, frequently amounting to jams." Further, San Antonio's compulsory vaccination ordinance had not been intended as a temporary measure but instead "purports to be in force and is intended to be in force all the time whether or not there is a single case of smallpox in said city, in said county or even within the State." Thus the city's requirement that she be vaccinated in order to attend public school represented an unreasonable infringement on Rosalyn Zucht's rights and violated the Fourteenth Amendment's guarantee that she receive equal protection under the law (260 U.S. 174).

The appellees, however, insisted that their actions did represent a legitimate exercise of the police power conferred on them by the state of Texas. Children, they contended, have "less resisting power to the ravages of the disease of smallpox" than adults do and thus requiring public school pupils to be vaccinated was justifiable. Even if smallpox was not actually present in the city at the time of Rosalyn Zucht's expulsion, the threat that it could enter the community at any time remained ongoing. San Antonio was "crowded with transients and strangers" who entered the vicinity from all parts of the nation but especially from Mexico, where smallpox "has been prevalent more or less at all times in the past and will continue in the future." Residents of the city's Mexican Quarter, they claimed, were very secretive about the presence of contagious disease, especially smallpox, among them and always attempted to hide any cases that appeared in their homes and neighborhoods. But the true danger to the public's well-being arose when these residents "permit the inmates of their houses to associate with other people, and permit their children to attend schools even when they have smallpox in the house or in the family." Thus, even in the absence of an actual outbreak, the *perceived threat* of smallpox remained ever-present in San Antonio, requiring that authorities act with "utmost vigilance and precaution to properly protect the health of its inhabitants." Compulsory vaccination was the best weapon available to city officials in their ongoing battle against smallpox contagion (260 U.S. 174).

The two parties to the case disagreed, not over local authorities' obligations to protect the community's health and safety, but rather over whether the unvaccinated body of Rosalyn Zucht posed a discernible threat requiring state action. A. D. Zucht believed that his daughter, raised in a neighborhood where the disease had never been present and currently enjoying a state of perfect health, did not represent a risk to others' well-being by attending school. The mere fact that his child had been singled out for expulsion for remaining unvaccinated had been construed as a derogation of her (and her parents') reputation in the community as well as a violation of her rights. The real threat to the community's health, the plaintiff's brief charged, was coming from the Mexican Quarter, where the inhabitants regularly engaged in unhealthy behaviors. Thus, his argument implied, the prophylactic of mandatory vaccination may be suitable for others, but not for his daughter. Interestingly, the defendants agreed with Zucht that the residents of San Antonio's Mexican Quarter posed a risk to the city's residents at large. In their construction, however, this risk was substantial enough to justify the compulsory vaccination of all public schoolchildren. The quarter's residents not only lived in less hygienic conditions, they argued, but they were also untrustworthy, uncooperative, and irresponsible; it was always possible that contagious disease could insinuate its way into the wider community's public schools. Although no smallpox was known to be present in San Antonio, the mere fact that people of such habits and disposition resided within its boundaries meant that danger always lurked just beneath the surface, and authorities must remain on the alert for an incipient outbreak at any time.

A. D. Zucht once again lost his case, and his subsequent appeal came before the U.S. Supreme Court in 1922. There Justice Louis Brandeis declined the high court's jurisdiction in the case on the basis that the San Antonio statute had been valid at the time Rosalyn was expelled from school and, further, that her father's petition had not presented a constitutional question of sufficient merit to warrant consideration by the Court. The question of whether or not compulsory vaccination violated individual civil liberties simply was no longer an issue for the justices in 1922. "Long before this suit was instituted," Brandeis wrote, "*Jacobson v. Massachusetts* had settled that it is within the police power of a State to provide for compulsory vaccination." From this founding precedent set in 1905, Brandeis continued, a long line of judicial decisions had established that "in the exercise of the police power reasonable classification may be freely applied" without violating the Fourteenth Amendment's guarantee of equal protection. Thus, the San Antonio ordinances conferred "not arbitrary power, but only that broad discretion required for the protection of public health." Brandeis's opinion suggested that, although it was possible to demarcate the limit of state power over the human body, the San Antonio vaccination ordinance did not cross the line (260 U.S. 174). The utilization of police power was justifiable because smallpox, although not actually present in the immediate vicinity, could be assumed to remain a potential hazard. The Court apparently accepted as reasonable officials' arguments that smallpox was *probably* already present in the Mexican Quarter, and if it were to become present in the future, residents there would be *likely* to act in an irresponsible manner and therefore threaten to spread contagion to the remainder of the community. The risk in San Antonio, therefore, came not so much from smallpox itself as from the residents of that city's Mexican Quarter. In that much, at least, all parties to the case appeared to be in agreement.

Although Justice Brandeis did not address the question of exactly how a state might determine that a particular individual or group posed a *potential* threat to public health and safety, he did affirm the power of the state to make "reasonable classification" among persons so perceived.

Mandatory Sterilization: Eugenics on Trial

Buck v. Bell (1927)

Five years later, the Supreme Court addressed the issue more bluntly. Carrie Buck was an eighteen-year-old Virginia resident who, in October 1927, was taken to a state institution where she was sterilized without her consent. Under Virginia law, Buck had been deemed in official proceedings to be the "probable potential parent of socially inadequate offspring" and had been ordered to undergo a salpingectomy, or the cutting and tying of the fallopian tubes to prevent conception. The leaders behind the Virginia law were state senator Aubrey Strode, a prominent politician with a strong reputation as a social reformer, and his close friend Albert Priddy, superintendent of the Virginia Colony for the Epileptic and Feeble-Minded, the institution in which Buck's sterilization took place. Anxious to ensure that the sterilization statute would hold up in court (Priddy had experienced legal difficulties after performing the operation on a married woman at the institution, when her husband had sued him for damages), Strode appealed the order to the Circuit Court of Amherst County, which, as he had hoped, upheld the sterilization order issued in Carrie Buck's case as legitimate.

As noted in Chapter 2, eugenicists argued that genetic deterioration had reached crisis proportions in the United States. In their view, the massive influx of eastern and southern European immigrants bearing criminal and imbecilic tendencies, the substantial proportion of the native-born population that was nonwhite (and thus self-evidently genetically contaminated), and the propensity of degenerates of various stripes to multiply at higher rates than their more desirable fellow citizens had all come together to create a national epidemic more insidious and more threatening to the public's well-being than any contagious disease. As early as 1880, Dr. Isaac Kerlin, at that time the nation's most respected physician in the field of mental retardation, had calculated that between 1870 and 1880, while the general population had increased by 30 percent, the increase in idiocy among Americans had skyrocketed a shocking 200 percent. To combat this alarming turn of events, in 1914 Harry Laughlin of the Eugenics Record Office of the Carnegie Institute of Washington, D.C., authored a study delineating "cacogenic," or undesirable, genetic traits and proposing measures to prevent their dissemination among the U.S. population. Laughlin's report included a model eugenic sterilization law that would establish in every state a special eugenics commission empowered by the legislature to order surgical sterilization for any patient in the state's custody whom the commission regarded as a potential threat to the gene pool. The Laughlin model became the template for the Virginia law that enabled the state to sterilize Carrie Buck (Lombardo 1982, 156–164).

It was within this context that Aubrey Strode defended Virginia's actions before the Circuit Court of Amherst County. He called neighbors and others who had come in contact with the family over the years to testify that Carrie Buck's mother had been slovenly, irresponsible, and sexually promiscuous, Carrie's brother had been "peculiar," and Carrie's illegitimate daughter, eight months old at the time of the trial, had a "look about it [sic] that is not quite normal." Although Carrie Buck herself was described as being capable of working constructively under supervision, a social worker asserted that the fact of her illegitimate pregnancy was strong evidence of Buck's feeblemindedness since "a feeble-minded girl is much more likely to go wrong." Having established in this manner that the Buck family fit the criteria for feeblemindedness, Strode brought in several expert witnesses to attest to the various classifications of mental defectiveness, the inheritability of feeblemindedness under the laws of genetics, and the benefits of sterilization to the individuals themselves as well as to society as a whole. Dr. J. S. De Jarnette, superintendent of Virginia's Western State Hospital, referred to the famous nineteenth-century studies of the Juke and Kallikak families that purported to demonstrate that mental disabilities were passed down to offspring in a virtually exponential manner. He also told the court that sterilization benefited society by allowing institutionalized inmates to return to the community, thereby making room for others of their kind, undoubtedly a vital concern for states' fiscal health if feeblemindedness were indeed reaching epidemic dimensions. Strode's next expert witness was Arthur Estabrook of the Carnegie Institute and the author of a 1915 follow-up study of the Jukes. Estabrook answered questions regarding the various classifications of mental defectives and assured the court that after examining both Carrie Buck and her mother, he could say with authority that they fit the criteria for feeblemindedness. Strode then read a deposition from Harry Laughlin, author of the model sterilization law, who pronounced them a clear case of genetically inherited mental incompetence, even though he had never actually seen any member of the Buck family. Irving Whitehead, Carrie Buck's attorney and a close friend of Aubrey Strode, called no expert witnesses of his own to counter the expert testimony of the eugenicists, nor did he call on personal acquaintances of Carrie Buck to testify that she was not mentally defective. After losing the case in the Circuit Court of Amherst County, Whitehead appealed to the Virginia Court of Appeals, which found the Virginia law a valid application of the state's police powers to protect public health and safety. Mindful of the need to close any constitutional loopholes not yet raised in the case, Strode himself orchestrated Carrie Buck's appeal to the U.S. Supreme Court (Lombardo 1982, 184–215).

The case of *Buck v. Bell* (Bell had become the superintendent of the Virginia Colony after Priddy's sudden death) was heard by the nation's high court in its October 1926 term. Seeming to borrow a page from the those opposing vaccination twenty years earlier, Irving Whitehead stressed that any intrusion by the state into the personal prerogatives of childbearing represented a violation of the Fourteenth Amendment, which protected the individual's "full bodily integrity." He told the Court that if such an intrusion were allowed, American citizens would be faced with a tyrannical "reign of doctors." Even more menacing, Whitehead continued, was the specter of a state holding unlimited power to "rid itself of those citizens deemed undesirable." Defending the Virginia statute once again was Aubrey Strode. Strode's argument rested on the precedent set by the Court in *Jacobson v. Massachusetts.* In each case, he insisted, the fundamental principle was the same: the state must be allowed broad authority to exercise its police powers whenever the safety and security of the public was at stake (Lombardo 1982, 215–220).

The legal viability of the Virginia compulsory sterilization statute, then, required that the Supreme Court accept as valid two medical arguments enjoying a great deal of popularity at the time: first, that the epidemic of feeblemindedness in the United States meant that the possible propagation of Carrie Buck's genes represented a clear threat to public well-being; and second, that sterilization was a safe and effective means of providing the necessary safeguards.

The cause of eugenic sterilization had an avid supporter in Justice Oliver Wendell Holmes, Jr., whose opinion in *Buck v. Bell* remains among the most striking—and controversial—in the Supreme Court's history. A eugenics enthusiast and a defender of social experimentation through legislation, Holmes's opinion in support of the Virginia sterilization law granted the eugenic movement a crucial aura of legitimacy at a time when its basic premises were coming under fire from many social scientists, physicians, and geneticists.

But Holmes chose not to consider any competing ideas regarding eugenics when he unequivocally pronounced that "the principle that sustains compulsory vaccination is broad enough to cover cutting the fallopian tubes. Three generations of imbeciles are enough." In fact, as Mary L. Dudziak has observed, Holmes's rhetoric in *Buck v. Bell* assumes that the facts as presented by Aubrey Strode defied contradiction (Dudziak 1986, 833–867). Carrie Buck's sterilization orders had been given in full compliance with Virginia law, Holmes stated, and her case had been duly reviewed by that state's courts. Ignoring the question of whether Carrie Buck's rights had been protected when her attorney failed to present evidence refuting either eugenic theory or her own diagnosis, Holmes categorically declared that "there can be no doubt that so far as procedure is concerned the rights of the patient are most carefully considered . . . there is no doubt that in that respect the plaintiff in error has had due process of law." Further, Holmes accepted as an established medical truth that the nation was threatened by an epidemic of mental incompetence and thus it was necessary to sustain the state's power to protect the public welfare by sterilizing the feebleminded. Drawing an analogy to those who gave their lives for the public good when called upon to defend the nation militarily, Holmes asserted that it would be "strange if [we] could not call upon those who already sap the strength of the State for these lesser sacrifices . . . in order to prevent our being swamped with incompetence" (275 U.S. 200).

Given this blessing by the U.S. Supreme Court, the state of Virginia went on to sterilize about 8,000 individuals between 1927 and 1972; the national figure would stand at more than 60,000. In 1974, the Virginia legislature repealed the compulsory sterilization law; *Buck v. Bell*, however, has never been overturned (Lombardo 1982, 1–2; 252–256).

In sanctioning the medical wisdom held by eugenic experts and then using eugenic theory as the basis for allowing the expansion of the state's authority over the human body, *Buck v. Bell* seems to be a manifestation of the antivaccination movement's worst nightmare come true. In less than twenty-five years, the border demarcating individual bodily autonomy and social claims on the human body had moved subtly but decidedly, and the conditions under which the state could legitimately exercise its power of regulation expanded as medical authority to define threats to the public's health and safety grew. Through the development of legal doctrine, the police powers awarded to health officials extended from compelling vaccination when contagious disease threatened the immediate community, to requiring the procedure when no disease was present in the community but a speculative threat emanated from particular members of the community, to enforcing sexual sterilization to contain a theoretically predicted threat to the nation's future health.

Skinner v. Oklahoma (1942)

Taking action on the eugenic theory, in 1935 Oklahoma enacted a statute requiring the sterilization of "habitual criminals," a class of offenders whom the state defined as persons convicted two or more times of "felonies involving moral turpitude." Although the law did not include a precise definition of "moral turpitude," it did expressly exempt "offenses arising out of the violation of the prohibitory laws, revenue acts, embezzlement or political offenses." The statute also created the process by which an individual would receive a jury trial for determining whether he or she was guilty of being a "habitual criminal," as well as whether the defendant might "be rendered sexually sterile without detriment to his or her general health." Those whom the jury determined to fit these criteria would be sterilized, using the prescribed procedures of vasectomy for males and salpingectomy for females (316 U.S. 535).

At the time the law was enacted, Jack Skinner was serving time in an Oklahoma prison for committing robbery with firearms, his third incarceration and second felony conviction. Skinner had been imprisoned in 1926 for stealing chickens and then again in 1929 for robbery with firearms. In 1936 the state's attorney general instituted proceedings for having Skinner declared a habitual criminal. At his trial, the judge instructed the jury that the crimes for which Skinner had been convicted did in fact fit the category of felonies involving moral turpitude, so the only question now before them was whether he could be sterilized without harm to his health. The jury determined that Skinner could be safely sterilized, and the court ordered him to receive a vasectomy, an order upheld by the Supreme Court of Oklahoma (316 U.S. 535).

Skinner argued before the U.S. Supreme Court that the Oklahoma law violated his rights on several constitutional grounds. First, the proceedings had provided no opportunity for the defendant to present his own evidence as to whether or not he was likely to produce socially undesirable offspring and thus represented a violation of due process of law under the Fourteenth Amendment. Second, Skinner argued that the sterilization order constituted cruel and unusual punishment, also in violation of the Fourteenth Amendment's prohibition against violations of civil liberties by the individual states. Finally, counsel for Skinner claimed that because the mandatory sterilization statute excluded certain crimes, it amounted to a violation of the Fourteenth Amendment's guarantee of equal protection under the laws.

It was the last argument that inspired comment from Justice William O. Douglas in his majority opinion declaring the Oklahoma statute unconstitutional. Douglas determined that the Oklahoma law did in fact infringe on the equal protection clause: "Sterilization of those who have thrice committed grand larceny, with immunity for those who are embezzlers is a clear, pointed, unmistakable discrimination," the justice wrote. "Oklahoma makes no attempt to say that he who commits larceny by trespass or trick or fraud has biologically inheritable traits which he who commits embezzlement lacks" (316 U.S. 535). The real problem, according to Douglas, lay in the seemingly arbitrary lines the Oklahoma legislature had drawn when distinguishing precisely which criminal conduct required the sterilization of the offender. Legal distinctions among "larceny," "fraud," and "embezzlement" were based on the point in time at which the offender intended to take property for his or her own use, classifications not rooted in any eugenic concept of criminal tendency. Although the criminal penalties for larceny and embezzlement were identical in Oklahoma, only the former warranted sterilizing the offender.

In a concurring opinion, Chief Justice Harlan F. Stone addressed a different constitutional dimension of Skinner's case. Stone commented that, if indeed it could be scientifically determined that Skinner's particular criminal tendencies could be passed to his potential offspring, the Oklahoma law need not pass any requirement that sterilization orders must be applied equally to all classes of criminals. Instead, Justice Stone expressed concern that because Skinner had not been allowed to present evidence that his own criminal tendencies did not belong in this class, the law had failed to protect his right to due process. (Interestingly, although Henning Jacobson had also been denied the opportunity to present evidence that the smallpox vaccination would make him sick, the *Skinner* opinion made no such comparison to *Jacobson v. Massachusetts*.) Instead, Stone contrasted Skinner's case with that of Carrie Buck, whose sterilization had come after an "appropriate inquiry" in which the court had determined her "socially injurious tendencies" (316 U.S. 535). In other words, although the proceedings in Buck's case had focused on the potential threat to the general welfare posed by Carrie Buck's individual body, taking her family history into account, Skinner's trial had merely determined that his actions placed him in a *class* of physical types that presented such a threat, without reference to his own genetic make-up.

In a separate concurring opinion, Justice Robert H. Jackson cautioned that, although not at issue here, at some future time the Court may be required to determine whether state eugenic laws exceeded the limits to which a "legislatively represented majority may conduct biological experiments at the expense of the dignity and personality and natural powers of a minority." Like Stone, Jackson contrasted Skinner's case with that of Carrie Buck, who was undeniably "an imbecile, a person with definite and observable characteristics, where the condition had persisted through three generations and afforded grounds for the belief that it was transmissible and would continue to manifest itself in generations to come" (316 U.S. 535). Thus although Justice Jackson acknowledged the dilemma of determining the boundaries between bodily autonomy and society's compelling interest in regulating the human body, he followed his colleagues in this and previous courts in accepting prevailing medical wisdom that feeblemindedness constituted an "inheritable disease" and as such posed a potential threat to community well-being.

Yet in another sense, Justice Douglas's opinion in *Skinner v. Oklahoma* also stands as a signpost in the development of twentieth-century legal doctrine concerning bodily autonomy. For the first time, the nation's highest court determined that procreation represented a core civil right granted to U.S. citizens. Surgical sterilization represented a gravely serious undertaking by the state, one that dramatically (and at the time, irreversibly) altered a fundamental physiological function of the human body. Although the Court allowed that the authority to sterilize its citizens fell within the reach of the state's police powers, its very seriousness required "strict scrutiny" by the Court in order to guard citizens from the potential harm that might result should such a power fall into "evil or reckless hands." The Oklahoma sterilization law, Justice Douglas asserted, concerned "one of the basic civil rights of man. Marriage and procreation are fundamental to the very existence and survival of the race." By constructing the ruling in this way, the Court in effect recognized a special zone of protection around the human body. A state law must now meet a higher standard (the Court's "strict scrutiny") demonstrating a compelling interest in protecting the public's health and safety in order to disregard the zone.

Contraception, Abortion, and the Right to Die: Privacy on Trial

Griswold v. Connecticut (1965)

More than twenty years later, Justice William O. Douglas again examined the boundaries between bodily autonomy and the legal regulation of the body, when the U.S. Supreme Court reviewed a Connecticut statute that prohibited the use of contraceptives by married couples. Enacted in 1879, the law was rooted in the theory that a state's police powers were broad enough to allow legislation designed to protect the moral purity of the population as well as its physical health and safety. The use of contraceptives, the Connecticut legislature had reasoned, separated sexual relations from procreation, thereby removing a powerful disincentive for engaging in sex in a casual or promiscuous manner. Late-nineteenth-century prohibitions on birth control had been part of a nationwide "vice control" campaign, in which state authorities had also outlawed prostitution and abortion in an attempt to introduce civic order into cities experiencing the tumult of expanding populations and the attendant social problems caused by rapid industrialization. By the second decade of the twentieth century, a small but tenacious movement to repeal laws prohibiting the use of contraceptives and the dissemination of birth control information argued that such restrictions constituted a denial of individual liberty, including the right to free speech (see Chapter 2). In 1942 the Birth Control Federation of America became the Planned Parenthood Federation of America, which began to promote birth control in support of families and healthy sexuality within marriage, rather than stressing sexuality as individual liberty. Married couples' freedom to decide the size of their "ideal" families gathered a great deal of public support during the 1950s. (In the "baby boom" decades, the ideal was four children.) The number of birth control clinics nationwide grew rapidly, and more than 80 percent of married white women of childbearing age were estimated to be using some form of contraception (May 2000, 512–513). In 1960, the federal Food and Drug Administration approved oral contraceptives, thereafter popularly known as "the pill." Although it promised to revolutionize Americans' beliefs and practices regarding sexuality and procreation, the pill still required prescription by a licensed health care practitioner. Despite prohibitions on the use of birth control in many states, individuals either using or dispensing contraceptives were rarely prosecuted for violating such statutes.

In Connecticut, the state's Planned Parenthood organization sought to have the 1879 law overturned. Estelle Griswold, the executive director of the Planned Parenthood League of Connecticut, along with the league's medical director, Dr. Thomas Buxton, were convicted as accessories to a crime by giving birth control information to a married woman at a New Haven clinic that had operated for ten days in November 1961. Under the Connecticut law, "any person who assists, abets, counsels, causes, hires or commands another to commit any offense may be prosecuted and punished as if he were the principal offender." Griswold and Buxton asserted that they had been found guilty of acting as accessories to a crime under a law that was unconstitutional to begin with. They alleged the Connecticut statute violated the Fourteenth Amendment's guarantee that states could not infringe upon citizens' rights to life, liberty, and property without due process of law. In 1965 the Supreme Court accepted their claim that they had standing to challenge the law on behalf of the married couples liable to prosecution under it because of the professional relationship between staff and clients at the clinic. The Court went on to rule the Connecticut law unconstitutional. But the import of the justices' decision in *Griswold v. Connecticut* went far beyond striking down a state law that was nearly 100 years old and rarely enforced. Justice Douglas framed the seven-to-two majority opinion in terms of a constitutional right to privacy, an entitlement of citizenship never actually enumerated in the Constitution itself.

How, then, could the Court determine the existence of such a right? For Douglas, the crucial idea was that the rights listed in the

Constitution necessarily require the existence of other, unlisted, ones that give them full meaning. Douglas took the First Amendment's protection of citizens' right to assemble peaceably as one case in point. More than merely the right to attend a meeting, the justice argued, this right "includes the right to express one's attitudes or philosophies by membership in a group or by affiliation with it or by other lawful means. Association in that context," he continued, "is a form of expression of opinion, and while it is not expressly included in the First Amendment, its existence is necessary in making the express guarantees fully meaningful." Douglas then cited other examples, such as parents' right to educate their children in a parochial school (*Pierce v. Society of Sisters,* 1925) and the right to read (*Martin v. Struthers,* 1943), that, even though not specifically mentioned in the Constitution itself, nevertheless make up the essence of what the right of free speech is meant to safeguard. In an unusual turn of phrase, Douglas wrote that such cases "suggest that specific guarantees in the Bill of Rights have penumbras, formed by emanations from those guarantees that help give them life and substance" (381 U.S. 479). The metaphor evoked an image of a gray area that surrounds a source of light and stands between the light and the outer darkness; a solar eclipse, for example, produces this phenomenon. It was within this partially illuminated area, then, that certain rights could be said to exist. And it was within this penumbra that Justice Douglas located a constitutional right to privacy.

In this case, the source of light consisted of a number of enumerated rights. The Third Amendment, for example, guarantees that Americans would not be required to quarter troops in their homes, and the Fourth Amendment affirms the right of citizens to be secure in their homes against "unreasonable searches and seizures" by the police. Even the Fifth Amendment's protection from self-incrimination, according to Douglas, contributed to the "zone of privacy" that the Constitution had constructed around the individual. But, although common law tradition had long held that private property merits special protection against governmental intrusion, the *Griswold* opinion recast the concept of privacy in terms of the *personal* rights belonging to individuals. The Connecticut anti–birth control statute dealt with "a right of privacy older than the Bill of Rights," Douglas declared. "Would we allow the police to search the sacred precincts of marital bedrooms for telltale signs of the use of contraceptives? The very idea is repulsive to the notions of privacy surrounding the marriage relationship" (381 U.S. 479). *Griswold's* assertion of a constitutional "right to privacy" was founded on the premise that the state of matrimony entitled couples to decide, free from intrusion by the state, whether sexual relations would result in reproduction. But such a privilege, like the right to procreate asserted in *Skinner v. Oklahoma,* also represented a fundamental right, and thus any action by government to encroach upon it required a higher standard of justification. Connecticut's purpose in prohibiting married couples from using birth control—guarding the community against vice—did not pass the "strict scrutiny" of the Court in the mid-1960s.

In a concurring opinion, Justice John M. Harlan suggested an even more sweeping notion of privacy rights. Harlan asserted that the due process clause of the Fourteenth Amendment alone protected citizens from government encroachment on their personal privacy. That amendment's guarantee that no state may infringe upon the individual's rights to life, liberty, and property without due process of law, Harlan claimed, represented all that was required to uphold the notion that the Constitution protects personal privacy. In Harlan's alternative rendering of the argument, privacy became a liberty interest belonging to all individuals rather than a special privilege of married couples. It is important to note the majority opinion in *Griswold v. Connecticut* would serve as a founding precedent for the expansion of personal autonomy rights over the next decade. Seven year later, for example, the Court found unconstitutional a Massachusetts statute making it a crime to "sell, lend, or give away any contraceptive drug, medicine, instrument, or article," unless it was to married persons by physicians and pharmacists. Writing for the majority opinion in *Eisenstadt v. Baird,* Justice William Brennan refuted Massachusetts's claim that its police powers gave it the authority to enact such legislation as a health measure, as a deterrent to fornication, or simply as a way to prevent the use of birth control. For Justice Brennan, the state had not proven a compelling interest in these matters, and thus the privacy rights they infringed must be protected. Further, according to the justice, the Massachusetts law treated married and unmarried persons unequally, and thus it also represented a violation of the Fourteenth Amendment's guarantee of equal protection under the law (405 U.S. 438).

The full emergence of a constitutional right of privacy then sprang from the intersection of legal and medical developments in the mid–twentieth century. Medical authority regarding the safety and efficacy of new contraceptives engendered a rethinking of Americans' constitutional rights to make decisions regarding whether and how to use birth control. Although in immediate terms, the *Griswold* decision threw out state laws that largely had laid dormant for years, the implications of this landmark opinion for the notion of bodily autonomy were much more profound. What other freedoms did citizens have regarding the choices they made concerning their own bodies? Critics of the decision feared that Justice Douglas's "penumbras" conceivably could be stretched to encompass the protection of nearly any and every physical behavior Americans chose to engage in. For these critics, the line between bodily autonomy and the authority of the state to regulate the human body had been drawn too far to the left.

Roe v. Wade (1973)

The most well-known—and controversial—of the post-*Griswold* personal autonomy decisions is the Court's opinion upholding a woman's right to terminate a pregnancy by abortion. Like prohibitions on birth control, laws barring the practice of abortion dated back to the nineteenth-century crusade against urban "vice." Laws criminalizing abortion were aimed primarily at driving out those who performed the procedure outside their regular medical practice and had the backing of physicians eager to distinguish their own medical services from those of their competitors, especially midwives. Women continued to seek abortions, however, frequently under circumstances that posed risks to their health or even their lives, since underground abortion practices were not subject to the same health and safety regulations governing other medical procedures. Wealthy women could escape these risks by seeking abortions outside the United States. In the late 1960s, access to abortion services became a rallying cry for a second-wave feminist movement that linked women's bodily autonomy to the realization of their equal rights under the law. A number of state legislatures enacted reforms to their century-old prohibitions, and in 1970 New York, along with Hawaii and Alaska, legalized abortion. Surveys demonstrated that thousands of women traveled to New York from throughout the country to have the operation performed. Meanwhile, many social and religious conservatives vociferously protested the growing social acceptance of abortion.

The challenge to remaining statutes prohibiting abortion came from Texas, where two lawyers, Linda Coffee and Sarah Weddington, had been working with a group of women's rights activists eager to see their state's law overturned. Coffee and Weddington filed two lawsuits, one on behalf of an impoverished single woman experiencing her third pregnancy, and one on behalf of a married couple. Pseudonyms were used to protect the litigants from media publicity. As events would show, it was a precaution much needed.

At the heart of what would become one of the most important cases ever to come before the Supreme Court was a woman who had faced her share of hardship. Norma McCorvey ("Jane Roe" revealed her own identity in 1984) had spent much of her early life in reform school and had become pregnant within weeks of her marriage at the age of sixteen. Fleeing her abusive husband, McCorvey gave birth to a daughter, who was given into the legal custody of McCorvey's mother. Several years later, McCorvey surrendered a second daughter to the custody of the baby's father, whom McCorvey had not married. Two years later, McCorvey was working in a traveling circus, when she discovered she was pregnant for a third time. She sought an abortion but was told that the practice was illegal in the state of Texas. McCorvey's case came to the attention of Coffee and Weddington through a lawyer who was arranging for the adoption of her unborn child. The lawyers met with McCorvey, and she agreed to serve as their plaintiff challenging the constitutionality of the Texas law on behalf of all pregnant women who wanted access to abortion in the state. A married couple also agreed to sue the state on the grounds that antiabortion laws would interfere with their right of marital privacy, should they wish to consider obtaining an abortion at some future date (Irons 1999, 430–432).

The Texas Supreme Court ruled that the married couple did not have standing to sue on behalf of all married couples in Texas, but Jane Roe's challenge was allowed to go before the U.S. Supreme Court. In Washington, D.C., the Texas case was tied to a nearly identical challenge coming from Georgia, *Doe v. Bolton*. (The *Doe* case involved statutory restrictions that Georgia placed on the practice of abortion in that state. For instance, the law required that abortions be performed in hospitals rather than clinics and that patients be residents of Georgia.) Oral arguments in *Roe v. Wade* were presented in December 1971 amid difficult circumstances. Justices Hugo Black and John Harlan had recently died, and their successors had not yet been seated. The seven justices remaining on the bench were painfully aware of the import of their decision in this landmark case, as well as the absolute necessity of clarifying the constitutional issues within the swirl of social and political controversy surrounding the subject of abortion. Adding to the difficulty, both sides stumbled in their oral arguments before the Court, muddying rather than clarifying the key constitutional issues (Irons 1999, 439). In June 1972, the justices notified the parties that they were to reargue *Roe v. Wade* in October.

With prodding from the justices, the second round of arguments focused more specifically on the constitutional definition of a "person," as expressed in the Fourteenth Amendment's guarantee that "all persons born in the United States . . . are citizens of the United States and of the state wherein they reside." Upon being questioned by Justice Byron White, Sara Weddington admitted that her case for the repeal of abortion laws would be made very difficult, should it be established under the law that an unborn fetus was indeed a person. If that were the case, then Texas would have a stronger basis for prohibiting abortion because of its compelling interest in safeguarding life. But when White posed the same question to Robert Flowers, the attorney for the state of Texas could not provide legal precedent supporting the idea that the Fourteenth Amendment was intended to include unborn fetuses within its definition of persons, thereby undermining his own argument. Nor could Flowers provide the Court with evidence of a medical consensus regarding "when life begins" (Irons 1999, 443–444). This highly significant exchange in the nation's highest court clearly demonstrated the critical ways in which legal doctrine and medical authority were intrinsically linked within the abortion issue.

Ultimately, the high court faced the task of balancing a woman's right to privacy with the state's compelling interest in protecting the health and safety of the mother and fetus. Writing for a seven-to-two majority, Justice Harry Blackmun worked through the equation. Building upon the *Griswold* decision's concept of privacy rooted in individual bodily autonomy, Blackmun asserted that the right to privacy is "broad enough to encompass a woman's decision whether or not to terminate her pregnancy." Blackmun then elaborated further:

The detriment that the State would impose upon the pregnant woman by denying this choice altogether is apparent. Specific and direct harm medically diagnosable even in early pregnancy may be involved.

Maternity, or additional offspring, may force upon the woman a distressful life and future. Psychological harm may be imminent. Mental and physical health may be taxed by child care. There is also the distress, for all concerned, associated with the unwanted child, and there is the problem of bringing a child into a family already unable, psychologically and otherwise, to care for it. In other cases, as in this one, the additional difficulties and continuing stigma of unwed motherhood may be involved. All these are factors the woman and her responsible physician necessarily will consider in consultation. (410 U.S. 113)

Still, the Court also acknowledged that the state may have a compelling interest of its own in regulating or even prohibiting the practice of abortion. "The Court's decisions recognizing a right of privacy also acknowledge that some state regulation in areas protected by that right is appropriate," Blackmun wrote. He noted that the Court had never acknowledged an "unlimited right to do with one's body as one pleases," citing both *Jacobson v. Massachusetts* upholding compulsory vaccination and *Buck v. Bell* in support of compulsory sterilization. Blackmun therefore concluded that "the right of personal privacy includes the abortion decision, but that this right is not unqualified and must be considered against important state interests in regulation" (410 U.S. 113). As in the two previous cases, the Court's challenge lay in defining the boundary between bodily autonomy and the state's authority to regulate the human body. In calculating where to draw this line, Justice Blackmun employed a standard medical framework that divided human pregnancy into three stages, or "trimesters." In the first trimester, he noted, a fetus is incapable of living as a separate entity outside the mother's body, and therefore a woman's privacy interest in making decisions regarding her own body may not be blocked by government. During the second trimester, however, as the fetus moves toward viability, states may regulate the practice of abortion in the interest of protecting the mother's health. In the final trimester, as the fetus becomes fully viable, states may prohibit abortions in the interest of protecting the fetus—unless continuation of the pregnancy would endanger the woman's life (410 U.S. 113). Thus, in *Roe v. Wade* the Court recognized abortion as a woman's right within the broader rubric of bodily autonomy but stopped short of according women an unqualified liberty interest in their bodies. Society, too, had a compelling interest in human reproduction.

William Rehnquist, one of the Court's two new appointees, filed a dissenting opinion. For Rehnquist, Blackmun's "trimester" scheme with its differentiated permissions for state action was not a matter for the Court to dictate at all. Rather, Rehnquist believed that these were matters best left to state legislatures. Justice Byron White agreed, and in a separate and much more strongly worded dissent argued that Blackmun's ruling imposed priorities on people who may "easily and heatedly differ" over the abortion question by "interposing a constitutional barrier to state efforts to protect human life and by investing mothers and doctors with the constitutionally protected right to exterminate it. This issue," White continued, "for the most part, should be left with the people and to the political processes the people have devised to govern their affairs." White labeled the decision "an exercise in raw judicial power" (410 U.S. 113). Although the majority opinion had left room for state legislatures to regulate the practice of abortion, the decision's minority view held that the Court had gone too far in extending a constitutional liberty interest to mean that abortion represents a fundamental right. Like many other landmark cases, the Court's decision in *Roe v. Wade* did not put to rest public controversy over the issue at hand; abortion continued to be a hotly debated topic, and numerous court challenges sought to reshape the original ruling over the next two decades.

In 1989, for example, the Court's opinion in *Webster v. Reproductive Services* allowed a Missouri statute that prohibited public employees from participating in and facilities from being used in abortions unless the operation was necessary to save the mother's life; the law also required physicians to ascertain whether a fetus of twenty or more weeks gestational age was viable before performing an abortion. In *Ohio v. Akron Center for Reproductive Health* (1990), the justices found constitutional a state law that placed particular requirements on unmarried minors requesting abortions. In 1992, a Pennsylvania abortion statute recently amended to place various restrictions on women's access to abortion (for example, that they give their consent at least twenty-four hours before the procedure is performed) was challenged by providers of abortion services. In a complex ruling, the high Court upheld certain provisions of the law and deemed others unconstitutional; the justices differed as to which provisions were acceptable and which were not. The key question in the complicated ruling in *Planned Parenthood v. Casey* was whether each of Pennsylvania's newly imposed requirements on women seeking abortions presented an "undue burden" to women exercising rights established nearly twenty years earlier in *Roe v. Wade.* The law's opponents charged that these "undue burdens" constituted violations of the due process clause of the Fourteenth Amendment because they amounted to an infringement on women's ability to exercise their liberties; its supporters disagreed.

A plurality of seven justices agreed that requirements of informed consent, a twenty-four-hour waiting period, and parental consent, as well as a statutory definition of "medical emergency," did not violate the due process clause of the Fourteenth Amendment because such requirements posed no undue burden on the woman seeking an abortion. Similarly, eight members agreed that certain requirements for record keeping and reporting did not violate the due process clause. By contrast, five justices found that a provision requiring a married woman to notify her spouse of her intentions before receiving an abortion did impose an undue burden in that it "enabled a husband to wield, in effect, an unconstitutional veto over his wife's decision concerning an abortion." But the more controversial part of the ruling came when five of the justices (David Souter, Blackmun, Sandra Day O'Connor, Anthony Kennedy, and John Paul Stevens) expressed their affirmation of the basic tenets of *Roe v. Wade,* whereas four (Rehnquist, White, Antonin Scalia, and Clarence Thomas) expressed the view that abortion is not a liberty protected by the Constitution at all. *Roe v. Wade,* they argued, was "plainly wrong, and the Supreme Court should get out of this area of the law, where it has no right to be" (112 S. Ct. 2791). The badly splintered Court reflected the sharp political divisions that had developed around abortion, as overturning *Roe* became a central tenet of conservative ideology. For conservatives, the boundaries of the due process clause had been stretched too far by the courts, creating personal autonomy "rights" unfounded in the Constitution. Abortion rights advocates feared that this ruling signaled the Court's desire to overturn *Roe v. Wade* at some future date.

Cruzan v. Director, Missouri Department of Public Health (1990)

Driving down a Missouri road in January 1983, twenty-five-year-old Nancy Cruzan lost control of her car and crashed. She was thrown from the car and landed face-down in a ditch, where a state trooper discovered her. She was unconscious, not breathing, and without a heartbeat. Paramedics revived Cruzan's heartbeat and breathing and transported her, still unconscious, to a hospital, where she was diagnosed with cerebral contusions and it was determined that she had suffered anoxia, or oxygen deprivation, for an estimated twelve to fourteen minutes, most probably resulting in permanent brain damage. She remained in a coma for weeks, and surgeons implanted tubes for nutrition and hydration. Over the next four months, she failed to respond to the hospital's rehabilitation efforts. Areas of her brain began to deteriorate, filling with cerebrospinal fluid. It became clear that she would not recover from her persistent vegetative state. Nancy's parents, Lester and Joyce Cruzan, requested the removal of the feeding and hydration tubes from their daughter's body.

But the hospital staff refused the request. Separating Nancy from the life-sustaining tubes would cause her to starve to death rather than die from her injuries, an action the doctors and nurses rejected as incompatible with their duty to care for their patients. The Cruzans then asked a judge to authorize their request. Citing a list of medical indicators that Nancy would never recover, the judge granted the request. Most important, the judge also took into account testimony by a former housemate that Nancy had previously expressed a desire never to be kept alive by artificial means. After a hearing in which each side presented arguments, the court determined that Nancy Cruzan had a fundamental right under both the Missouri and federal constitutions to direct the withdrawal of "death prolonging procedures," which she had done in her previous conversation with her housemate. When the hospital appealed, the Supreme Court of Missouri reversed the lower court's decision, ruling that Cruzan was not dead under Missouri's statutory definition of the word (she was capable of breathing on her own, for example, and still responded to certain stimuli), nor was she terminally ill. Although the court found the housemate's testimony too unreliable as proof of Cruzan's wishes (she had signed no formal decree, such as a "living will," to document her desires), it further asserted that Missouri's compelling interest in preserving life ultimately outweighed Cruzan's right to refuse treatment (760 SW2d 408). When *Cruzan v. Director, Missouri Department of Public Health* came before the U.S. Supreme Court in 1990, Nancy Cruzan had lain in the hospital in a persistent vegetative state for seven years. For the first time in its history, the Court was being asked to consider the very profound dilemma of whether an individual in Nancy's circumstances had a "right to die." Once again, the case was argued and deliberated within the framework of the Fourteenth Amendment's due process clause. The key question this time was whether Missouri's statutory provisions for terminating life-sustaining technology represented an infringement on Cruzan's right to make decisions regarding her body. In other words, did Missouri's requirement that a patient sign a formal document such as a "living will" interfere with Cruzan's wish, expressed orally but not in writing, not to be kept alive by artificial means?

And once again, the justices were sharply divided. In a five-to-four majority opinion written by Chief Justice Rehnquist, the high Court ruled that Missouri's requirements did not unduly interfere with Nancy Cruzan's right to bodily autonomy. A state such as Missouri, Rehnquist wrote, had a legitimate interest in wanting to safeguard the health and life of an incompetent individual and could therefore impose "heightened evidentiary requirements" of the individual's wishes. Family members or legal guardians might be unavailable to make such crucial decisions on behalf of the patient, the Chief Justice pointed out, or might even wish to act against the patient's own best interests. The Missouri statute had erected a legitimate process for hearing requests for the termination of life support and for appealing the trial court's decision, and the state supreme court also had acted legitimately in ruling that there was insufficient evidence of Cruzan's wishes, given that she had never discussed the actual circumstances she had tragically fallen under, specifically the withdrawal of hydration and nutrition, even though she could still breathe on her own. Justice Rehnquist found that, absent a clear directive from the patient herself, the courts were not required to defer to the wishes of the patient's family.

In a concurring opinion, Justice Sandra Day O'Connor clarified her position that the due process clause did protect an individual's personal decision to refuse medical treatment, including the artificial delivery of food and water into her body. The problem here was the lack of sufficient evidence demonstrating this was in fact what Nancy Cruzan wanted to do. In supporting Missouri's interest in protecting the life of an incompetent individual in this instance, Justice O'Connor emphasized, the Court was not saying that states could not also develop means for protecting such individuals' liberty interest in refusing medical treatment. Although Justice Scalia went along with the majority in supporting Missouri's statute, he pointedly disagreed that a refusal by Nancy Cruzan to receive food and water would be tantamount to refusing medication. In fact, Scalia saw such a refusal as "indistinguishable from ordinary suicide," and U.S. law had always accorded states the power to prevent suicide—even by force if necessary. Because the Constitution made no mention of a "right" to end one's own life—by any means, including refusing food and water—Scalia would leave the determination of whether the law would allow this to "the citizens of Missouri to decide, through their elected representatives" (497 U.S. 261). As he would do two years later in *Planned Parenthood v. Casey*, Scalia argued that the Constitution awards no broad rights to do what one pleases with one's body and therefore challenges of this nature do not even belong before the Court. Rather, the issues being raised in these cases are solely for state legislatures to determine. The dissenting opinion in *Cruzan* was written by Justice William Brennan, who was joined by Thurgood Marshall and Harry Blackmun. These three justices found that Nancy Cruzan did in fact have a "fundamental right, under the due process clause, to be free of unwanted artificial nutrition and hydration," a right that "is not outweighed by any interests of the State." In contrast to Massachusetts' successful arguments in *Jacobson v. Massachusetts* that Henning Jacobson's refusal to be vaccinated against smallpox constituted a threat to public health, Missouri had not demonstrated that a benefit to society as a whole would result from Nancy being fed artificially. The guarantee of due process, in fact, would *require* a state to allow a decision regarding bodily autonomy to be granted to the patient's family or a chosen proxy rather than to the state itself. The justices disagreed with Scalia's argument that refusing to be fed artificially is tantamount to suicide, since the insertion of the feeding tubes into Nancy's body required surgery and continued maintenance by trained medical staff to ensure against physical complications (such as leakage of the stomach's contents into the lungs) and thus could not be considered "normal" feeding. Under these circumstances, they asserted, a person may very well want to forgo nutrition and hydration. "A quiet, proud death, bodily integrity intact, is a matter of extreme consequence," Brennan concluded, adding that Nancy Cruzan is "entitled to choose to die with dignity." A separate dissent written by Justice John Paul Stevens put the case for Cruzan's right to bodily autonomy with equal force. Stevens claimed that the Constitution required Missouri to care for Cruzan's life "in a way that gave appropriate respect to the woman's own best interests," but the Missouri statute failed to do so. According to Stevens, Missouri's actions suggested that chronically incompetent people such as Nancy Cruzan "had no constitutionally cognizable interests at all, and so were not persons within the meaning of the Constitution" (497 U.S. 261). The ability to control what happens to one's body was, for Stevens, inexorably tied to what it meant to be a "person."

Ultimately, then, the Supreme Court's decision in the Cruzan case both acknowledged a right to bodily autonomy—rooted in an individual's liberty interest and protected by the Fourteenth Amendment—and supported the state's interest in protecting human life. Missouri's statute was allowed to stand, but the justices had left open the possibility that, should Lester and Joyce Cruzan be able to provide evidence of their daughter's desires regarding the control of her own body that met Missouri's provisional standards, their request to have her removed from the feeding and hydration tubes might be granted. Taking this opening, the Cruzans went before the original trial judge again, this time bringing testimony from additional witnesses regarding the wishes Nancy had expressed to them. The state of Missouri chose to withdraw all opposition from the case since, according to the state's attorney general, its original challenge to the Cruzan's request had been about upholding Missouri's statute—and that had been accomplished by the Supreme Court's decision. On December 15, 1990, the tubes were removed, and Nancy Cruzan died the day after Christmas (Filene 1998, 181–182).

Conclusion

In his concurring opinion, Justice Scalia acknowledged that the justice's varying views in Nancy Cruzan's case "portray quite clearly the difficult, indeed agonizing, questions that are presented by the constantly increasing power of science to keep the human body alive for longer than any reasonable person would want to inhabit it" (497 U.S. 261). As historian Peter Filene has pointed out, there is a striking irony in the fact that Nancy Cruzan's parents had to argue for their daughter's right to bodily self-determination while she lay hospitalized in a persistent vegetative state, kept alive by feeding and hydration tubes (Filene 1998, 179). By century's end, medical technologies had created a world in which a physical body could continue to live far longer than the apparent consciousness of the person inhabiting it. The body and the self now could be thought of as completely separate entities. In this new world, what did it actually mean to say that the individual possessed a right of bodily autonomy? And how far did the state's authority to regulate the human body extend? Like Justice Scalia, Justice Brennan also considered the far-reaching implications of Nancy Cruzan's case. If the state could keep such a person alive despite her wishes, Brennan worried, "Perhaps the State could lawfully remove more vital organs for transplanting into others who would then be cured of their ailments, provided the State placed Nancy on some other life-support equipment to replace the lost function." The justice even speculated about "too brave a new world," in which the state might "perform medical experiments on her body, experiments that might save countless lives, and would cause her no greater burden than she already bears by being fed through the gastrostomy tube." Yet by century's end, rapid developments in bioengineering brought these very issues into the arena of public debate.

References and Further Reading

Chase, Allan. 1982. *Magic Shots*. New York: William Morrow.

Dudziak, Mary L. 1986. "Oliver Wendell Holmes as a Eugenic Reformer: Rhetoric in the Writing of Constitutional Law." *Iowa Law Review* 71, no. 3 (March): 833–867.

Filene, Peter G. 1998. *In the Arms of Others: A Cultural History of the Right to Die in America*. Chicago: Ivan R. Dee.

Irons, Peter. 1999. *A People's History of the Supreme Court*. New York: Penguin Books.

Kevles, Daniel J. 1985. *In the Name of Eugenics: Genetics and the Uses of Human Heredity*. New York: Alfred A. Knopf.

Kline, Wendy. 2001. *Building a Better Race: Gender, Sexuality, and Eugenics from the Turn of the Century to the Baby Boom*. Berkeley: University of California Press.

Lombardo, Paul A. 1982. "Eugenic Sterilization in Virginia: Aubrey Strode and the Case of *Buck v. Bell*." Ph.D. diss., University of Virginia.

May, Elaine Tyler. 2000. "Pushing the Limits 1940–1961." Pp. 473–528 in Nancy F. Cott, ed., *No Small Courage: A History of Women in the United States*. Oxford: Oxford University Press.

Mohr, James C. 1978. *Abortion in America: The Origins and Evolution of National Policy, 1800–1900*. New York: Oxford University Press.

Reagan, Leslie J. 1997. *When Abortion Was a Crime: Women, Medicine, and Law in the United States, 1867–1973.* Berkeley: University of California Press.

U.S. Supreme Court. 1903. *Transcripts of Records and File Copies of Briefs,* vol. 14, case nos. 65–73. Washington, DC: Judd and Detweiler.

Weddington, Sarah. 1993. *A Question of Choice.* New York: Penguin Books.

4

Legacy and Impact

End-of-Life Issues on Trial

On March 22, 2002, Judge Robert E. Jones heard final arguments in his Portland, Oregon, courtroom. The case centered around that state's Death with Dignity Act, which was enacted in 1994 and took effect in 1997. The law permits patients with less than six months to live and certifications from two physicians to obtain lethal medication. Doctors may provide the medication but must not administer it. At the time of the Portland trial, ninety-one people had taken their lives under the statute's provisions. Among the spectators in the courtroom that day was James Romney, a patient suffering from Lou Gehrig's disease (amyotrophic lateral sclerosis), who was a plaintiff in the case. On behalf of terminally ill patients, a nonprofit organization called the Compassion in Dying Federation, along with the state of Oregon and several medical doctors, had brought suit seeking relief from a directive to overturn the law issued by U.S. attorney general John Ashcroft. "I want to die with dignity," Romney told reporters from the *New York Times*. "I'm devastated that my own federal government is trying to take that choice away from me." The liberty to decide what medical procedures Americans choose to use was on trial once again.

The Oregon case casts the question we have been exploring in this volume into full relief: Where do we draw the line between an individual's right to bodily autonomy and the state's authority to regulate the human body? The "right to die" is a disturbing, emotionally charged issue that Americans continue to debate in both public and private forums, from a variety of personal, cultural, and religious perspectives. As we have seen, underlying the current discussion is a long history of interrelated medical and legal developments that have shaped the issues as we understand them today. Both parties in the Oregon case sought support from medical authority, judicial precedent, and the U.S. Constitution to make their arguments before Judge Jones's court.

As the nation's chief law enforcement officer, Attorney General Ashcroft ordered the state of Oregon to cease applying the statute because it stood in contradiction to federal law. Specifically, Ashcroft argued that the assisted-suicide law violated the Controlled Substances Act (CSA), passed by Congress in 1970. The regulations for the act's enforcement state in part that:

A medical prescription for a controlled substance to be effective must be issued for a legitimate medical purpose by an individual practitioner acting in the usual course of his professional practice. The responsibility for the proper prescribing and dispensing of controlled substances is upon the prescribing practitioner, but a corresponding responsibility rests with the pharmacist who fills the prescription. An order purporting to be a prescription issued not in the usual course of professional treatment or in legitimate and authorized research is not a prescription within the meaning of the Act . . . and the person knowingly filling such a purported prescription, as well as the person issuing it, shall be subject to the penalties provided for violations of the provisions of law relating to controlled substances. (21 C. F. R. 1306.04[a])

Language in the Controlled Substances Act affirmed the police powers awarded to the federal government. Regulating drugs fell within the legislative branch's authority because their improper use "has a substantial and detrimental effect on the health and general welfare of the American people" (21 U. S. C. 801[2]). In other words, the CSA empowered the federal government to regulate or prohibit certain drugs on behalf of the public's health and safety. But the Oregon case was not about trafficking in narcotics. Attorney General Ashcroft claimed that the state's law, by permitting doctors to issue prescriptions for medication they know will be used by patients to end their own lives, has the effect of subverting the CSA because such a prescription is not intended for a "legitimate medical purpose" and is not issued by a doctor "in the usual course of professional treatment." Ashcroft asserted that a physician's actions in writing the prescription could be considered "inconsistent with the public interest"—more specifically, the citizens' interest in not being prescribed substances that will kill them. The attorney general determined that, although prescribing powerful and perhaps even toxic drugs for the management of a medical condition or of the pain associated with that condition represents a physician's legitimate responsibility, prescribing lethal drugs expressly for the purpose of aiding a patient to commit suicide is *not* an accepted standard within current medical practice. Such actions by a physician, therefore, may be prohibited under the CSA, and Oregon's Death with Dignity Act cannot interfere with prosecution of medical practitioners who violate a federal law.

But the plaintiffs challenging the attorney general's directive argued that "terminal sedation" is in fact accepted by the American Medical Association, as well other professional medical organizations such as the American Nurses Association and the American Psychiatric Association. "Terminal sedation" refers to the practice of sedating a patient into unconsciousness and then withholding food and water until death ensues. The plaintiffs maintained that the Death with Dignity Act offered *patients* the choice of requesting from their physicians what is already considered a legitimate medical procedure within the medical community. The attorney general's directive, in their view, ignored "both the reality of modern medicine and how it has changed the process of dying." Further, they charged, the attorney general does not have the authority to determine what is or is not legitimate medical practice, since its regulation has always been left to the states (Patient Plaintiffs' Brief). The Supreme Court's decision in *Cruzan* affirmed that, in difficult end-of-life cases, "the . . . challenging task of crafting appropriate procedures for safeguarding . . . liberty interests is entrusted to the laboratory of the States in the first interest" (521 U.S. 702). Congress's exercise of police powers in enacting the Controlled Substances Act pertained to protecting the public from physicians trafficking in illegal narcotics, not to determining what is and what is not an acceptable standard in medical care.

As in the cases we saw in Chapter 3, the Oregon court was engaged in the process of determining what is and is not legitimate medical theory. In 1905, for example, Henning Jacobson claimed before the U.S. Supreme Court that a smallpox vaccination would make him sick, whereas in 1942 the state of Oklahoma argued that sterilizing Jack Skinner was essential to prevent him from passing on his criminal tendencies to his offspring. In *Roe v. Wade,* supporters of legal abortion asserted that, when performed in a legitimate hospital or clinical setting, the procedure was a safe and effective means of ending a pregnancy and thus legalization avoided the possible injuries or even death that might result when abortions were performed under illicit conditions. In the Oregon case, Judge Jones faced a particularly difficult question: Is there a legal difference between a physician knowingly prescribing therapeutic medication that *may* cause death to the patient and prescribing one *expressly for the purpose* of ending an individual's life? Both parties in the case turned to recent rulings by the U.S. Supreme Court for support in answering this complex question.

On June 27, 1997, the high Court had issued rulings in two separate but closely related cases originating from two different states. *Quill v. Vacco* challenged a 1994 New York statute making it a felony for a person to intentionally aid another person's attempt to commit suicide on the grounds that the statute violated the equal protection clause of the Fourteenth Amendment. The second case, *Washington v. Glucksberg,* challenged a Washington State law that also made aiding or promoting a suicide attempt a felony, this time on the grounds that the statute violated the due process clause of the Fourteenth Amendment. Coming before the Court at the close of the twentieth century, these cases stood on a large body of legal precedent and medical authority stretching back to the Reverend Jacobson's claim that the Constitution protected his liberty to determine what course of medical treatment he would or would not receive and the state's counterargument that this liberty may be curtailed on behalf of the general welfare. Once again, the Court considered where to draw the line between an individual's bodily autonomy and a state's authority to place limitations on that right.

Timothy E. Quill, Samuel C. Klagsburn, and Howard A. Grossman were physicians who brought suit against New York's attorney general, charging that the state's ban on assisted suicide deterred them from prescribing lethal medication for terminally ill patients in great pain who desired a doctor's help in ending their own lives, even though the current standards of U.S. medical practice allowed them to do so. The physicians originally had been joined in their suit by three terminally ill patients who desired assisted suicide, but all three had died before the case came before the court. The plaintiffs based their challenge on the Fourteenth Amendment's equal protection clause. Because the New York law permitted a competent person to refuse medical treatment that would sustain his or her life, banning physician-assisted suicide—which the plaintiffs claimed was essentially the same thing—amounted to unequal treatment under the law.

The nine justices, however, disagreed. Chief Justice William Rehnquist's majority opinion concluded that the New York statute neither "burdens a fundamental right nor targets a suspect class" and therefore did not violate the equal protection clause. But Rehnquist focused most of his opinion on the plaintiffs' claim that withdrawing life support and assisting suicide were essentially the same thing. The chief justice countered that making a distinction between these two actions was not only important and rational but also a difference recognized in the traditions of both medicine and law.

In calculating where to draw the line between bodily autonomy and the state's authority to regulate the human body, Rehnquist used the age-old legal principles of causation and intent. According to the first principle, when a patient refuses medical treatment necessary to sustain his life, he dies from his illness, whereas when a patient takes lethal medication, he is killed by that medication. Thus there is a vital difference in the actual *cause* of death occurring in each case. Further, according to the second principle, when a physician honors a patient's request to withdraw medical treatment, she is respecting her patient's wishes, which may have a wide variety of motivations that are not primarily a desire to die, even though both doctor and patient may be aware that death may be the result of ending treatment. The patient may wish to be freed from the burdens of intrusive machines attached to his body, for example, or he may wish to cease ingesting a drug that interferes with his ability to communicate lucidly with his loved ones in his final days. In such cases, the chief justice stated, the physician's intent is to conform to her patient's request to die in the manner of the patient's choosing, and both legal tradition and current medical standards accept "*letting* the patient die" as an appropriate course of action (or nonaction) a doctor may take in caring for her patient. By contrast, if the doctor prescribes her patient a lethal dose of medication, her sole intent is "*making* the patient die," which is not accepted in law or medicine, and therefore a state may declare such an action to be illegal. New York's law making it a felony to assist in a suicide, therefore, did not violate the requirements of the equal protection clause. Finally, Rehnquist pointed out that in enacting laws governing end-of-life issues, the majority of state legislatures had made these critical distinctions regarding causation and intent (521 U.S. 793).

The chief justice's assertion that the New York statute did not represent an undue burden on a fundamental right highlights the core question raised in the second case, *Washington v. Glucksberg:* Is there a constitutionally protected right to die? The Ninth Circuit Court of Appeals had answered "yes," and now the state of Washington sought a reversal of that decision. As in the New York suit, the original plaintiffs, now known as "respondents" because they had won their case in the lower court, were physicians (Harold Glucksberg, Abigail Halperin, Thomas Preston, and Peter Shalit), joined by several anonymous terminally ill individuals and the Compassion in Dying Federation. The claim they brought before the high court was that the Fourteenth Amendment's due process clause guaranteed a right to die in its protections of individual liberty. A patient who is both mentally competent and terminally ill possesses a "liberty interest in controlling the time and manner of [his or her] own death." Such a liberty must include the option of receiving assistance when carrying out the choice to die, the coalition claimed. Therefore, Washington's ban on assisted suicide was unconstitutional.

In constructing their argument, the respondents relied upon the Supreme Court's previous decisions in *Cruzan v. Director, Missouri Department of Public Health* (1990) and *Planned Parenthood v. Casey* (1992; see Chapter 3). First, they asserted that the *Cruzan* opinion recognized that, because "informed consent" is generally required for receiving medical treatment, the same principle could apply to rejecting the same treatment. Had Nancy Cruzan, prior to the accident that caused her persistent vegetative state, made clear and convincing statements to the effect that she would not wish to receive life-supporting interventions under such conditions, her wishes could have been respected by medical personnel without rendering them liable to criminal prosecution. From this premise, the respondents concluded that "the constitutional principle behind recognizing the patient's liberty to direct the withdrawal of artificial life support applies at least as strongly to the choice to hasten death by consuming lethal medication." They were now asking the Court to make explicit the recognition that, if individuals possess a liberty interest in controlling the timing and manner of their deaths, then they also enjoy a right to willfully take lethal medication and, by implication, to receive the assistance of a doctor in prescribing the drugs. But the respondents were also asking the justices to go a step further. If it has been established that individuals do indeed possess a right to die, then according to *Casey*, a state legislature may not impose any "undue burden" on persons wishing to exercise their right. Washington State's prohibition against doctors prescribing lethal medication to a terminally ill patient who wishes to end his life would constitute just such an undue burden, the respondents claimed. "It is a promise of the Constitution," their brief stated, "that there is a realm of personal liberty which the government cannot enter." This realm encompasses "basic and intimate exercises of personal autonomy," and thus "protects the liberty of competent, terminally-ill adults to make end-of-life decisions free of undue government interference" (521 U.S. 702).

As it indicated in its *Quill* decision, however, the Court rejected the argument that assisted suicide constituted a fundamental right deserving protection under the Constitution. Once again writing for a unanimous majority, Chief Justice Rehnquist insisted that the *Cruzan* case had not established a right to die at all and, in fact, involved particular circumstances that made it quite distinct from the case now before the Court. Once again, Rehnquist looked to a long history of determining causation and intent: although a decision to refuse unwanted medical treatment could be supported by legal tradition upholding the right to refuse medication, assisted suicide enjoyed no such support. In *Cruzan*, Rehnquist pointed out, "we recognized that most States outlawed assisted suicide—and even more do today—and we certainly gave no intimation that the right to refuse unwanted medical treatment could be somehow transmuted into a right to assistance in committing suicide. . . . The history of the law's treatment of assisted suicide in this country has been and continues to be one of the rejection of nearly all efforts to permit it. That being the case," the chief justice continued, "our decisions lead us to conclude that the asserted 'right' to assistance in committing suicide is not a fundamental liberty interest protected by the Due Process Clause" (521 U.S. 702).

Nor did he accept the respondent's claim that the "undue burden" standard articulated in the *Casey* decision was applicable to the Washington law. The constitution mandates that a state must demonstrate a legitimate interest when enacting or enforcing laws that curtail individual liberties. For the chief justice, the states retain numerous legitimate interests in prohibiting assisted suicide, including their interests in preserving life; protecting vulnerable individuals from arbitrary, unfair, or undue influence in making end-of-life decisions; protecting family members and loved ones of the terminally ill; upholding the integrity of the medical profession; and holding firm against a policy slide toward the practice of euthanasia. (These issues had recently come under intense public scrutiny after a series of notorious cases involving the controversial Michigan doctor, Jack Kevorkian, who helped individuals to die with the aid of a machine he had constructed himself. Kevorkian was eventually sentenced to prison for his actions.) Because it emerges from these and other legitimate state interests, the Washington law presents no "undue burden" on individuals who wish to commit suicide with the assistance of a doctor.

In 1997, then, the U.S. Supreme Court in two unanimous decisions seemingly put to rest the idea of a right to die. Or did it? Five years later, another group of physicians and terminally ill patients, once again assisted by the Compassion in Dying Federation, went before an Oregon court asking it to uphold the individual's liberty to die by doctor-assisted suicide, this time as a right safeguarded under their state's Death with Dignity Act. That right, they contended, was now being infringed by the U.S. attorney general's directive that the Oregon law could not be enforced. Interestingly, the Oregon plaintiffs found support for their position in none other than the Supreme Court's opinion in *Quill v. Vacco* and *Washington v. Glucksberg.*

As we have seen, the justices had ruled *against* the existence of a constitutionally protected right to die in both cases Why, then, would the Oregon plaintiffs feel they had found support in these decisions? The answer lies in the concurrences delivered along with Justice Rehnquist's majority opinion. Reading carefully into these texts, supporters of the Oregon Death with Dignity Act found enough "play in the joints" to support their assertions. Opinions written by Justices David Souter, Ruth Bader Ginsberg, Stephen Breyer, Sandra Day O'Connor, and John Paul Stevens all indicated their apparent willingness to have the Court explore these questions further. For example, although she refuted the legitimacy of a fundamental right to die, Justice O'Connor drew upon Justice Louis Brandeis's often-quoted declaration that the *states* are the appropriate "laboratory" in which "extensive and serious evaluation of physician-assisted suicide and other related issues" should take place. "There is no reason to think," O'Connor observed, "that the democratic process will not strike the proper balance between the interests of terminally ill, mentally competent individuals who would seek to end their suffering and the State's interests in protecting those who might seek to end life mistakenly or under pressure" (*Washington v. Glucksberg*, 521 U.S. 702). In conceding this much to the states, Justice O'Connor gave the supporters of the Oregon law reason to believe the statute would receive due consideration in the courts.

Justice John Paul Stevens appeared to open the door to physician-assisted suicide even wider. Also concurring in *Glucksberg* and agreeing that the Constitution does not guarantee a right to assisted suicide, the justice went on to express his desire "to make it clear that there is also room for further debate about the limits that the Constitution places on the power of the States to punish the practice [of assisted suicide]." Stevens expressed the view that the majority's finding in *Glucksberg* was correct within the specific context of the case, leaving open the possibility that the court might find otherwise in a future case in which the facts are different. Stevens compared assisted suicide with capital punishment, which the Supreme Court has determined to be constitutional but has also at times ruled to be "impermissibly cruel" in its application. The Court must acknowledge, he asserted, "that there are situations in which an interest in hastening death is legitimate. Indeed, not only is that interest sometimes legitimate, I am also convinced that there are times when it is entitled to constitutional protection" (521 U.S. 702).

Justice Stevens construed the liberty interest in refusing medical treatment that the Court acknowledged in *Cruzan* in a much more sweeping—and potentially more revolutionary—way than Justice Rehnquist had offered in his more circumscribed discussion of common law tradition. Nancy Cruzan's right to refuse medical treatment, Stevens contended, embraced "her interest in dignity, and in determining the character of the memories that will survive long after her death. . . . While I agree with the Court that *Cruzan* does not decide the [right to die] issue presented by these cases," Stevens argued,

> *Cruzan* did give recognition, not just to vague, unbridled notions of autonomy, but to the more specific interest in making decisions about

how to confront an imminent death. Although there is no absolute right to physician-assisted suicide, *Cruzan* makes it clear that some individuals who no longer have the option of deciding whether to live or to die because they are already on the threshold of death have a constitutionally protected interest that may outweigh the State's interest in preserving life at all costs. The liberty interest at stake in a case like this differs from, and is stronger than, both the common-law right to refuse medical treatment and the unbridled interest in deciding whether to live or die. It is an interest in deciding how, rather than whether, a critical threshold shall be crossed. (521 U.S. 702)

Stevens also addressed the contentious question of whether prescribing lethal medicine for the purpose of a patient's suicide represented legitimate medical practice. For some terminally ill patients in unbearable pain, he argued, "it would be a physician's refusal to dispense medication to ease their suffering and make their death tolerable and dignified that would be inconsistent with the healing role. . . . Because physicians are already involved in making decisions that hasten the death of terminally ill patients—through termination of life support, withholding medical treatment, and terminal sedation—there is in fact significant tension between the traditional view of the physician's role and the actual practice in a growing number of cases" (521 U.S. 702). Stevens's written statement here included a footnote citing evidence from various professional medical organizations that testified to their growing acceptance of assisted suicide as a part of modern medical practice.

Justices O'Connor's and Stevens's nods toward the notion that there may exist an individual liberty interest in choosing the manner of one's own death opened the possibility of the U.S. Supreme Court revisiting the issue at some future date. As the *Glucksberg* and *Quill* decisions also demonstrate, in any future case the justices will be required to carefully consider and weigh the evolving legal doctrine of bodily autonomy within the context of changing medical beliefs and practices about caring for the human body. Even the meaning of the term *medical care* has come into question, as Americans continue to debate medical practitioners' obligations toward their terminally ill patients. For some, the physician's role as caregiver must extend to enabling terminally ill patients suffering unbearable pain to exercise their liberty to end their own lives. Others counter that government has a responsibility to protect weak and vulnerable patients against potential abuse by those whose own interests may be in conflict with the patient's right to life. The skyrocketing costs of medical care and increased pressures to contain them, opponents of assisted suicide point out, may put significant pressures on family members and hospital staffs to place economic considerations over the fundamental right to life. Would the precedent set when one patient exercises his *right* to commit assisted suicide become another patient's *obligation* to end her life when she faces the same circumstances? As one constitutional historian has observed, "bright line tests do not work well" in the area of physician-assisted suicide because "we cannot generalize from one case" (Urofsky 2000, 18). Whether the latest challenge arising from the enforcement of Oregon's Death with Dignity Act will conclude with another landmark decision by the nation's highest court remains to be seen.

Biotechnology on Trial

As Americans consider the legal and constitutional dimensions of recent changes in medical practices that affect the way life ends, new issues at the beginning of human life have come under unprecedented public scrutiny as well. Rapid advances in the science of genetic engineering demand that we address anew the question of where to draw the line between individual bodily autonomy and the state's authority to regulate the human body in the name of protecting the health and welfare of the wider society.

Some have questioned, for example, how many of the legal and historical precedents reviewed in this volume might be applied to the thorny issue of genetically enhancing our own children. If *Skinner v. Oklahoma* established a "right to reproduce" and *Roe v. Wade* a woman's right to terminate a pregnancy, does it follow that the government must also stay out of deeply personal decisions parents might make to ensure that their children do not carry a potentially devastating genetic defect such as spina bifida? If this is so, does it also mean that parents have a fundamental liberty interest in being able to choose to produce only tall, or green-eyed, or dark-skinned children? May the state exercise its police powers to prohibit "designer babies" in the interest of protecting the public welfare—by maintaining the diversity of the human gene pool, for example, or ensuring a balanced ratio of males and females? Alternatively, does the state have a compelling interest in regulating how genetic engineering is practiced in order to protect the life and health of the future offspring? Does genetic engineering infringe upon the bodily autonomy of the people who would be produced by these technologies? Which scientific and medical theories regarding human genetic engineering will be accepted as authoritative by the courts, and which will be found invalid? If history offers us a guide, the answers to these questions will be answered neither quickly nor easily.

Likewise, with the successful cloning of a number of animal species, the possibility of human cloning in the near future has simultaneously raised both expectations for a healthier populace and fears about potential abuses of this practice. Although many Americans argue that cloning entire or parts of human beings could provide life-saving benefits for thousands (patients who today are condemned to wait in vain for an organ transplant, for example), others counter that cloning—even for therapeutic purposes—undermines the dignity of human life and presents a threat to the very order of nature. Liberal U.S. senators Ted Kennedy and Dianne Feinstein have proposed legislation that would allow medical researchers to clone human cells for research, even as an unusually broad coalition of environmental activists, feminists, religious leaders, and political conservatives are urging Congress to take preemptive action to ban all human cloning. In this ongoing debate, individual liberty interests in reproductive choice clash with the specter of a new eugenics and anxieties about repeating the horrors of such practices taken to extremes, such as in Germany's Third Reich. As we have seen, abuses of medical sterilization of those deemed "unworthy" to reproduce were carried out in the United States as well, and Justice Holmes's opinion supporting states' power to sterilize the "unfit" to protect public health and safety has never been overturned. In the brave new world of biotechnology, the boundaries between bodily autonomy and society's claims on the human body appear more blurred than ever.

Americans have also found themselves suddenly confronted with the possible threat of "bioterrorism," the use of biological weapons to harm or kill large numbers of the population. On September 11, 2001, terrorists using commercial jet airliners attacked the World Trade Center in New York City and the Pentagon in Washington, D.C. Another jet believed to be part of the planned assault crashed in an open field in Pennsylvania. Approximately 2,700 people died in the attacks. President George W. Bush labeled these as acts of war. Even while a traumatized nation tried to cope with these devastating events,

Americans learned that anthrax had been disseminated through the nation's postal service, resulting in twenty-two infections and five deaths. Anthrax is a livestock disease that cannot be passed from one person to another but is nevertheless quite deadly if its spores are contacted directly by the skin or inhaled into the lungs. In this case, the disease had been spread via a powdery substance mailed in postal envelopes, raising anxieties that the nation might be facing a new and terrifying kind of biological warfare. (As of this writing, however, many key details about the precise nature of the incident remain unconfirmed.) Since the early 1990s, U.S. military personnel have been routinely vaccinated against anthrax as a precaution against its possible use in a military confrontation. Soldiers refusing to be vaccinated, in fact, are subject to strict military discipline. But in the fall of 2001, the apparent use of anthrax to inflict harm on the civilian population raised the issue of diseases as weapons of mass destruction to an unprecedented level of public attention.

The national discourse quickly turned to the question of whether other deadly illnesses might be employed as weapons, diseases such as plague or Ebola or even the ancient scourge of smallpox. And if this fear should become reality, what should the response be from local, state, and national governments? As we have seen, the idea that governments are empowered to enact quarantines to protect the public health and safety is an ancient one. But what does this mean for Americans living in the twenty-first century? The Associated Press reported that at least twenty state public health departments had begun investigating their options in the event of an epidemic of contagious disease. But because mass quarantines had not been employed in the United States for decades, new questions have arisen about the form and substance of such measures, as well as who possessed the authority to direct them. Should local police be empowered to enforce compliance with quarantines? Would states be enabled to call up the National Guard, or even the U.S. military? In response to the sudden dilemma, the Centers for Disease Control and Prevention, along with a number of public health institutions, initiated the development of a sample law that states could use as a template for enacting their own measures. Mindful of the long history of controversy surrounding quarantines, the model law directs state and local governments to employ the least restrictive measures necessary and to go beyond simply isolating affected persons to ensure that they receive adequate medical care.

But, as we have seen, compulsory vaccination has been an equally contested notion in U.S. history. The last mandatory smallpox immunization laws in the United States expired in 1972, and it remains unclear whether individuals who received vaccinations more than ten years ago are still being afforded protection. Thus it is probable that many Americans today are without immunities to the disease. For many years, medical authorities were confident that smallpox had been eradicated not only from the United States but also from most of the Earth, in large measure because of massive efforts organized by the World Health Organization. Live smallpox virus continued to be stored in at least one U.S. research laboratory. In 1992, a defector from the former Soviet Union confirmed the existence of stocks of the virus in weapons research laboratories there as well. Although for years the American public had not seemed unduly concerned about these remaining stores of a deadly contagion, national security anxieties engendered by the September 11 attacks reanimated the debate about whether or not compulsory vaccination measures should be undertaken. And once again, the issue was framed by the tensions between bodily autonomy and the state's duty to protect the public health and safety. How plausible was it that the smallpox virus could be somehow released into the general population? Was it prudent to vaccinate the general public if a massive smallpox epidemic represented a distinct threat but not a likely one? Could individual American citizens be forced to comply?

Many Americans believe that their country has been fundamentally changed by the events of September 11, 2001. In the months following the attack, they considered threats to the health and safety of the general public in an entirely different way. As in past crises, they have looked to their government to fulfill its duty in protecting them from bodily harm. And yet, twenty-first century Americans are also the heirs to a well-established legal doctrine of bodily autonomy. They have come to regard the freedom to make choices concerning their own bodies as a fundamental—and highly valued—right. In fact, these beliefs have become so central to the American sense of citizenship that they have entered into policy discussions about national security. A number of medical authorities have argued that the health risks posed by smallpox vaccines warrant extreme caution in implementing a large-scale vaccination program. Dr. Anthony S. Fauci, the director of the National Institute of Allergies and Infectious Diseases, recommended that, in the formulation of a national policy regarding vaccination against smallpox, the American public "should be given an opportunity to hear an open debate" among those holding differing views about the safety and efficacy of the procedure (Kolata 2002). Nearly 100 years after Reverend Jacobson argued unsuccessfully before the U.S. Supreme Court that he had a right to refuse vaccination because he believed it would make him sick, the potentially severe health risks posed by the smallpox vaccine are widely acknowledged in contemporary policy deliberations.

As we have seen in this volume, American notions of bodily autonomy have in large measure been shaped by a series of decisions handed down by the U.S. Supreme Court over the course of the twentieth century. The safeguards the Constitution affords to life and liberty have been extended to derive rights to reproduce, prevent conception, terminate a pregnancy, and refuse life support. At the same time, the Court has also upheld society's claims on the human body. It has established that the state, acting on behalf of the general welfare, holds a compelling interest in mandating vaccination, compelling sterilization, and prohibiting physician-assisted suicide. But the Court's deliberations in determining the boundary between bodily autonomy and the state's power to regulate the human body have taken place within a context of medical understanding that has itself continually evolved. It is a process that continues today. New contingencies and unforeseen challenges will require that we examine the boundaries again. The past will serve as our guide.

References and Further Reading

Associated Press. 2002. "States Revisit Old-Style Quarantines." *New York Times,* January 28.

Berry, Robert. 1998. "From Involuntary Sterilization to Genetic Enhancement: The Unsettled Legacy of *Buck v. Bell." Notre Dame Journal of Ethics and Public Policy* 12: 401–448.

Dworkin, Ronald. 1993. *Life's Dominion: An Argument about Abortion, Euthanasia, and Individual Freedom.* New York: Vintage Books.

Kolata, Gina. 2002. "With Vaccine Available, Smallpox Debate Shifts." *New York Times,* March 30.

McKibben, Bill. 2002. "Unlikely Allies against Cloning." *New York Times,* March 27.

Tucker, Jonathan B. 2001. *Scourge: The Once and Future Threat of Smallpox.* New York: Atlantic Monthly Press.

Urofsky, Melvin I. 2000. "Justifying Assisted Suicide: Comments on the Ongoing Debate." *Notre Dame Journal of Ethics and Public Policy* 14: 893–943.

Part Two

Part Two

Documents

Fourteenth Amendment to the U.S. Constitution

Ratified in 1868, the Fourteenth Amendment to the Constitution both defined U.S. citizenship and guaranteed citizens protections from infringements of their rights by individual states. Nineteenth-century courts tended to interpret the amendment conservatively, narrowly circumscribing individual rights. Over the course of the twentieth century, however, the amendment's due process and equal protection clauses became central to the development of legal doctrines deriving the constitutional right of privacy and the liberty interest individuals hold in making choices regarding their bodies.

Section 1. All persons born or naturalized in the United States, and subject to the jurisdiction thereof, are citizens of the United States and of the State wherein they reside. No State shall make or enforce any law which shall abridge the privileges or immunities of citizens of the United States; nor shall any State deprive any person of life, liberty, or property, without due process of law; nor deny to any person within its jurisdiction the equal protection of the laws.

"Anti-Vaccination Circular, Distributed during the Epidemic of Small Pox in Boston, 1901"

In the late nineteenth and early twentieth centuries, antivaccination-ists vigorously protested compulsory vaccination. A loosely organized group, activists opposed vaccination on various grounds, arguing that this method of controlling epidemics was ineffective at least and lethal at most. For some, like the Reverend Henning Jacobson, the point was not so much the safety and efficacy of smallpox vaccines as it was the individual's liberty to decide for himself what medical treatment he will undergo. As was typical of antivaccination literature, this pamphlet circulated widely in Boston and Cambridge, Massachusetts, during the 1901–1902 smallpox epidemic.

Vaccination Is the Curse of Childhood: Important Facts for Parents and Guardians, and for the People

What Is Vaccine Virus?

The viruses injected into the human for the alleged purpose of preventing small-pox, may be any one, or combination, of the following *pus products:*

(1) The original Horse-grease Cow-pox of Jenner; (2) A combination of Cow-pox and Small-pox virus; (3) Swine-pox; (4) Horse-pox; (5) Spontaneous Cow-pox; (6) Small-pox matter passed through the cow; (7) Donkey-lymph; (8) Buffalo-lymph; and many more pus products of disease, having passed through various animal and human bodies, and carrying with them the seeds of *erysipelas, scrofula, consumption, eczema, leprosy, syphilis,* and other loathsome diseases. No physician can tell you, for a certainty, *what it is* which he advises you to have injected into the arm of your child.

What is the New Glycerinated Calf Lymph so much boasted of, and styled "pure vaccine lymph"?

It is the vaccine matter described above, mixed with *glycerin,* which is a substance especially adapted for the growth of the seeds of disease. Deadly diseases have been and are transmitted by its use. It has been condemned by expert witnesses before the English Royal Commission of 1889–1896 (Drs. Barlow and Acland); by Sir George Buchanan, M.D., F.R.S.; the *Indian Lancet* and many others. There is and *can be no such thing* as "pure vaccine lymph."

What are the Results of Vaccination?

Disease, constitutional debility, death. Many a sufferer from debility and blood deterioration can trace that condition to vaccination; and many other like sufferers from vaccination are not aware of the real cause of their condition. The cause of such sickness and death is too often *concealed under some other name.*

The people have sifted this matter, and have learned these facts concerning vaccination:

1. That no number of vaccination "marks" will prevent small-pox; the vaccinated and re-vaccinated in civil life, and in the army, everywhere, have the disease.
2. That it does not mitigate small-pox; the vaccinated frequently die of the most malignant kind, while the unvaccinated as well as the vaccinated experience the mildest form.
3. That small-pox vaccination (or "inoculation") gives small-pox instead of preventing it; while Cow-pox vaccination cannot prevent small-pox, since it *bears no relation to that disease.*
4. That the vaccination imposture is, in times of small-pox "scare," a great source of revenue to doctors, many of whom really believe in a delusion they have not the energy or courage to investigate.
5. That the inoculation craze is extending to many other diseases, and we are threatened with a general blood-poisoning crusade with the so-called "Antitoxins" of cholera, consumption, "hydrophobia," yellow fever, diphtheria, etc.
6. That compulsory vaccination, or the forcible implantation of disease into a body, on the theory that it may in the future prevent some other disease, is an ATROCIOUS CRIME, which has no place in the laws of the civilized community and is inherently a *violation of the Constitution of the United States.*
7. That Sanitation—which means good drainage, good ventilation, pure water, and healthy food—is the only preventive of small-pox and other epidemics. . . .

Do not Allow your Child to be Vaccinated

In Boston, within the past few months, numerous cases of serious illness and blood-poisoning, and several deaths, have been the result of vaccination. In the fatal cases the real facts are concealed from the public, some disease, WHICH HAS BEEN THE DIRECT RESULT OF VACCINATION, being given as the cause of death.

You say, "My child will not be allowed to attend the public schools of Massachusetts unless vaccinated." *That is a mistake.* The following is from Public Statutes for 1894; Chapter 515, Sect. 2:

"All children who shall present a certificate, signed by a regular practicing physician, that they are unfit subjects for vaccination, shall not be subject to the provisions of section 9 of chapter 47 of the public statutes, excluding unvaccinated children from public schools, and all children upon such a certificate shall be exempted from the provisions of this act."

There are hundreds of physicians in Massachusetts who are well aware of the uselessness and evil effects of vaccination. Apply to any one of them for certificate of exemption for your child.

Write to Room 77, No. 1 Beacon St., Boston, for names of such physicians if they are unknown to you.

Reprinted from "Anti-Vaccination Circular, Distributed during the Epidemic of Small Pox in Boston, 1901." Countway Library of Medicine, Harvard University.

Jacobson v. Massachusetts (1905)

Henning Jacobson was one of several citizens arrested for refusing to comply with a compulsory vaccination order issued by health authorities during a smallpox epidemic in Cambridge, Massachusetts. Appealing his case to the U.S. Supreme Court, Jacobson argued that because he was healthy, he posed no threat to the health and safety of the community. Further, he insisted that a previous vaccination had made him sick and thus it was his right to choose whether to undergo the procedure. Jacobson argued that the Fourteenth Amendment's guarantee of liberty protected his freedom to make this choice concerning his own body.

October Term, 1904
  Brief of Argument
  Revised Laws, Ch. 75, Sec. 137, are as follows:
  "The Board of Health of a city or town if, in its opinion, it is necessary for the public health or safety, shall require and enforce the vaccination and revaccination of all the inhabitants thereof and shall provide them with the means of free vaccination. Whoever, being over twenty-one years of age and not under guardianship, refuses or neglects to comply with such requirement shall forfeit five dollars." ...
  The plaintiff in error ... respectfully submits that said section is unconstitutional:
  1. Because it is contrary to the preamble of the Constitution of the United States, which declares that the Constitution is ordained and established to promote the general welfare, and secure the blessings of liberty to ourselves and our posterity.

2. Because it is contrary to the Fourteenth Amendment of the Constitution, to wit, Sec. 1 thereof, which provides that "No state shall make or enforce any law which shall abridge the privileges or immunities of citizens of the United States; nor shall any state deprive any person of life, liberty, or property, without due process of law, nor deny to any person within its jurisdiction the equal protection of the laws." . . .

The state intervenes to secure the personal health, preservation and comfort of its citizens, and punishes those who violate it. But except under compulsory vaccination laws it has not yet undertaken to attack the health of individuals.

The plaintiff in error does not deny the right to the exercise of the police power within any accepted definition of that power. . . . While the police power might properly be exercised to protect this plaintiff in error as a citizen of the United States from compulsion from any source, even the state itself, to be inoculated with a disease, no constitutional precedent can be found which justifies the exercise of the police power to compel a citizen to submit himself to an assault and to inoculation with a disease. . . .

The plaintiff in error . . . does not deny that if he or his property be infected with contagious or infectious disease, or if he commits any noxious act, it is the right and duty of the state to defend the rest of the community against him as a public, or even as a private nuisance, but nowhere within this decision, or any other which has been made by this Court can he be constitutionally made subject to such criminal prosecution when he is in health and does no act whatever which can offend his fellow-citizens.

The police power rests upon well-founded principles, all of which have their basis and reason in existing offensive acts or conditions. Offensive trades, noisome occupations, pollution of air or water, unsafe or unhealthy buildings, burials, transportation of dead bodies, cemeteries, burning fluids and adulteration of food or drink contain present conditions which are a menace to the public health or safety. The regulation of medicine and dentistry and similar occupations is based upon the protection of the community from unskillfulness in those who undertake to deal with the bodies or health of the people. . . . But this court has not yet decided that the police power can be imposed upon healthy citizens, merely because as human beings they have the potentiality of contracting contagious diseases. . . .

The plaintiff in error disclaims any objection to voluntary vaccination, which should be open to the citizens from free choice if he believes in its efficacy and desires to undergo its dangers. It is against the compulsory feature of the Massachusetts law that the plaintiff protests. A compulsory vaccination law, like that involved in the case at bar, is founded upon unreasonable and false theories in many respects.

It is not a reasonable or legitimate exercise of legislative power, because it undertakes to compel a man to do for the protection of other men what other men can voluntarily do to protect themselves. The law, therefore, is predicated upon a failure of its own enforcement, for if all the people of Massachusetts except the plaintiff in error were vaccinated and, therefore, immune, the plaintiff could do no harm to the rest of the community, and if he were neglectful of his own health the penalty would fall upon himself. The only possible victims of the plaintiff's failure to be vaccinated would be those who had themselves failed or refused to be vaccinated. In other words, who had themselves violated the law.

Is it possible that an exercise of the police power of the state can be predicated upon the protection of those who are themselves violating the law which calls forth such an exercise of power?

Viewed from the standpoint of the individual to be protected, may it not fairly be asked, if I, who neglect to be vaccinated, have a right to demand of my neighbor that he be vaccinated to protect me? Clearly if the method is effective I have it in my power to protect myself. Viewed from the standpoint of the community at large, if I am the only unvaccinated person, I suffer alone and others, who have become immune, are in no danger. The only answer to this proposition is that vaccination is but a partial remedy; this is but an argument against the law itself which, to obtain doubtful results, insists that the citizen should introduce into his own healthy system, and the systems of his children or wards, a disease which may produce ill-health and death. In any event, considering it as a partial remedy, every person in the community can avail himself by his voluntary act of whatever protection it affords, and I, in declining to avail myself of the same protection, am at best a possible and not a present menace to their health. . . .

By what precedent of Constitutional or Statutory law can a citizen be punished who menaces no present injury to his fellow-men, and who objects to a present injury to himself, inflicted upon the order of the state for the purpose of protecting others from possible injury.

Wherein has a citizen violated the law upon which the police power is based, viz.: That he shall so use his own as not to injure others. Surely in going about in the community, healthy and law-abiding, he does no injury to the community or the state, and the plaintiff in error challenges upon any theory of the legislative power in this Republic the right of the state to penalize him for preserving his health, even against the admonition of the state.

The preamble of the Constitution declares it to be one of the purposes of the instrument to "secure the blessings of liberty to ourselves and our posterity." Liberty of the citizen in the very first analysis is immunity of his person from seizure or injury, except for the commission of an offence against the state, and the vaccination law of Massachusetts is a violation of his fundamental right to liberty as guaranteed to English speaking peoples from the Magna Charta, through the Constitution of the United States to the Fourteenth Amendment. . . .

In the early twentieth century, Henning Jacobson's Fourteenth Amendment liberty argument fell on deaf ears, and the U.S. Supreme Court ruled that compulsory vaccination statutes represented a constitutional use of states' police powers. Although individuals cannot be forced to submit to vaccination, Justice John Marshall Harlan wrote, the Massachusetts law's imposition of fine or imprisonment was not an excessive infringement of individual liberty.

Argued December 6, 1904.

Decided February 20, 1905.

MR. JUSTICE HARLAN delivered the opinion of the court:

We pass without extended discussion the suggestion that the particular section of the statute of Massachusetts now in question (137, chap. 75) is in derogation of rights secured by the preamble of the Constitution of the United States. Although that preamble indicates the general purposes for which the people ordained and established the Constitution, it has never been regarded as the source of any substantive power conferred on the government of the United States, or on any of its departments. Such powers embrace only those expressly granted in the body of the Constitution, and such as may be implied from those so granted. Although, therefore, one of the declared objects of the Constitution was to secure the blessings of liberty to all under the sovereign jurisdiction and authority of the United States, no power can be exerted to that end by the United States, unless, apart from the preamble, it be found in some express delegation of power, or in some power to be properly implied therefrom. . . .

What, according to the judgment of the state court, are the scope and effect of the statute? What results were intended to be accomplished by it? . . . Is the statute, so construed, therefore, inconsistent with the liberty which the Constitution of the United States secures to every person against deprivation by the state?

The authority of the state to enact this statute is to be referred to what is commonly called the police power,—a power which the state did not surrender when becoming a member of the Union under the Constitution. Although this court has refrained from any attempt to define the limits of that power, yet it has distinctly recognized the authority of a state to enact quarantine laws and "health laws of every description;" indeed, all laws that relate to matters completely within its territory and which do not by their necessary operation affect the people of other states. According to settled principles, the police power of a state must be held to embrace, at least, such reasonable regulations established directly by legislative enactment as will protect the public health and the public safety. It is equally true that the state may invest local bodies called into existence for purposes of local administration with authority in some appropriate way to safeguard the public health and the public safety. The mode or manner in which those results are to be accomplished is within the discretion of the state, subject, of course, so far as Federal power is concerned, only to the condition that no rule prescribed by a state, nor any regulation adopted by a local governmental agency acting under the sanction of state legislation, shall contravene the Constitution of the United States, nor infringe any right granted or secured by that instrument. A local enactment or regulation, even if based on the acknowledged police powers of a state, must always yield in case of conflict with the exercise by the general government of any power it possesses under the Constitution, or with any right which that instrument gives or secures.

We come, then, to inquire whether any right given or secured by the Constitution is invaded by the statute as interpreted by the state court. The defendant insists that his liberty is invaded when the state subjects him to fine or imprisonment for neglecting or refusing to submit to vaccination; that a compulsory vaccination law is unreasonable, arbitrary, and oppressive, and, therefore, hostile to the inherent right of every freeman to care for his own body and health in such way as to him seems best; and that the execution of such a law against one who objects to vaccination, no matter for what reason, is nothing short of an assault upon his person. But the liberty secured by the Constitution of the United States to every person within its jurisdiction does not import an absolute right in each person to be, at all times and in all circumstances, wholly freed from restraint. There are manifold restraints to which every person is necessarily subject for the common good. On any other basis organized society could not exist with safety to its members. Society based on the rule that each one is a law unto himself would soon be confronted with disorder and anarchy. Real liberty for all could not exist under the operation of a principle which recognizes the right of each individual person to use his own, whether in respect of his person or his property, regardless of the injury that may be done to others. This court has more than once recognized it as a fundamental principle that "persons and property are subjected to all kinds of restraints and burdens in order to secure the general comfort, health, and prosperity of the state; of the perfect right of the legislature to do which no question ever was, or upon acknowledged general principles ever can be, made, so far as natural persons are concerned." . . . Even liberty itself, the greatest of all rights, is not unrestricted license to act according to one's own will. It is only freedom from restraint under conditions essential to the equal enjoyment of the same right by others. It is, then, liberty regulated by law. In the Constitution of Massachusetts adopted in 1780 it was laid down as a fundamental principle of the social compact that the whole people covenants with each citizen, and each citizen with the whole people, that all shall be governed by certain laws for "the common good," and that government is instituted "for the common good, for the protection, safety, prosperity, and happiness of the people, and not for the profit, honor, or private interests of any one man, family, or class of men." The good and welfare of the commonwealth, of which the legislature is primarily the judge, is the basis on which the police power rests in Massachusetts.

Applying these principles to the present case, it is to be observed that the legislature of Massachusetts required the inhabitants of a city or town to be vaccinated only when, in the opinion of the board of health, that was necessary for the public health or the public safety. The authority to determine for all what ought to be done in such an emergency must have been lodged somewhere or in some body; and surely it was appropriate for the legislature to refer that question, in the first instance, to a board of health composed of persons residing in the locality affected, and appointed, presumably, because of their fitness to determine such questions. To invest such a body with authority over such matters was not an unusual, nor an unreasonable or arbitrary, requirement. Upon the principle of self-defense, of paramount necessity, a community has the right to protect itself against an epidemic of disease which threatens the safety of its members. It is to be observed that when the regulation in question was adopted, smallpox, according to the recitals in the regulation adopted by the board of health, was prevalent to some extent in the city of Cambridge, and the disease was increasing. If such was the situation,—and nothing is asserted or appears in the record to the contrary,—if we are to attach, any value whatever to the knowledge which, it is safe to affirm, in common to all civilized peoples touching smallpox and the methods most usually employed to eradicate that disease, it cannot be adjudged that the present regulation of the board of health was not necessary in order to protect the public health and secure the public safety. Smallpox being prevalent and increasing at Cambridge, the court would usurp the functions of another branch of government if it adjudged, as matter of law, that the mode adopted under the sanction of the state, to protect the people at large was arbitrary, and not justified by the necessities of the case. We say necessities of the case, because it might be that an acknowledged power of a local community to protect itself against an epidemic threatening the safety of all might be exercised in particular circumstances and in reference to particular persons in such an arbitrary, unreasonable manner, or might go so far beyond what was reasonably required for the safety of the public, as to authorize or compel the courts to interfere for the protection of such persons. . . . If the mode adopted by the commonwealth of Massachusetts for the protection of its local communities against smallpox proved to be distressing, inconvenient, or objectionable to some,—if nothing more could be reasonably affirmed of the statute in question,—the answer is that it was the duty of the constituted authorities primarily to keep in view the welfare, comfort, and safety of the many, and not permit the interests of the many to be subordinated to the wishes or convenience of the few. There is, of course, a sphere within which the individual may assert the supremacy of his own will, and rightfully dispute the authority of any human government,—especially of any free government existing under a written constitution, to interfere with the exercise of that will. But it is equally true that in every well-ordered society charged with the duty of conserving the safety of its members the rights of the individual in respect of his liberty may at times, under the pressure of great dangers, be subjected to such restraint, to be enforced by reasonable regulations, as the safety of the general public may demand. . . .

It is said, however, that the statute, as interpreted by the state court, although making an exception in favor of children certified by a registered physician to be unfit subjects for vaccination, makes no exception in case of adults in like condition. But this cannot be deemed a denial of the equal protection of the laws to adults; for the statute is applicable equally to all in like condition, and there are obviously reasons why regulations may be appropriate for adults which could not be safely applied to persons of tender years.

Looking at the propositions embodied in the defendant's rejected offers of proof, it is clear that they are more formidable by their number than by their inherent value. Those offers in the main seem to have had no purpose except to state the general theory of those of the medical profession who attach little or no value to vaccination as a means of preventing the spread of smallpox, or who think that vaccination causes other diseases of the body. What everybody knows the court must know, and therefore the state court judicially knew, as this court knows, that an opposite theory accords with the common belief, and is maintained by high medical authority. We must assume that, when the statute in question was passed, the legislature of Massachusetts was not unaware of these opposing theories, and was compelled, of necessity, to choose between them. It was not compelled to commit a matter involving the public health and safety to the final decision of a court or jury. It is no part of the function of a court or a jury to determine which one of two modes was likely to be the most effective for the protection of the public against disease. That was for the legislative department to determine in the light of all the information it had or could obtain. It could not properly abdicate its function to guard the public health and safety. The state legislature proceeded upon the theory which recognized vaccination as at least an effective, if not the best-known, way in which to meet and suppress the evils of a smallpox epidemic that imperiled an entire population. Upon what sound principles as to the relations existing between the different departments of government can the court review this action of the legislature? If there is any such power in the judiciary to review legislative action in respect of a matter affecting the general welfare, it can only be when that which the legislature has done comes within the rule that, if a statute purporting to have been enacted to protect the public health, the public morals, or the public safety, has no real or substantial relation to those objects, or is, beyond all question, a plain, palpable invasion of rights secured by the fundamental law, it is the duty of the courts to so adjudge, and thereby give effect to the Constitution.

Whatever may be thought of the expediency of this statute, it cannot be affirmed to be, beyond question, in palpable conflict with the Constitution. Nor, in view of the methods employed to stamp out the disease of smallpox, can anyone confidently assert that the means prescribed by the state to that end has no real or substantial relation to the protection of the public health and the public safety. . . .

In a free country, where the government is by the people, through their chosen representatives, practical legislation admits of no other standard of action, for what the people believe is for the common welfare must be accepted as tending to promote the common welfare, whether it does in fact or not. Any other basis would conflict with the spirit of the Constitution, and would sanction measures opposed to a Republican form of government. While we do not decide, and cannot decide, that vaccination is a preventive of small-pox, we take judicial notice of the fact that this is the common belief of the people of the state, and, with this fact as a foundation, we hold that the statute in question is a health law, enacted in a reasonable and proper exercise of the police power. . . .

The defendant offered to prove that vaccination "quite often" caused serious and permanent injury to the health of the person vaccinated; that the operation "occasionally" resulted in death; that it was "impossible" to tell "in any particular case" what the results of vaccination would be, or whether it would injure the health or result in death; that "quite often" one's blood is in a certain condition of impurity when it is not prudent or safe to vaccinate him; that there is no practical test by which to determine "with any degree of certainty" whether one's blood is in such condition of impurity as to render vaccination necessarily unsafe or dangerous; that vaccine matter is "quite often" impure and dangerous to be used, but whether impure or not cannot be ascertained by any known practical test; that the defendant refused to submit to vaccination for the reason that he had, "when a child," been caused great and extreme suffering for a long period by a disease produced by vaccination; and that he had witnessed a similar result of vaccination, not only in the case of his son, but in the cases of others.

These offers, in effect, invited the court and jury to go over the whole ground gone over by the legislature when it enacted the statute in question. . . .

The matured opinions of medical men everywhere, and the experience of mankind, as all must know, negate the suggestion that it is not possible in any case to determine whether vaccination is safe. Was defendant exempted from the operation of the statute simply because of his dread of the same evil results experienced by him when a child, and which he had observed in the cases of his son and other children? Could he reasonably claim such an exemption because "quite often," or "occasionally," injury had resulted from vaccination, or because it was impossible, in the opinion of some, by any practical test, to determine with absolute certainty whether a particular person could be safely vaccinated? It seems to the court that an affirmative answer to these questions would practically strip the legislative department of its function to care for the public health and the public safety when endangered by epidemics of disease. Such an answer would mean that compulsory vaccination could not, in any conceivable case, be legally enforced in a community, even at the command of the legislature, however widespread the epidemic of smallpox, and however deep and universal was the belief of the community and of its medical advisers that a system of general vaccination was vital to the safety of all. . . .

Before closing this opinion we deem it appropriate, in order to prevent misapprehension as to our views, to observe—perhaps to repeat a thought already sufficiently expressed, namely—that the police power of a state, whether exercised directly by the legislature, or by a local body acting under its authority, may be exerted in such circumstances, or by regulations so arbitrary and oppressive in particular cases, as to justify the interference of the courts to prevent wrong and oppression. Extreme cases can be readily suggested. Ordinarily such cases are not safe guides in the administration of the law. It is easy, for instance, to suppose the case of an adult who is embraced by the mere words of the act, but yet to subject whom to vaccination in a particular condition of his health or body would be cruel and inhuman in the last degree. We are not to be understood as holding that the statute was intended to be applied to such a case, or, if it was so intended, that the judiciary would not be competent to interfere and protect the health and life of the individual concerned. . . .

No such case is here presented. It is the cause of an adult who, for aught that appears, was himself in perfect health and a fit subject of vaccination, and yet, while remaining in the community, refused to obey the statute and the regulation adopted in execution of its provisions for the protection of the public health and the public safety, confessedly endangered by the presence of a dangerous disease. We now decide only that the statute covers the present case, and that nothing clearly appears that would justify this court in holding it to be unconstitutional and inoperative in its application to the plaintiff in error.

The judgment of the court below must be affirmed.

It is so ordered.

Mr. Justice Brewer and Mr. Justice Peckham dissent.

Zucht v. King (1922)

The Supreme Court revisited the issue of compulsory vaccination in the 1922 case Zucht v. King. *This time, the circumstances of the case were different, since the San Antonio school board's mandate that all public school students be vaccinated applied at a time when no smallpox was present; in fact, the disease had not appeared in ten years. But the school board insisted that there was a threat to the general health and safety because children came in contact with communities likely to be infected with communicable diseases. After losing her case in the lower court in Texas, Rosalyn Zucht appealed to the U.S. Supreme Court. This excerpt from the Application to the Court for Writ of Certiorari illustrates Zucht's argument that children attending school are exposed to no more risk of communicable disease than others throughout the community. Further, the conditions in which Rosalyn lived made it unlikely, in her estimation, that she would ever come into contact with the disease. Therefore, she claimed, the school board's mandate was not a valid exercise of police powers as a measure to protect the public's health.*

Application for Writ of Certiorari in the Supreme Court of the United States

4: The said City of San Antonio is a city having over 100,000 inhabitants and has a street car system operating on and over its principal streets transporting passengers on its cars during each and every day and for the greater part of each and every night, which cars have seats where the passengers, consisting of men, women, and children, are seated in closest juxtaposition; and said cars are daily and nightly crowded with passengers to such an extent frequently that there is hardly standing room in such cars; the passengers being almost literally packed in said cars. Said City has also a great number of theaters and other buildings where public shows are daily and nightly conducted and where great crowds of men, women, and children gather daily and nightly for entertainment, and are seated in close personal contact. Likewise said City has a great number of churches where crowds of people, consisting of men, women, and children are in personal contact at least once a week and frequently oftener. Said City also has within its limits quite a number of railway passenger depots where large crowds of people, consisting of men, women, and children assemble in close personal contact daily and nightly. There is also in said City a public monitor car service operating on a number of principal streets daily and nightly transporting passengers, consisting of men, women, and children which passengers are in the closest personal contact frequently sitting on each other's laps. There are also in said City a large number of factories where large numbers of men, women, and children are employed in close personal contact each and every day of the week except Sundays. There are in said City a large number of laundries where large numbers of men, women, boys and girls are employed working daily in close personal contact. There is also in said City what is known as the Mexican quarter where the Sanitary conditions are not good and where approximately 20,000 of the inhabitants of said City reside closely crowded and where large crowds assemble in close personal contact daily and frequently at night. Said City also has a number of public parks where crowds of men, women, and children gather frequently for recreation and where there are swimming pools in which great crowds of men, women, and children bathe daily and nightly during the summer season. And on the principle streets of said City there are great crowds of people on the sidewalks daily and nightly in close personal contact, frequently amounting to jams. Said City has a large number of private educational institutions within its limits where children and persons over the age of twenty-one years are educated. There are also have been [sic] for many years a great number of public free school buildings in said City where public free schools are conducted for the benefit of the children who are entitled to attend the same for educational purposes under the constitution and laws of the State and under the provisions of the special act of the Legislature incorporating the said San Antonio Independent School District. Said public free schools are under the exclusive control and management of the said San Antonio School Board under the law of this State. There are and have been for many years in said City a large number of private schools and institutions where great numbers of pupils both under the age of twenty one years and over the age of twenty-one years constantly attend now and have constantly attended and are taught and have been taught in various branches of learning and skill, and there are now and have been many other persons employed in, connected with, and attendant upon said private institutions. . . .

9: The said public free schools in said district are conducted in a thoroughly sanitary manner and every reasonable precaution has been taken to protect the health of the pupils attending the same. The grounds and buildings of said public free school in said district are in most excellent sanitary condition and are so kept all the time. All the public free school buildings in said district are provided with separate individual seats on which the pupils and all other persons connected with said schools are seated separate and apart from each other and are not in personal contact. The same is true with reference to the private schools and other educational institutions in said City.

10: The said City and its said City Council have never attempted to enforce vaccination generally among the inhabitants of said city nor even among the children generally of said city, but undertook to arbitrarily discriminate against the pupils who attended the schools and educational institutions in said city and the persons connected with said schools and institutions in said city, including the pupils attending the same and the other persons connected therewith, by adopting an ordinance as follows:

"Section 25. NO child or other person shall be permitted to attend any of the public schools, or any place of education within its city, unless such child or other person shall first present certificate from some duly qualified physician to the city physician that such child, or other person, has been successfully vaccinated within six years preceding the time at which said child, or other person, desires to attend school. Such certificate shall give a description of such child, or person, age and nativity, and kind of virus used, for which purpose the city physician shall furnish the necessary blanks to all persons requiring the same." . . .

11: No valid reason existed or does exist for said discrimination. But on the contrary, there was and is much more danger of the contagion of small-pox (which the advocates of vaccination claim vaccination will prevent) spreading from the close personal contact of persons in the assemblages and in the places other than the schools and educational institutions of said city hereinbefore named than there is such danger from the contact of the pupils, teachers, employees and other persons in said schools and educational institutions. Especially is this the case in the said Mexican Quarter of said city where the danger of the breaking out of the disease called small pox is infinitely greater than in the said schools and educational institutions.

12: The said ordinance is not and was not intended to be a mere temporary measure to be in force only when there is an epidemic of smallpox in said city or when such an epidemic is imminent; but purports to be in force and is intended to be in force all the time whether or not there is a single case of smallpox in said city, in said county, or even within the State....

15. The said Rosalyn Zucht never has been vaccinated nor is she willing to be vaccinated nor are her parents willing that she should submit to vaccination because she and her parents fear that vaccination will endanger her health and life....

She and her parents have a permanent home and reside in a locality in said City where there has never been single [*sic*] case of smallpox, and they have continuously resided in said locality, for many years. She has never been exposed to the contagion of smallpox, and the sanitary conditions in said locality where she and her parents have their said home are excellent, being a quiet residence portion of said city where the inhabitants own their own homes and there is no crowding of houses close together and no crowds gather on the streets or elsewhere in said locality....

17: Yet, on, to-wit: March 3rd, 1919, the present year, the defendants hereinbefore named conspired together to expel her from school, and said defendants and each of them, acting wantonly and maliciously, expelled her, the said Rosalyn Zucht, from said school; and the said defendants and each of them, acting wantonly and maliciously refuse to permit her to attend said school any longer and prevent her from attending said school or any other public school in said city any longer unless she will submit to vaccination and the said defendants and each of them have thereby deprived her of the benefits of an education and of the benefits of her proportionate part of said public free school fund provided by the Constitution and Laws of Texas....

22. The said ordinance, by reason of discriminating against the pupils and the other persons connected with said schools and other

educational institutions in said city and undertaking to compel the pupils attending and the other persons connected therewith to submit to vaccination as a condition precedent to their being permitted to attend such schools and other educational institutions or to be connected therewith . . . is unreasonable, deprives such pupils and other persons, including plaintiff, of their rights and privileges without due course of the law of the land in violation of Section 19 of Article 1 of the Constitution of the State of Texas; and said ordinance denies to such pupils including plaintiff herein, and other persons connected with said schools and other educational institutions in said city the equal protection of the laws in violation of the XIV Amendment to the Constitution of the United States of America and said ordinance is, therefore, absolutely void. . . .

Writing for the majority in Zucht v. King, *Justice Louis Brandeis upheld the precedent set in* Jacobson *and allowed health authorities to retain a great deal of discretionary authority in determining when a public health threat was significant enough to warrant mandatory preventive measures.*

Argued October 20, 1922
    November 13, 1922, Decided
    MR. JUSTICE BRANDEIS delivered the opinion of the Court.
    Ordinances of the City of San Antonio, Texas, provide that no child or other person shall attend a public school or other place of education without having first presented a certificate of vaccination. Purporting to act under these ordinances, public officials excluded Rosalyn Zucht from a public school because she did not have the required certificate and refused to submit to vaccination. They also caused her to be excluded from a private school. Thereupon Rosalyn brought this suit against the officials in a court of the State. The bill charges that there was then no occasion for requiring vaccination; that the ordinances deprive plaintiff of her liberty without due process of law by, in effect, making vaccination compulsory; and, also, that they are void because they leave to the Board of Health discretion to determine when and under what circumstances the requirement shall be enforced without providing any rule by which that board is to be guided in its action and without providing any safeguards against partiality and oppression. The prayers were for an injunction against enforcing the ordinances, for a writ of mandamus to compel her

admission to the public school, and for damages. A general demurrer to the bill of complaint was sustained by the trial court; and, plaintiff having declined to amend, the bill was dismissed. This judgment was affirmed by the Court of Civil Appeals for the Fourth Supreme Judicial District. . . . The case is now here on writ of error granted by the Chief Justice of the Court of Civil Appeals. It is assigned as error that the ordinances violate the due process and equal protection clauses of the Fourteenth Amendment; and that as administered they denied to plaintiff equal protection of the laws.

The validity of the ordinances under the Federal Constitution was drawn in question by objections properly taken below. . . .

But, although the validity of a law was formally drawn in question, it is our duty to decline jurisdiction whenever it appears that the constitutional question presented is not, and was not at the time of granting the writ, substantial in character. Long before this suit was instituted, *Jacobson v. Massachusetts*, 197 U.S. 11, had settled that it is within the police power of a State to provide for compulsory vaccination. That case and others had also settled that a State may, consistently with the Federal Constitution, delegate to a municipality authority to determine under what conditions health regulations shall become operative. And still others had settled that the municipality may vest in its officials broad discretion in matters affecting the application and enforcement of a health law. A long line of decisions by this Court had also settled that in the exercise of the police power reasonable classification may be freely applied and that regulation is not violative of the equal protection clause merely because it is not all-embracing. In view of these decisions we find in the record no question as to the validity of the ordinance sufficiently substantial to support the writ of error . . . [T]hese ordinances confer not arbitrary power, but only that broad discretion required for the protection of public health.

Buck v. Bell (1927)

Carrie Buck was determined to be "feebleminded" by a Virginia court. The label rendered her a "fit subject" for sterilization, according to Virginia law. This excerpt from the transcripts of Carrie Buck's hearing demonstrate the nature of eugenic thought in the 1920s, the authority of scientific "experts," and the character of the evidence used to determine her status as "feebleminded."

Statement of Evidence, November 18, 1924

Miss Caroline E. Wilhelm, a witness of lawful age, having been first duly sworn, testified as follows:

Direct examination by Col. Strode.

Q. Miss Wilhelm, what is your occupation?

A. I am a social worker of the Red Cross. Secretary superintendent of public welfare at Albemarle County.

Q. Have you any record of this girl, Carrie Buck?

A. Yes, sir.

Q. What is her record?

A. I came to Charlottesville about February of this year, and just before that time the case had been reported to Miss Duke, who was in charge temporarily in the office as Secretary, that Mr. Dobbs, who had charge of the girl, had taken her when a small child, had reported to Miss Duke that the girl was pregnant and that he wanted to have her committed somewhere—to have her sent to some institution, and wanted Miss Duke to have that brought about. The matter was not put through until I was in the office, and officially I brought Carrie Buck over to the Colony at Lynchburg.

Q. You know that Carrie was not married?

A. No, she was not.

Q. Was that child born?

A. Yes, sir.

Q. She had an illegitimate child?

A. Yes, sir.

Q. And her character was such that you had her committed to the institution at Lynchburg?

A. Yes, sir. There was a commission held and she was committed to the Colony.

Q. From your experience as a social worker, if Carrie were discharged from the colony still capable of child-bearing, is she likely to become the parent of a defective child?

A. I should judge so. I think a girl of her mentality is more or less at the mercy of other people, and this girl particularly, from her past record. Her mother had three illegitimate children, and I should say that Carrie would be very likely to have illegitimate children.

Q. So that the only way that she could be likely kept from increasing her own kind would be either segregation or something that would stop her power to propagate. Is she an asset or a liability to society?

A. A distinct liability, I should say.

Q. Did you have any personal dealings with Carrie?

A. Just a few weeks between the time when the commission was held and when I brought her to Lynchburg.

Q. Was she obviously feeble-minded?

A. I should say so, as a social worker.

Q. Did you know her mother?

A. No, I never saw her mother.

Q. Where is the child?

A. The child is with Mr. and Mrs. Dobbs. They kept the child.

Q. How old is the child?

A. It is not quite eight months old.

Q. Have you any impression about the child?

A. It is difficult to judge prob-ilities [*sic*] of a child as young as that, but it seems to me not quite a normal baby.

Q. You don't regard the child as a normal baby?

A. In its appearance—I should say that perhaps my knowledge of the mother may prejudice me in that regard, but I saw the child at the same time as Mrs. Dobbs' daughter's baby, which is only three days older than this one, and there is a very decided difference in the development of the babies. That was about two weeks ago.

Q. You would not judge the child as a normal baby?

A. There is a look about it that is not quite normal, but just what it is, I can't tell. . . .

Cross-examination.

By Mr. Whitehead:

Q. This baby you are talking about now is Carrie Buck's baby?

A. Yes, sir.

Q. What other baby was the comparison made by?

A. Mr. and Mrs. Dobbs' who have had Carrie since she was three years old. They have a daughter who has a baby three days older than Carrie's.

Q. You say the baby of Carrie's does not measure up to the Dobbs'?

A. Not nearly.

Q. Neither one of them can talk.

A. No.

Q. Can they walk?

A. No.

Q. In what way do they differ?

A. The children—Mrs. Dobbs's daughter's baby is a very responsive baby. When you play with it, or try to attract its attention—it is a baby that you can play with. The other baby is not. It seems very apathetic and not responsive. . . .

Q. Now, there are records down in Charlottesville in connection with social work—have any records against Carrie Buck, the girl here, which would tend to show she was feeble-minded, or unsocial, or anti-social, or whatever the term is, other than the birth of the child?

A. No, sir, our record begins on the 17th of January of this year, and that is the first knowledge we have of her.

Q. Basing your opinion that the girl is unsocial, or antisocial, on the fact that she had an illegitimate child—the point I am getting at is this—are you basing your opinion on that?

A. On that fact, and that as a social worker I know what girls of that type—

Q. But the question of pregnancy is not evidence of feeble-mindedness, is it—the fact that, as we say, she made a miss-step—went wrong—is that evidence of feeble-mindedness?

A. No, but a feeble-minded girl is much more likely to go wrong. . . .

Dr. J. S. DeJarnette, a witness of lawful age, having been first duly sworn, testified as follows:

Direct examination by Col. Strode:

Q. Doctor, where do you live, and what is your occupation?

A. Staunton, and my occupation is Superintendent of the Western State Hospital at Staunton.

Q. What class of patients?

A. Chiefly the insane. We take also the habitual drunkards and dopers—drug addicts.

Q. How long have you been officially connected with the hospital at Staunton?

A. Thirty-six years. . . .

Q. What would you say is a feeble-minded person?

A. I would say a feeble-minded person was one who, on account of his mental condition, was unable to take care of himself properly.

Q. Mental condition in what way?

A. Any way that occurs from his birth or the failure develope [sic] of his mind, would strictly come within the definition. Of course, insanity would cover the whole thing.

Q. I understand that insanity may supervene upon a mind of normal development, but mental defectives—

A. That is feeble from birth.

Q. Now, feeblemindedness is—

A. Is inherited and acquired.

Q. Is it curable?

A. No, sir.

Q. It is an incurable mental defect?

A. Yes, sir.

Q. Therefore it is judicially ascertainable, whether or not any particular individual is feebleminded, is it?

A. It is.

Q. In your experience, and in your studies, have you reached any conclusion as to whether there are laws of heredity which are ascertainable and which may be relied on in determining whether or not a feeble-minded patient is likely to be a potential parent of socially inadequate offspring?

A. Yes, sir.

Q. I will ask you to enlarge on that. I wish you would give the Court some benefit of your observation. Give them the family history, to a degree, of one of the feeble-minded patients—how far can you foresee of they will probably propagate?

A. Well, you find feeblemindedness runs in families. That is, if the parents are feebleminded and the children are feebleminded, you have every right to believe it is from inheritance. Occasionally a feebleminded child may be from an injury, which will not affect its offspring—this is, if it is accidental. . . .

Q. Naturally, it is provided that this operation [vasectomy or salpingectomy] should be performed only for the welfare of society. In what way would you say the welfare of society would be promoted by it?

A. The standard of general intelligence would be lifted, the crimes that they are liable to produce, as there are larger and larger percentage of feeble-minded in prison and as it affects that, it would lower the number of criminals. . . .

Q. You have heard the evidence tending to show that this girl, Carrie Buck, is herself feeble-minded; that her mother is also an inmate of the same institution and is feeble-minded; and that Carrie has an illegitimate child, who, though only eight months old, does not appear to be normal. Taking those facts into consideration with the other evidence you have heard in regard to her, what would you say as to whether or not she is the probable potential parent of socially inadequate offspring, by the laws of heredity?

A. I think so.

Q. You think she might be sterilized without detriment to her general health?

A. I do.

Q. Do you think her welfare and the welfare of society would be promoted by her sterilization?

A. I do.

Cross-examination by Mr. Whitehead.

Q. Doctor, what is, in your opinion as a physician and from your experience as superintendent of that hospital, what in your opinion is the greatest cause of insanity?

A. Inheritance. . . .

Q. It is a question of selective breeding, in other words. You are cutting out the unfit by breaking up the source?

A. Yes, sir, and you are raising the standard of intelligence in the state. . . .

Q. Do you weigh [Carrie Buck's] sexual gratification and liberty as against her becoming, as Dr. Drury calls them, a fire-ship?

A. I do. . . .

Q. And you say society would be benefited by turning her out?

A. It benefits society by taking care of them, and by the work they do. They are hewers of wood and drawers of water, and there is not very much more likelihood that they would spread venereal disease if sterilized than if they were not. And then it is only for one generation, and the state is not able to pay for segregating them, and by having an in and out method, that is to take these feeble-minded; put them in for a month or two; sterilize them and turn them out; you can get most of them sterilized, whereas the state would keep all of them in.

Q. Therefore your idea is that the State Hospital, say it can only care for one hundred—it takes one hundred and sterilizes them, and turns them out and takes another hundred, and so forth?

A. Yes.

Buck v. Bell *remains among the most controversial opinions handed down by the Supreme Court. Oliver Wendell Holmes, Jr., used the precedent set more than twenty years earlier in* Jacobson v. Massachusetts *to determine that Virginia's compulsory sterilization law represented a valid exercise of police powers to protect the public health and safety from potential damage caused by the passing of "bad genes" down through the generations.*

Argued April 22, 1927.

Decided May 2, 1927.

MR. JUSTICE HOLMES delivered the opinion of the Court.

This is a writ of error to review a judgment of the Supreme Court of Appeals of the State of Virginia, affirming a judgment of the Circuit Court of Amherst County, by which the defendant in error, the superintendent of the State Colony for Epileptics and Feeble Minded, was ordered to perform the operation of salpingectomy upon Carrie Buck, the plaintiff in error, for the purpose of making her sterile. The case comes here upon the contention that the statute authorizing the judgment is void under the Fourteenth Amendment as denying to the plaintiff in error due process of law and the equal protection of the laws.

Carrie Buck is a feeble-minded white woman who was committed to the State Colony above mentioned in due form. She is the daughter of a feeble-minded mother in the same institution, and the mother of an illegitimate feeble-minded child. She was eighteen years old at the time of the trial of her case in the Circuit Court in the latter part of 1924. An Act of Virginia approved March 20, 1924 (Laws 1924, c. 394) recites that the health of the patient and the welfare of society may be promoted in certain cases by the sterilization of mental defectives, under careful safeguard, etc.; that the sterilization may be effected in males by vasectomy and in females by salpingectomy, without serious pain or substantial danger to life; that the Commonwealth is supporting in various institutions many defective persons who if now discharged would become [274 U.S. 200, 206] a menace but if incapable of procreating might be discharged with safety and become self-supporting with benefit to themselves and to society; and that experience has shown that heredity plays an important part in the transmission of insanity, imbecility, etc. The statute then enacts that whenever the superintendent of certain institutions including the above named State Colony shall be of opinion that it is for the best interest of the patients and of society that an inmate under his care should be sexually sterilized, he may have the operation performed upon any patient afflicted with hereditary forms of insanity, imbecility, etc., on complying with the very careful provisions by which the act protects the patients from possible abuse. . . .

The attack is not upon the procedure but upon the substantive law. It seems to be contended that in no circumstances could such an order be justified. It certainly is contended that the order cannot be justified upon the existing grounds. The judgment finds the facts that have been recited and that Carrie Buck "is the probable potential parent of socially inadequate offspring, likewise afflicted, that she may be sexually sterilized without detriment to her general health and that her welfare and that of society will be promoted by her sterilization," and thereupon makes the order. In view of the general declarations of the Legislature and the specific findings of the Court obviously we cannot say as matter of law that the grounds do not exist, and if they exist they justify the result. We have seen more than once that the public welfare may call upon the best citizens for their lives. It would be strange if it could not call upon those who already sap the strength of the State for these lesser sacrifices, often not felt to be such by those concerned, in order to prevent our being swamped with incompetence. It is better for all the world, if instead of waiting to execute degenerate offspring for crime, or to let them starve for their imbecility, society can prevent those who are manifestly unfit from continuing their kind. The principle that sustains compulsory vaccination is broad enough to cover cutting the Fallopian tubes. . . . Three generations of imbeciles are enough. But, it is said, however it might be if this reasoning were applied generally, it fails when it is confined to the small number who are in the institutions named and is not applied to the multitudes outside. It is the usual last resort of constitutional arguments to point out shortcomings of this sort. But the answer is that the law does all that is needed when it does all that it can, indicates a policy, applies it to all within the lines, and seeks to bring within the lines all similarly situated so far and so fast as its means allow. Of course so far as the operations enable those who otherwise must be kept confined to be returned to the world, and thus open the asylum to others, the equality aimed at will be more nearly reached.

Judgment affirmed.

Mr. Justice BUTLER dissents.

Skinner v. Oklahoma (1942)

Justice William O. Douglas's opinion overturned an Oklahoma law that mandated sterilization for three-time offenders convicted of certain felonies on the grounds that, because it rather arbitrarily included some crimes and not others, it violated the equal protection clause of the Fourteenth Amendment. More importantly, the decision defined human procreation as a fundamental right, thereby requiring states to demonstrate a compelling interest when enacting laws designed to regulate or prohibit it.

Argued and Submitted May 6, 1942.

Decided June 1, 1942.

MR. JUSTICE DOUGLAS delivered the opinion of the Court.

This case touches a sensitive and important area of human rights. Oklahoma deprives certain individuals of a right which is basic to the perpetuation of a race—the right to have offspring. Oklahoma has decreed the enforcement of its law against petitioner, overruling his claim that it violated the Fourteenth Amendment. Because that decision raised grave and substantial constitutional questions, we granted the petition for certiorari.

The statute involved is Oklahoma's Habitual Criminal Sterilization Act. That Act defines an "habitual criminal" as a person who, having been convicted two or more times for crimes "amounting to felonies involving moral turpitude" either in an Oklahoma court or in a court of any other State, is thereafter convicted of such a felony in Oklahoma and is sentenced to a term of imprisonment in an Oklahoma penal institution. Machinery is provided for the institution by the Attorney General of a proceeding against such a person in the Oklahoma courts for a judgment that such person shall be rendered sexually sterile. Notice, an opportunity to be heard, and the right to a jury trial are provided. The issues triable in such a proceeding are narrow and confined. If the court or jury finds that the defendant is an "habitual criminal" and that he "may be rendered sexually sterile without detriment to his or her general health," then the court "shall render judgment to the effect that said defendant be rendered sexually sterile," by the operation of vasectomy in case of a male and of salpingectomy in case of a female. Only one other provision of the Act is material here and that is 195 which provides that "offenses arising out of the violation of the prohibitory laws, revenue acts, embezzlement, or political offenses, shall not come or be considered within the terms of this Act."

Petitioner was convicted in 1926 of the crime of stealing chickens and was sentenced to the Oklahoma State Reformatory. In 1929 he was convicted of the crime of robbery with fire arms and was sentenced to the reformatory. In 1934 he was convicted again of robbery with firearms and was sentenced to the penitentiary. He was confined there in 1935 when the Act was passed. In 1936 the Attorney General instituted proceedings against him. Petitioner in his answer challenged the Act as unconstitutional by reason of the Fourteenth Amendment. A jury trial was had. The court instructed the jury that the crimes of which petitioner had been convicted were felonies involving moral turpitude and that the only question for the jury was whether the operation of vasectomy could be performed on petitioner without detriment to his general health. The jury found that it could be. A judgment directing that the operation of vasectomy be performed on petitioner was affirmed by the Supreme Court of Oklahoma by a five to four decision.

Several objections to the constitutionality of the Act have been pressed upon us. It is urged that the Act cannot be sustained as an exercise of the police power in view of the state of scientific authorities respecting inheritability of criminal traits. It is argued that due process is lacking because under this Act, unlike the act upheld in *Buck v. Bell,* the defendant is given no opportunity to be heard on the issue as to whether he is the probable potential parent of socially undesirable offspring. It is also suggested that the Act is penal in character and that the sterilization provided for is cruel and unusual punishment and violative of the Fourteenth Amendment.

We pass those points without intimating an opinion on them, for there is a feature of the Act which clearly condemns it. That is its failure to meet the requirements of the equal protection clause of the Fourteenth Amendment.

We do not stop to point out all of the inequalities in this Act. A few examples will suffice. In Oklahoma grand larceny is a felony. Larceny is grand larceny when the property taken exceeds $20 in value. Embezzlement is punishable "in the manner prescribed for feloniously stealing property of the value of that embezzled." Hence he who embezzles property worth more than $20 is guilty of a felony. A clerk who appropriates over $20 from his employer's till and a stranger who steals the same amount are thus both guilty of felonies. If the latter repeats his act and is convicted three times, he may be sterilized. But the clerk is not subject to the pains and penalties of the Act no matter how large his embezzlements nor how frequent his convictions. A person who enters a chicken coop and steals chickens commits a felony; and he may be sterilized if he is thrice convicted. If, however, he is a bailee of the property and fraudulently appropriates it, he is an embezzler. Hence no matter how habitual his proclivities for embezzlement are and no matter how often his conviction, he may not be sterilized. Thus the nature of the two crimes is intrinsically the same and they are punishable in the same manner.

Furthermore, the line between them follows close distinctions— distinctions comparable to those highly technical ones which shaped the common law as to "trespass" or "taking." There may be larceny by fraud rather than embezzlement even where the owner of the person- al property delivers it to the defendant, if the latter has at that time "a fraudulent intention to make use of the possession as a means of con- verting such property to his own use, and does so convert it." If the fraudulent intent occurs later and the defendant converts the property, he is guilty of embezzlement. Whether a particular act is larceny by fraud or embezzlement thus turns not on the intrinsic quality of the act but on when the felonious intent arose—a question for the jury under appropriate instructions.

It was stated in *Buck v. Bell*, supra, that the claim that state legisla- tion violates the equal protection clause of the Fourteenth Amend- ment is "the usual last resort of constitutional arguments." Under our constitutional system the States in determining the reach and scope of particular legislation need not provide "abstract symmetry." They may mark and set apart the classes and types of problems according to the needs and as dictated or suggested by experience. . . . Only recent- ly we reaffirmed the view that the equal protection clause does not prevent the legislature from recognizing "degrees of evil" by our rul- ing that "the Constitution does not require things which are different in fact or opinion to be treated in law as though they were the same." Thus, if we had here only a question as to a State's classification of crimes, such as embezzlement or larceny, no substantial federal ques- tion would be raised. For a State is not constrained in the exercise of its police power to ignore experience which marks a class of offenders or a family of offenses for special treatment. Nor is it prevented by the equal protection clause from confining "its restrictions to those class- es of cases where the need is deemed to be clearest." As stated in *Buck v. Bell*, " . . . the law does all that is needed when it does all that it can, indicates a policy, applies it to all within the lines, and seeks to bring within the lines all similarly situated so far and so fast as its means allow." But [this] legislation runs afoul of the equal protection clause, though we give Oklahoma that large deference which the rule of the foregoing cases requires. We are dealing here with legislation which involves one of the basic civil rights of man. Marriage and procreation are fundamental to the very existence and survival of the race. The power to sterilize, if exercised, may have subtle, far-reaching and devastating effects. In evil or reckless hands it can cause races or types which are inimical to the dominant group to wither and disappear. There is no redemption for the individual whom the law touches.

Any experiment which the State conducts is to his irreparable injury. He is forever deprived of a basic liberty. We mention these matters not to reexamine the scope of the police power of the States. We advert to them merely in emphasis of our view that strict scrutiny of the classification which a State makes in a sterilization law is essential, lest unwittingly or otherwise invidious discriminations are made against groups or types of individuals in violation of the constitutional guaranty of just and equal laws. The guaranty of "equal protection of the laws is a pledge of the protection of equal laws." When the law lays an unequal hand on those who have committed intrinsically the same quality of offense and sterilizes one and not the other, it has made as an invidious a discrimination as if it had selected a particular race or nationality for oppressive treatment. Sterilization of those who have thrice committed grand larceny with immunity for those who are embezzlers is a clear, pointed, unmistakable discrimination. Oklahoma makes no attempt to say that he who commits larceny by trespass or trick or fraud has biologically inheritable traits which he who commits embezzlement lacks. Oklahoma's line between larceny by fraud and embezzlement is determined, as we have noted, "with reference to the time when the fraudulent intent to convert the property to the taker's own use" arises. We have not the slightest basis for inferring that that line has any significance in eugenics nor that the inheritability of criminal traits follows the neat legal distinctions which the law has marked between those two offenses. In terms of fines and imprisonment the crimes of larceny and embezzlement rate the same under the Oklahoma code. Only when it comes to sterilization are the pains and penalties of the law different. The equal protection clause would indeed be a formula of empty words if such conspicuously artificial lines could be drawn. In *Buck v. Bell,* the Virginia statute was upheld though it applied only to feebleminded persons in institutions of the State. But it was pointed out that "so far as the operations enable those who otherwise must be kept confined to be returned to the world, and thus open the asylum to others, the equality aimed at will be more nearly reached." Here there is no such saving feature. Embezzlers are forever free. Those who steal or take in other ways are not. If such a classification were permitted, the technical common law concept of a "trespass" based on distinctions which are "very largely dependent upon history for explanation" could readily become a rule of human genetics. . . .

We have therefore a situation where the Act as construed and applied to petitioner is allowed to perpetuate the discrimination which we have found to be fatal. Whether the severability clause would be so applied as to remove this particular constitutional objection is a question which may be more appropriately left for adjudication by the Oklahoma court. That is reemphasized here by our uncertainty as to what excision, if any, would be made as a matter of Oklahoma law. It is by no means clear whether if an excision were made, this particular constitutional difficulty might be solved by enlarging on the one hand or contracting on the other the class of criminals who might be sterilized.

REVERSED.

Mr. Chief Justice STONE concurring.

I concur in the result, but I am not persuaded that we are aided in reaching it by recourse to the equal protection clause. If Oklahoma may resort generally to the sterilization of criminals on the assumption that their propensities are transmissible to future generations by inheritance, I seriously doubt that the equal protection clause requires it to apply the measure to all criminals in the first instance, or to none.

Moreover, if we must presume that the legislature knows—what science has been unable to ascertain—that the criminal tendencies of any class of habitual offenders are transmissible regardless of the varying mental characteristics of its individuals, I should suppose that we must likewise presume that the legislature, in its wisdom, knows that the criminal tendencies of some classes of offenders are more likely to be transmitted than those of others. And so I think the real question we have to consider is not one of equal protection, but whether the wholesale condemnation of a class to such an invasion of personal liberty, without opportunity to any individual to show that his is not the type of case which would justify resort to it, satisfies the demands of due process.

There are limits to the extent to which the presumption of constitutionality can be pressed, especially where the liberty of the person is concerned and where the presumption is resorted to only to dispense with a procedure which the ordinary dictates of prudence would seem to demand for the protection of the individual from arbitrary action. Although petitioner here was given a hearing to ascertain whether sterilization would be detrimental to his health, he was given none to discover whether his criminal tendencies are of an inheritable type. Undoubtedly a state may, after appropriate inquiry, constitutionally interfere with the personal liberty of the individual to prevent the transmission by inheritance of his socially injurious tendencies.

But until now we have not been called upon to say that it may do so without giving him a hearing and opportunity to challenge the existence as to him of the only facts which could justify so drastic a measure.

Science has found and the law has recognized that there are certain types of mental deficiency associated with delinquency which are inheritable. But the State does not contend—nor can there be any pretense—that either common knowledge or experience, or scientific investigation, has given assurance that the criminal tendencies of any class of habitual offenders are universally or even generally inheritable. In such circumstances, inquiry whether such is the fact in the case of any particular individual cannot rightly be dispensed with. Whether the procedure by which a statute carries its mandate into execution satisfies due process is a matter of judicial cognizance. A law which condemns, without hearing, all the individuals of a class to so harsh a measure as the present because some or even many merit condemnation, is lacking in the first principles of due process. And so, while the state may protect itself from the demonstrably inheritable tendencies of the individual which are injurious to society, the most elementary notions of due process would seem to require it to take appropriate steps to safeguard the liberty of the individual by affording him, before he is condemned to an irreparable injury in his person, some opportunity to show that he is without such inheritable tendencies. The state is called on to sacrifice no permissible end when it is required to reach its objective by a reasonable and just procedure adequate to safeguard rights of the individual which concededly the Constitution protects.

Mr. Justice JACKSON, concurring.

I join the CHIEF JUSTICE in holding that the hearings provided are too limited in the context of the present Act to afford due process of law. I also agree with the opinion of Mr. Justice DOUGLAS that the scheme of classification set forth in the Act denies equal protection of the law. I disagree with the opinion of each in so far as it rejects or minimizes the grounds taken by the other.

Perhaps to employ a broad and loose scheme of classification would be permissible if accompanied by the individual hearings indicated by the CHIEF JUSTICE. On the other hand, narrow classification with reference to the end to be accomplished by the Act might justify limiting individual hearings to the issue whether the individual belonged to a class so defined. Since this Act does not present these questions, I reserve judgment on them. I also think the present plan to sterilize the individual in pursuit of a eugenic plan to eliminate from the race characteristics that are only vaguely identified and which in our present state of knowledge are uncertain as to transmissibility presents other constitutional questions of gravity.

This Court has sustained such an experiment with respect to an imbecile, a person with definite and observable characteristics where the condition had persisted through three generations and afforded grounds for the belief that it was transmissible and would continue to manifest itself in generations to come.

There are limits to the extent to which a legislatively represented majority may conduct biological experiments at the expense of the dignity and personality and natural powers of a minority—even those who have been guilty of what the majority define as crimes. But this Act falls down before reaching this problem, which I mention only to avoid the implication that such a question may not exist because not discussed. On it I would also reserve judgment.

Griswold v. Connecticut (1965)

These excerpts from briefs filed by Planned Parenthood in Griswold v. Connecticut *reveal the growing authority of medical opinion in the 1960s. Physicians widely agreed that regular sexual relations between married couples were fundamental for maintaining both physical and psychological health. Therefore, Planned Parenthood argued, Connecticut's statute outlawing the distribution of contraception and birth control information represented an unconstitutional infringement of individual liberty.*

Brief as *Amicus Curiae* for Planned Parenthood Federation of America, Inc.

(f) Abridgment of the Right to Practice Medicine in Accordance with Accepted Scientific Principles.

As we have stressed throughout this brief, the Connecticut statutes run squarely counter to all accepted medical opinion and practice. They prohibit physicians from employing methods dictated by scientific knowledge. They require the use of practices which students and practitioners of medicine virtually unanimously condemn as unscientific and harmful; indeed use of such methods in other States might well in some cases render a physician guilty of malpractice. They hamper further inquiry and foreclose experimentation in new techniques for the solution of human and social problems. At the time the statutes were enacted the science of medicine had not reached the stage where the legislature could be aware of all these considerations, or at least of their full impact. But they cannot be ignored now. . . .

(g) Irrationality In Relation to Other Laws.

Judged by the policy expressed in other Connecticut legislation, the restrictions imposed by the statutes involved in this case are wholly irrational:

Under the Connecticut abortion law a physician may abort a patient when "necessary to preserve her life or that of her unborn child." Conn. Gen. Stats., Sec. 53-29. So, too, a woman may "produce upon herself miscarriage or abortion" where necessary for the same reasons. Conn. Gen. Stats., Sec. 53-30. But under the anti-contraceptive statutes they are forbidden to take effective measures to prevent the conception, even though they know a later abortion will be necessary.

Under other Connecticut laws sterilization—an operation in which an "instrument" is used "for the purpose of preventing conception"—may be performed upon inmates of the State Prison or of State mental hospitals in certain medically prescribed situations where that operation "is a medical necessity." Conn. Gen. Stats., Sec. 17-19 and 53-33. But less permanent measures for achieving the same purpose are not allowed.

Under the statutes applied to these appellants, contraceptives can be prescribed, sold or used for the prevention of disease (see Statement of the Case, *supra.*), but not for the protection of life.

None of these distinctions makes sense, either in moral terms or in practical terms. If moral principles require that never, under any circumstances, can life be thwarted by extrinsic aids to avoid conception, how can the State justify the more serious denial of life by abortion or sterilization? And how can it justify the same thwarting of life in order to prevent the less serious results of venereal disease? The statutes challenged here are not the outcome of any exercise of rational judgment. They are, by the most elementary meaning, arbitrary and capricious.

(h) Irrationalities In Operation

The Connecticut statutes operate in an irrational manner in at least four important respects:

(1) The statutes, so far as enforced, would always be applicable to married persons and seldom applicable to unmarried persons engaging in sexual relations. This paradox arises from the fact that, as just stated, it is not unlawful for persons to use otherwise forbidden devices for the purpose of preventing disease although by so doing they also prevent conception. The Connecticut law requires a serological test and a certification that the parties are free from venereal disease before a marriage certificate can be obtained. Conn. Gen. Stats., Sec 46-5(b). When married, presumably the parties are healthy in this respect and, if they are faithful to each other, will have no occasion to use contraceptives for the prevention of disease. Persons engaged in extra-marital intercourse cannot be expected to have the assurance of a physician's certificate that they will not risk infection. Consequently, they may legally employ the devices forbidden to married couples. . . .

III. Opinions of Medical Text Writers and Authorities as to the Medical Necessity for Contraceptive Measures

The clear consensus among distinguished medical authorities on the medical need for contraception is evidenced by the treatment of contraception in authoritative obstetrical and gynecological texts over a period of nearly forty years. The following are some of the most important statements from these authorities, beginning with the most recent: *Benson, Ralph C.,* M.D. Professor of Obstetrics and Gynecology and Chairman, Department of Obstetrics and Gynecology University of Oregon Medical School, Hospitals, and Clinic—*Handbook of Obstetrics and Gynecology* (Lange Medical Publications, Los Altos, California, 1964, p. 602): "The voluntary and temporary prevention of pregnancy may be indicated or desirable for any of the following reasons: Socio-economic (spacing children to raise the standard of living and prevent overgrowth of population); medical (improving maternal health during the treatment for diseases such as tuberculosis, renal disease, diabetes); eugenic (avoiding the perpetuation of undesirable traits, e.g., hereditary diseases such as amaurotic familial idiocy); and personal (couples who do not wish children)"; *Reynolds, Edward T.,* M.D., F.A.C.S., and *Macomber, Gerald,* M.D., F.A.C.S.—*Fertility and Sterility in Human Marriage* (Philadelphia, W. B. Saunders Company, 1924, p. 211): "Complete restraint in a couple who are living together in the daily contacts of marital life is, however, so unnatural that it is almost inevitably followed by disturbances in their sexual organs. In point of fact, it can hardly exist between normal individuals without verging upon the third and most extreme mistake of habit: No condition is so harmful to the organs as continued presence of desire without gratification. Any frequent excitation of this condition inevitably leads to chronic and unusually severe congestion"; *Child, Charles Gardner, Jr.—Sterility and Fertility* (New York, Appleton, 1922, p. 201): "We know that for many women further pregnancies are simply out of the question. With such it is but foolish to advise continence, for married life without intercourse is hardly to be realized"; *Ellis, Havelock*—"Studies in the Psychology of Sex," Vol. VI. *"Sex in Relation to Society"* (Philadelphia, F. A. Davis Company, 1910, p. 182): "Krafft-Ebing showed that sexual abstinence could produce a state of general nervous excitement.... Schrenck Notzing regards sexual abstinence as a cause of extreme sexual hyperaesthesia and of nervous perversions." ...

The landmark opinion by Justice William O. Douglas overturned Connecticut's law banning contraception. But more importantly, the justice asserted that a right to privacy may be derived from the "penumbras" surrounding other, enumerated rights in the Constitution.

Mr. Justice DOUGLAS delivered the opinion of the court.

... Coming to the merits, we are met with a wide range of questions that implicate the Due Process Clause of the Fourteenth Amendment. ... We do not sit as a super-legislature to determine the wisdom, need, and propriety of laws that touch economic problems, business affairs, or social conditions. This law, however, operates directly on an intimate relation of husband and wife and their physician's role in one aspect of that relation. The association of people is not mentioned in the Constitution nor in the Bill of Rights. The right to educate a child in a school of the parents' choice—whether public or private or parochial—is also not mentioned. Nor is the right to study any particular subject or any foreign language. Yet the First Amendment has been construed to include certain of those rights. By *Pierce v. Society of Sisters,* supra, the right to educate one's children as one chooses is made applicable to the States by the force of the First and Fourteenth Amendments. By *Meyer v. Nebraska,* supra, the same dignity is given the right to study the German language in a private school. In other words, the State may not, consistently with the spirit of the First Amendment, contract the spectrum of available knowledge. The right of freedom of speech and press includes not only the right to utter or to print, but the right to distribute, the right to receive, the right to read and freedom of inquiry, freedom of thought, and freedom to teach—indeed the freedom of the entire university community. Without those peripheral rights the specific rights would be less secure. . . .

In *NAACP v. Alabama,* 357 U.S. 449, 462, we protected the "freedom to associate and privacy in one's associations," noting that freedom of association was a peripheral First Amendment right. Disclosure of membership lists of a constitutionally valid association, we held, was invalid "as entailing the likelihood of a substantial restraint upon the exercise by petitioner's members of their right to freedom of association." In other words, the First Amendment has a penumbra where privacy is protected from governmental intrusion. In like context, we have protected forms of "association" that are not political in the customary sense but pertain to the social, legal, and economic benefit of the members. In *Schware v. Board of Bar Examiners,* 353 U.S. 232, we held it not permissible to bar a lawyer from practice, because he had once been a member of the Communist Party. The man's "association with that Party" was not shown to be "anything more than a political faith in a political party" (id., at 244) and was not action of a kind proving bad moral character. Those cases involved more than the "right of assembly"—a right that extends to all irrespective of their race or ideology. The right of "association," like the right of belief, is more than the right to attend a meeting; it includes the right to express one's attitudes or philosophies by membership in a group or by affiliation with it or by other lawful means.

Association in that context is a form of expression of opinion; and while it is not expressly included in the First Amendment its existence is necessary in making the express guarantees fully meaningful.

The foregoing cases suggest that specific guarantees in the Bill of Rights have penumbras, formed by emanations from those guarantees that help give them life and substance.

Various guarantees create zones of privacy. The right of association contained in the penumbra of the First Amendment is one, as we have seen. The Third Amendment in its prohibition against the quartering of soldiers "in any house" in time of peace without the consent of the owner is another facet of that privacy. The Fourth Amendment explicitly affirms the "right of the people to be secure in their persons, houses, papers, and effects, against unreasonable searches and seizures." The Fifth Amendment in its Self-Incrimination Clause enables the citizen to create a zone of privacy which government may not force him to surrender to his detriment. . . .

These cases bear witness that the right of privacy which presses for recognition here is a legitimate one.

The present case, then, concerns a relationship lying within the zone of privacy created by several fundamental constitutional guarantees. And it concerns a law which, in forbidding the use of contraceptives rather than regulating their manufacture or sale, seeks to achieve its goals by means having a maximum destructive impact upon that relationship. Such a law cannot stand in light of the familiar principle, so often applied by this Court, that a "governmental purpose to control or prevent activities constitutionally subject to state regulation may not be achieved by means which sweep unnecessarily broadly and thereby invade the area of protected freedoms." Would we allow the police to search the sacred precincts of marital bedrooms for telltale signs of the use of contraceptives? The very idea is repulsive to the notions of privacy surrounding the marriage relationship.

We deal with a right of privacy older than the Bill of Rights—older than our political parties, older than our school system. Marriage is a coming together for better or for worse, hopefully enduring, and intimate to the degree of being sacred. It is an association that promotes a way of life, not causes; a harmony in living, not political faiths; a bilateral loyalty, not commercial or social projects. Yet it is an association for as noble a purpose as any involved in our prior decisions.

REVERSED.

MR. JUSTICE GOLDBERG, whom THE CHIEF JUSTICE and MR. JUSTICE BRENNAN join, concurring.

I agree with the Court that Connecticut's birth-control law unconstitutionally intrudes upon the right of marital privacy, and I join in its opinion and judgment. Although I have not accepted the view that "due process" as used in the Fourteenth Amendment incorporates all of the first eight Amendments, I do agree that the concept of liberty protects those personal rights that are fundamental, and is not confined to the specific terms of the Bill of Rights. My conclusion that the concept of liberty is not so restricted and that it embraces the right of marital privacy though that right is not mentioned explicitly in the Constitution is supported both by numerous decisions of this Court, referred to in the Court's opinion, and by the language and history of the Ninth Amendment. In reaching the conclusion that the right of marital privacy is protected, as being within the protected penumbra of specific guarantees of the Bill of Rights, the Court refers to the Ninth Amendment, I add these words to emphasize the relevance of that Amendment to the Court's holding. . . .

This Court, in a series of decisions, has held that the Fourteenth Amendment absorbs and applies to the States those specifics of the first eight amendments which express fundamental personal rights. The language and history of the Ninth Amendment reveal that the Framers of the Constitution believed that there are additional fundamental rights, protected from governmental infringement, which exist alongside those fundamental rights specifically mentioned in the first eight constitutional amendments.

The Ninth Amendment simply shows the intent of the Constitution's authors that other fundamental personal rights should not be denied such protection or disparaged in any other way simply because they are not specifically listed in the first eight constitutional amendments. I do not see how this broadens the authority of the Court; rather it serves to support what this Court has been doing in protecting fundamental rights. . . .

In sum, the Ninth Amendment simply lends strong support to the view that the "liberty" protected by the Fifth and Fourteenth Amendments from infringement by the Federal Government or the States is not restricted to rights specifically mentioned in the first eight amendments.

In determining which rights are fundamental, judges are not left at large to decide cases in light of their personal and private notions. Rather, they must look to the "traditions and [collective] conscience of our people" to determine whether a principle is "so rooted [there] . . . as to be ranked as fundamental." The inquiry is whether a right involved "is of such a character that it cannot be denied without violating those 'fundamental principles of liberty and justice which lie at the base of all our civil and political institutions.'" . . .

The entire fabric of the Constitution and the purposes that clearly underlie its specific guarantees demonstrate that the rights to marital privacy and to marry and raise a family are of similar order and magnitude as the fundamental rights specifically protected. Although the Constitution does not speak in so many words of the right of privacy in marriage, I cannot believe that it offers these fundamental rights no protection. The fact that no particular provision of the Constitution explicitly forbids the State from disrupting the traditional relation of the family—a relation as old and as fundamental as our entire civilization—surely does not show that the Government was meant to have the power to do so. Rather, as the Ninth Amendment expressly recognizes, there are fundamental personal rights such as this one, which are protected from abridgment by the Government though not specifically mentioned in the Constitution.

My Brother STEWART, while characterizing the Connecticut birth control law as "an uncommonly silly law," would nevertheless let it stand on the ground that it is not for the courts to "'substitute their social and economic beliefs for the judgment of legislative bodies, who are elected to pass laws.'" . . .

The logic of the dissents would sanction federal or state legislation that seems to me even more plainly unconstitutional than the statute before us. Surely the Government, absent a showing of a compelling subordinating state interest, could not decree that all husbands and wives must be sterilized after two children have been born [381 U.S. 479, 497] to them. Yet by their reasoning such an invasion of marital privacy would not be subject to constitutional challenge because, while it might be "silly," no provision of the Constitution specifically prevents the Government from curtailing the marital right to bear children and raise a family. While it may shock some of my Brethren that the Court today holds that the Constitution protects the right of marital privacy, in my view it is far more shocking to believe that the personal liberty guaranteed by the Constitution does not include protection against such totalitarian limitation of family size, which is at complete variance with our constitutional concepts. Yet, if upon a showing of a slender basis of rationality, a law outlawing voluntary birth control by married persons is valid, then, by the same reasoning, a law requiring compulsory birth control also would seem to be valid. In my view, however, both types of law would unjustifiably intrude upon rights of marital privacy which are constitutionally protected. . . .

Although the Connecticut birth-control law obviously encroaches upon a fundamental personal liberty, the State does not show that the law serves any "subordinating [state] interest which is compelling" or that it is "necessary [381 U.S. 479, 498] . . . to the accomplishment of a permissible state policy." The State, at most, argues that there is some rational relation between this statute and what is admittedly a legitimate subject of state concern—the discouraging of extra-marital relations. It says that preventing the use of birth-control devices by married persons helps prevent the indulgence by some in such extramarital relations. The rationality of this justification is dubious, particularly in light of the admitted widespread availability to all persons in the State of Connecticut, unmarried as well as married, of birth-control devices for the prevention of disease, as distinguished from the prevention of conception. But, in any event, it is clear that the state interest in safeguarding marital fidelity can be served by a more discriminately tailored statute, which does not, like the present one, sweep unnecessarily broadly, reaching far beyond the evil sought to be dealt with and intruding upon the privacy of all married couples. . . .

Finally, it should be said of the Court's holding today that it in no way interferes with a State's proper regulation of sexual promiscuity or misconduct. . . .

In sum, I believe that the right of privacy in the marital relation is fundamental and basic—a personal right "retained by the people" within the meaning of the Ninth Amendment. Connecticut cannot constitutionally abridge this fundamental right, which is protected by the Fourteenth Amendment from infringement by the States. I agree with the Court that petitioners' convictions must therefore be reversed.

Roe et al. v. Wade (1973)

This decision remains one of the most significant—and controversial—rendered by the Supreme Court. By the 1970s, abortions performed in hospitals and clinics had become safe, but many states continued to prohibit them. The State of Texas argued that it had a compelling interest in safeguarding the life of the fetus. Attorneys for "Jane Roe" argued that a woman's liberty to decide whether or not to carry a pregnancy to term must be preserved. Justice Harry Blackmun's opinion attempted to find a balance between the two interests, utilizing the "trimester" framework of pregnancy employed in medicine. In the first trimester a woman's liberty interest is paramount, Justice Blackmun determined, but the state also has a compelling interest in preserving life and therefore may regulate abortion as the fetus moves toward viability—or the ability to survive independently of the mother's body.

Argued December 13, 1971
  Reargued October 11, 1972
  Decided January 22, 1973
  MR. JUSTICE BLACKMUN delivered the opinion of the Court.

This Texas federal appeal and its Georgia companion, *Doe v. Bolton,* present constitutional challenges to state criminal abortion legislation. The Texas statutes under attack here are typical of those that have been in effect in many States for approximately a century. The Georgia statutes, in contrast, have a modern cast and are a legislative product that, to an extent at least, obviously reflects the influences of recent attitudinal change, of advancing medical knowledge and techniques, and of new thinking about an old issue.

We forthwith acknowledge our awareness of the sensitive and emotional nature of the abortion controversy, of the vigorous opposing views, even among physicians, and of the deep and seemingly absolute convictions that the subject inspires. One's philosophy, one's experiences, one's exposure to the raw edges of human existence, one's religious training, one's attitudes toward life and family and their values, and the moral standards one establishes and seeks to observe, are all likely to influence and to color one's thinking and conclusions about abortion. In addition, population growth, pollution, poverty, and racial overtones tend to complicate and not to simplify the problem.

Our task, of course, is to resolve the issue by constitutional measurement, free of emotion and of predilection. We seek earnestly to do this, and, because we do, we inquired into, and in this opinion place some emphasis upon, medical and medical-legal history and what that history reveals about man's attitudes toward the abortion procedure over the centuries. . . .

Jane Roe, a single woman who was residing in Dallas County, Texas, instituted this federal action in March 1970 against the District Attorney of the county. She sought a declaratory judgment that the Texas criminal abortion statutes were unconstitutional on their face, and an injunction restraining the defendant from enforcing the statutes.

Roe alleged that she was unmarried and pregnant; that she wished to terminate her pregnancy by an abortion "performed by a competent, licensed physician, under safe, clinical conditions"; that she was unable to get a "legal" abortion in Texas because her life did not appear to be threatened by the continuation of her pregnancy; and that she could not afford to travel to another jurisdiction in order to secure a legal abortion under safe conditions. She claimed that the Texas statutes were unconstitutionally vague and that they abridged her right of personal privacy, protected by the First, Fourth, Fifth, Ninth, and Fourteenth Amendments. By an amendment to her complaint Roe purported to sue "on behalf of herself and all other women" similarly situated. . . .

It perhaps is not generally appreciated that the restrictive criminal abortion laws in effect in a majority of States today are of relatively recent vintage. Those laws, generally proscribing abortion or its attempt at any time during pregnancy except when necessary to preserve the pregnant woman's life, are not of ancient or even of common-law origin. Instead, they derive from statutory changes effected, for the most part, in the latter half of the 19th century. . . . It is undisputed that at common law, abortion performed before "quickening"—the first recognizable movement of the fetus in utero, appearing usually from the 16th to the 18th week of pregnancy—was not an indictable offense. The absence of a common-law crime for pre-quickening abortion appears to have developed from a confluence of earlier philosophical, theological, and civil and canon law concepts of when life begins. These disciplines variously approached the question in terms of the point at which the embryo or fetus became "formed" or recognizably human, or in terms of when a "person" came into being, that is, infused with a "soul" or "animated." . . .

In this country, the law in effect in all but a few States until mid-19th century was the pre-existing English common law. . . .

It is thus apparent that at common law, at the time of the adoption of our Constitution, and throughout the major portion of the 19th century, abortion was viewed with less disfavor than under most American statutes currently in effect. Phrasing it another way, a woman enjoyed a substantially broader right to terminate a pregnancy than she does in most States today. At least with respect to the early stage of pregnancy, and very possibly without such a limitation, the opportunity to make this choice was present in this country well into the 19th century. Even later, the law continued for some time to treat less punitively an abortion procured in early pregnancy. . . .

Three reasons have been advanced to explain historically the enactment of criminal abortion laws in the 19th century and to justify their continued existence. It has been argued occasionally that these laws were the product of a Victorian social concern to discourage illicit sexual conduct. Texas, however, does not advance this justification in the present case, and it appears that no court or commentator has taken the argument seriously. The appellants and amici contend, moreover, that this is not a proper state purpose at all and suggest that, if it were, the Texas statutes are overbroad in protecting it since the law fails to distinguish between married and unwed mothers.

A second reason is concerned with abortion as a medical procedure. When most criminal abortion laws were first enacted, the procedure was a hazardous one for the woman. This was particularly true prior to the development of antisepsis. Antiseptic techniques, of course, were based on discoveries by Lister, Pasteur, and others first announced in 1867, but were not generally accepted and employed until about the turn of the century. Abortion mortality was high. Even after 1900, and perhaps until as late as the development of antibiotics in the 1940s, standard modern techniques such as dilation and curettage were not nearly so safe as they are today. Thus, it has been argued that a State's real concern in enacting a criminal abortion law was to protect the pregnant woman, that is, to restrain her from submitting to a procedure that placed her life in serious jeopardy.

Modern medical techniques have altered this situation. Appellants and various amici refer to medical data indicating that abortion in early pregnancy, that is, prior to the end of the first trimester, although not without its risk, is now relatively safe. Mortality rates for women undergoing early abortions, where the procedure is legal, appear to be as low as or lower than the rates for normal childbirth. Consequently, any interest of the State in protecting the woman from an inherently hazardous procedure, except when it would be equally dangerous for her to forgo it, has largely disappeared. Of course, important state interests in the areas of health and medical standards do remain. The State has a legitimate interest in seeing to it that abortion, like any other medical procedure, is performed under circumstances that insure maximum safety for the patient. This interest obviously extends at least to the performing physician and his staff, to the facilities involved, to the availability of after-care, and to adequate provision for any complication or emergency that might arise. The prevalence of high mortality rates at illegal "abortion mills" strengthens, rather than weakens, the State's interest in regulating the conditions under which abortions are performed.

Moreover, the risk to the woman increases as her pregnancy continues. Thus, the State retains a definite interest in protecting the woman's own health and safety when an abortion is proposed at a late stage of pregnancy.

The third reason is the State's interest—some phrase it in terms of duty—in protecting prenatal life. Some of the argument for this justification rests on the theory that a new human life is present from the moment of conception. The State's interest and general obligation to protect life then extends, it is argued, to prenatal life. Only when the life of the pregnant mother herself is at stake, balanced against the life she carries within her, should the interest of the embryo or fetus not prevail.

Logically, of course, a legitimate state interest in this area need not stand or fall on acceptance of the belief that life begins at conception or at some other point prior to live birth. In assessing the State's interest, recognition may be given to the less rigid claim that as long as at least potential life is involved, the State may assert interests beyond the protection of the pregnant woman alone.

Parties challenging state abortion laws have sharply disputed in some courts the contention that a purpose of these laws, when enacted, was to protect prenatal life. Pointing to the absence of legislative history to support the contention, they claim that most state laws were designed solely to protect the woman. Because medical advances have lessened this concern, at least with respect to abortion in early pregnancy, they argue that with respect to such abortions the laws can no longer be justified by any state interest. There is some scholarly support for this view of original purpose.

The few state courts called upon to interpret their laws in the late 19th and early 20th centuries did focus on the State's interest in protecting the woman's health rather than in preserving the embryo and fetus. Proponents of this view point out that in many States, including Texas, by statute or judicial interpretation, the pregnant woman herself could not be prosecuted for self-abortion or for cooperating in an abortion performed upon her by another. They claim that adoption of the "quickening" distinction through received common law and state statutes tacitly recognizes the greater health hazards inherent in late abortion and impliedly repudiates the theory that life begins at conception.

It is with these interests, and the weight to be attached to them, that this case is concerned. . . .

This right of privacy, whether it be founded in the Fourteenth Amendment's concept of personal liberty and restrictions upon state action, as we feel it is, or, as the District Court determined, in the Ninth Amendment's reservation of rights to the people, is broad enough to encompass a woman's decision whether or not to terminate her pregnancy. The detriment that the State would impose upon the pregnant woman by denying this choice altogether is apparent. Specific and direct harm medically diagnosable even in early pregnancy may be involved. Maternity, or additional offspring, may force upon the woman a distressful life and future. Psychological harm may be imminent. Mental and physical health may be taxed by child care. There is also the distress, for all concerned, associated with the unwanted child, and there is the problem of bringing a child into a family already unable, psychologically and otherwise, to care for it. In other cases, as in this one, the additional difficulties and continuing stigma of unwed motherhood may be involved. All these are factors the woman and her responsible physician necessarily will consider in consultation.

On the basis of elements such as these, appellant and some amici argue that the woman's right is absolute and that she is entitled to terminate her pregnancy at whatever time, in whatever way, and for whatever reason she alone chooses. With this we do not agree. Appellant's arguments that Texas either has no valid interest at all in regulating the abortion decision, or no interest strong enough to support any limitation upon the woman's sole determination, are unpersuasive. The Court's decisions recognizing a right of privacy also acknowledge that some state regulation in areas protected by that right is appropriate. As noted above, a State may properly assert important interests in safeguarding health, in maintaining medical standards, and in protecting potential life. At some point in pregnancy, these respective interests become sufficiently compelling to sustain regulation of the factors that govern the abortion decision. The privacy right involved, therefore, cannot be said to be absolute. In fact, it is not clear to us that the claim asserted by some amici that one has an unlimited right to do with one's body as one pleases bears a close relationship to the right of privacy previously articulated in the Court's decisions. The Court has refused to recognize an unlimited right of this kind in the past. *Jacob-*

son v. Massachusetts, 197 U.S. 11 (1905) (vaccination); *Buck v. Bell,* 274 U.S. 200 (1927) (sterilization).

We, therefore, conclude that the right of personal privacy includes the abortion decision, but that this right is not unqualified and must be considered against important state interests in regulation. . . .

Where certain "fundamental rights" are involved, the Court has held that regulation limiting these rights may be justified only by a "compelling state interest," and that legislative enactments must be narrowly drawn to express only the legitimate state interests at stake. . . .

The appellee and certain amici argue that the fetus is a "person" within the language and meaning of the Fourteenth Amendment. In support of this, they outline at length and in detail the well-known facts of fetal development. If this suggestion of personhood is established, the appellant's case, of course, collapses, for the fetus' right to life would then be guaranteed specifically by the Amendment. The appellant conceded as much on reargument. On the other hand, the appellee conceded on reargument that no case could be cited that holds that a fetus is a person within the meaning of the Fourteenth Amendment.

The Constitution does not define "person" in so many words . . . the use of the word is such that it has application only postnatally. None indicates, with any assurance, that it has any possible pre-natal application. All this, together with our observation, supra, that throughout the major portion of the 19th century prevailing legal abortion practices were far freer than they are today, persuades us that the word "person," as used in the Fourteenth Amendment, does not include the unborn. . . .

This conclusion, however, does not of itself fully answer the contentions raised by Texas, and we pass on to other considerations. . . .

The pregnant woman cannot be isolated in her privacy. She carries an embryo and, later, a fetus, if one accepts the medical definitions of the developing young in the human uterus. The situation therefore is inherently different from marital intimacy, or bedroom possession of obscene material, or marriage, or procreation, or education, with which Eisenstadt and Griswold, Stanley, Loving, Skinner, and Pierce and Meyer were respectively concerned. As we have intimated above, it is reasonable and appropriate for a State to decide that at some point in time another interest, that of health of the mother or that of potential human life, becomes significantly involved. The woman's privacy is no longer sole and any right of privacy she possesses must be measured accordingly.

Texas urges that, apart from the Fourteenth Amendment, life begins at conception and is present throughout pregnancy, and that, therefore, the State has a compelling interest in protecting that life from and after conception. We need not resolve the difficult question of when life begins. When those trained in the respective disciplines of medicine, philosophy, and theology are unable to arrive at any consensus, the judiciary, at this point in the development of man's knowledge, is not in a position to speculate as to the answer. It should be sufficient to note briefly the wide divergence of thinking on this most sensitive and difficult question. There has always been strong support for the view that life does not begin until live birth. This was the belief of the Stoics. It appears to be the predominant, though not the unanimous, attitude of the Jewish faith. It may be taken to represent also the position of a large segment of the Protestant community, insofar as that can be ascertained; organized groups that have taken a formal position on the abortion issue have generally regarded abortion as a matter for the conscience of the individual and her family. As we have noted, the common law found greater significance in quickening. Physicians and their scientific colleagues have regarded that event with less interest and have tended to focus either upon conception, upon live birth, or upon the interim point at which the fetus becomes "viable," that is, potentially able to live outside the mother's womb, albeit with artificial aid. Viability is usually placed at about seven months (28 weeks) but may occur earlier, even at 24 weeks. . . .

Substantial problems for precise definition of this view are posed, however, by new embryological data that purport to indicate that conception is a "process" over time, rather than an event, and by new medical techniques such as menstrual extraction, the "morning-after" pill, implantation of embryos, artificial insemination, and even artificial wombs. In areas other than criminal abortion, the law has been reluctant to endorse any theory that life, as we recognize it, begins before live birth or to accord legal rights to the unborn except in narrowly defined situations and except when the rights are contingent upon live birth. For example, the traditional rule of tort law denied recovery for prenatal injuries even though the child was born alive. That rule has been changed in almost every jurisdiction. . . . Similarly, unborn children have been recognized as acquiring rights or interests by way of inheritance or other devolution of property, and have been represented by guardians ad litem. Perfection of the interests involved, again, has generally been contingent upon live birth. In short, the unborn have never been recognized in the law as persons in the whole sense.

In view of all this, we do not agree that, by adopting one theory of life, Texas may override the rights of the pregnant woman that are at stake. We repeat, however, that the State does have an important and legitimate interest in preserving and protecting the health of the pregnant woman, whether she be a resident of the State or a nonresident who seeks medical consultation and treatment there, and that it has still another important and legitimate interest in protecting the potentiality of human life. These interests are separate and distinct. Each grows in substantiality as the woman approaches term and, at a point during pregnancy, each becomes "compelling."

With respect to the State's important and legitimate interest in the health of the mother, the "compelling" point, in the light of present medical knowledge, is at approximately the end of the first trimester. This is so because of the now-established medical fact, referred to above . . . that until the end of the first trimester mortality in abortion may be less than mortality in normal childbirth. It follows that, from and after this point, a State may regulate the abortion procedure to the extent that the regulation reasonably relates to the preservation and protection of maternal health. Examples of permissible state regulation in this area are requirements as to the qualifications of the person who is to perform the abortion; as to the licensure of that person; as to the facility in which the procedure is to be performed, that is, whether it must be a hospital or may be a clinic or some other place of less-than-hospital status; as to the licensing of the facility; and the like.

This means, on the other hand, that, for the period of pregnancy prior to this "compelling" point, the attending physician, in consultation with his patient, is free to determine, without regulation by the State, that, in his medical judgment, the patient's pregnancy should be terminated. If that decision is reached, the judgment may be effectuated by an abortion free of interference by the State.

With respect to the State's important and legitimate interest in potential life, the "compelling" point is at viability. This is so because the fetus then presumably has the capability of meaningful life outside the mother's womb. State regulation protective of fetal life after viability thus has both logical and biological justifications. If the State is interested in protecting fetal life after viability, it may go so far as to proscribe abortion during that period, except when it is necessary to preserve the life or health of the mother.

Measured against these standards, Art. 1196 of the Texas Penal Code, in restricting legal abortions to those "procured or attempted by medical advice for the purpose of saving the life of the mother," sweeps too broadly. The statute makes no distinction between abortions performed early in pregnancy and those performed later, and it limits to a single reason, "saving" the mother's life, the legal justification for the procedure. The statute, therefore, cannot survive the constitutional attack made upon it here. . . .

This holding, we feel, is consistent with the relative weights of the respective interests involved, with the lessons and examples of medical and legal history, with the lenity of the common law, and with the demands of the profound problems of the present day. The decision leaves the State free to place increasing restrictions on abortion as the period of pregnancy lengthens, so long as those restrictions are tailored to the recognized state interests. The decision vindicates the right of the physician to administer medical treatment according to his professional judgment up to the points where important state interests provide compelling justifications for intervention. Up to those points, the abortion decision in all its aspects is inherently, and primarily, a medical decision, and basic responsibility for it must rest with the physician. If an individual practitioner abuses the privilege of exercising proper medical judgment, the usual remedies, judicial and intra-professional, are available. . . .

Bowers, Attorney General of Georgia v. Hardwick, et al. (1986)

This case originated in a Georgia statute making it a criminal offense, punishable by up to 20 years' imprisonment, to commit sodomy. Michael Hardwick was caught engaging in sodomy with a consenting male adult in the bedroom of his home by police who had entered on an unrelated warrant. Hardwick challenged the statute criminalizing consensual sodomy on the grounds that it violated the Fourteenth Amendment's protection of individual liberty. He won the case in an appellate court, which also ruled that Georgia had to prove both a compelling interest in regulating such activities and that the law would achieve that end without overbroad interference in private consensual sexual behavior. The U.S. Supreme Court, however, reversed, holding that the Fourteenth Amendment does not grant fundamental rights to engage in sodomy. Four justices dissented, asserting that the constitutional right to privacy does extend to protecting intimate associations and in fact gives special protections to the privacy of the home. Justices Blackmun, Brennan, Marshall, and Stevens rejected Georgia's claim that such a law was allowable because it protected the public's health and welfare. The badly split decision illustrates the continued difficulties of drawing a clear line between the right to bodily autonomy and the state's interest in regulating the human body.

Argued, March 31, 1986

  Decided, June 30, 1986

  JUSTICE WHITE delivered the opinion of the Court:

This case does not require a judgment on whether laws against sodomy between consenting adults in general, or between homosexuals in particular, are wise or desirable. It raises no question about the right or propriety of state legislative decisions to repeal their laws that criminalize homosexual sodomy, or of state-court decisions invalidating those laws on state constitutional grounds. The issue presented is whether the Federal Constitution confers a fundamental right upon homosexuals to engage in sodomy and hence invalidates the laws of the many States that still make such conduct illegal and have done so for a very long time. The case also calls for some judgment about the limits of the Court's role in carrying out its constitutional mandate. . . . [R]espondent would have us announce, as the Court of Appeals did, a fundamental right to engage in homosexual sodomy. This we are quite unwilling to do. It is true that despite the language of the Due Process Clauses of the Fifth and Fourteenth Amendments, which appears to focus only on the processes by which life, liberty, or property is taken, the cases are legion in which those Clauses have been interpreted to have substantive content, subsuming rights that to a great extent are immune from federal or state regulation or proscription. Among such cases are those recognizing rights that have little or no textual support in the constitutional language. . . .

The Court is most vulnerable and comes nearest to illegitimacy when it deals with judge-made constitutional law having little or no cognizable roots in the language or design of the Constitution. That this is so was painfully demonstrated by the face-off between the

Executive and the Court in the 1930's, which resulted in the repudiation of much of the substantive gloss that the Court had placed on the Due Process Clauses of the Fifth and Fourteenth Amendments. There should be, therefore, great resistance to expand the substantive reach of those Clauses, particularly if it requires redefining the category of rights deemed to be fundamental. Otherwise, the Judiciary necessarily takes to itself further authority to govern the country without express constitutional authority. The claimed right pressed on us today falls far short of overcoming this resistance.   Respondent, however, asserts that the result should be different where the homosexual conduct occurs in the privacy of the home. He relies on *Stanley v. Georgia*, 394 U.S. 557 (1969), where the Court held that the First Amendment prevents conviction for possessing and reading obscene material in the privacy of one's home: "If the First Amendment means anything, it means that a State has no business telling a man, sitting alone in his house, what books he may read or what films he may watch." *Stanley* did protect conduct that would not have been protected outside the home, and it partially prevented the enforcement of state obscenity laws; but the decision was firmly grounded in the First Amendment. The right pressed upon us here has no similar support in the text of the Constitution, and it does not qualify for recognition under the prevailing principles for construing the Fourteenth Amendment. Its limits are also difficult to discern. Plainly enough, otherwise illegal conduct is not always immunized whenever it occurs in the home. Victimless crimes, such as the possession and use of illegal drugs, do not escape the law where they are committed at home. *Stanley* itself recognized that its holding offered no protection for the possession in the home of drugs, firearms, or stolen goods. And if respondent's submission is limited to the voluntary sexual conduct between consenting adults, it would be difficult, except by fiat, to limit the claimed right to homosexual conduct while leaving exposed to prosecution adultery, incest, and other sexual crimes even though they are committed in the home. We are unwilling to start down that road.   Even if the conduct at issue here is not a fundamental right, respondent asserts that there must be a rational basis for the law and that there is none in this case other than the presumed belief of a majority of the electorate in Georgia that homosexual sodomy is immoral and unacceptable. This is said to be an inadequate rationale to support the law. The law, however, is constantly based on notions of morality, and if all laws representing essentially moral choices are to be invalidated under the Due Process

Clause, the courts will be very busy indeed. Even respondent makes no such claim, but insists that majority sentiments about the morality of homosexuality should be declared inadequate. We do not agree, and are unpersuaded that the sodomy laws of some 25 States should be invalidated on this basis. Accordingly, the judgment of the Court of Appeals is *Reversed.*

DISSENT: JUSTICE BLACKMUN, with whom JUSTICE BREN-NAN, JUSTICE MARSHALL, and JUSTICE STEVENS join, dissenting:

This case is no more about "a fundamental right to engage in homosexual sodomy," as the Court purports to declare, *ante,* at 191, than *Stanley v. Georgia,* 394 U.S. 557 (1969), was about a fundamental right to watch obscene movies, or *Katz v. United States,* 389 U.S. 347 (1967), was about a fundamental right to place interstate bets from a telephone booth. Rather, this case is about "the most comprehensive of rights and the right most valued by civilized men," namely, "the right to be let alone." *Olmstead v. United States,* 277 U.S. 438, 478 (1928) (Brandeis, J., dissenting). The statute at issue, Ga. Code Ann. § 16-6-2 (1984), denies individuals the right to decide for themselves whether to engage in particular forms of private, consensual sexual activity. The Court concludes that § 16-6-2 is valid essentially because "the laws of . . . many States . . . still make such conduct illegal and have done so for a very long time." *Ante,* at 190. But the fact that the moral judgments expressed by statutes like § 16-6-2 may be "'natural and familiar . . . ought not to conclude our judgment upon the question whether statutes embodying them conflict with the Constitution of the United States.'" *Roe v. Wade,* 410 U.S. 113, 117 (1973), quoting *Lochner v. New York,* 198 U.S. 45, 76 (1905) (Holmes, J., dissenting). Like Justice Holmes, I believe that "[it] is revolting to have no better reason for a rule of law than that so it was laid down in the time of Henry IV. It is still more revolting if the grounds upon which it was laid down have vanished long since, and the rule simply persists from blind imitation of the past." Holmes, *The Path of the Law,* 10 Harv. L. Rev. 457, 469 (1897). I believe we must analyze respondent Hardwick's claim in the light of the values that underlie the constitutional right to privacy. . . . The Court's failure to comprehend the magnitude of the liberty interests at stake in this case leads it to slight the question whether petitioner, on behalf of the State, has justified Georgia's infringement on these interests. I believe that neither of the two general justifications for § 16-6-2 that petitioner has advanced warrants dismissing respondent's challenge for failure to state a claim. First, petitioner asserts that the acts made criminal by the statute may have serious adverse consequences for "the general public health and welfare," such as spreading communicable diseases or fostering other criminal activity. . . . In light of the state of the record, I see no justification for the Court's attempt to equate the private, consensual sexual activity at issue here with the "possession in the home of drugs, firearms, or stolen goods," *ante,* at 195, to which *Stanley* refused to extend its protection. 394 U.S., at 568, n. 11. None of the behavior so mentioned in *Stanley* can properly be viewed as "[victimless]," *ante,* at 195: drugs and weapons are inherently dangerous, see, *e. g., McLaughlin v. United States,* 476 U.S. 16 (1986), and for property to be "stolen," someone must have been wrongfully deprived of it. Nothing in the record before the Court provides any justification for finding the activity forbidden by § 16-6-2 to be physically dangerous, either to the persons engaged in it or to others. The core of petitioner's defense of § 16-6-2 , however, is that respondent and others who engage in the conduct prohibited by § 116-6-2 interfere with Georgia's exercise of the "'right of the Nation and of the States to maintain a decent society,'" *Paris Adult Theatre I v. Slaton,* 413 U.S., at 59–60, quoting *Jacobellis v. Ohio,* 378 U.S. 184, 199 (1964) (Warren, C. J., dissenting). Essentially, petitioner argues, and the Court agrees, that the fact that the acts described in § 16-6-2 "for hundreds of years, if not thousands, have been uniformly condemned as immoral" is a sufficient reason to permit a State to ban them today. . . . I cannot agree that either the length of time a majority has held its convictions or the passions with which it defends them can withdraw legislation from this Court's scrutiny. . . . It is precisely because the issue raised by this case touches the heart of what makes individuals what they are that we should be especially sensitive to the rights of those whose choices upset the majority. Nor can § 16-6-2 be justified as a "morally neutral" exercise of Georgia's power to "protect the public environment," *Paris Adult Theatre I,* 413 U.S., at 68–69. Certainly, some private behavior can affect the fabric of society as a whole. Reasonable people may differ about whether particular sexual acts are moral or immoral, but "we have ample evidence for believing that people will not abandon morality, will not think any better of murder, cruelty and dishonesty, merely because some private sexual practice which they abominate is not

punished by the law." H. L. A. Hart, *Immorality and Treason,* reprinted in *The Law as Literature* 220, 225 (L. Blom-Cooper ed. 1961). Petitioner and the Court fail to see the difference between laws that protect public sensibilities and those that enforce private morality.
Statutes banning public sexual activity are entirely consistent with
protecting the individual's liberty interest in decisions concerning sexual relations: the same recognition that those decisions are intensely
private which justifies protecting them from governmental interference can justify protecting individuals from unwilling exposure to the
sexual activities of others. But the mere fact that intimate behavior
may be punished when it takes place in public cannot dictate how
States can regulate intimate behavior that occurs in intimate places....
This case involves no real interference with the rights of others, for the
mere knowledge that other individuals do not adhere to one's value
system cannot be a legally cognizable interest ... let alone an interest
that can justify invading the houses, hearts, and minds of citizens who
choose to live their lives differently.

Webster, et al. v. Reproductive Health Services, et al. (1989)

*A 1986 Missouri statute amended that state's existing abortion laws.
The new statute included a preamble establishing that the Missouri
legislature had determined that human life begins at conception and
that unborn children have interests that may be protected by the
states. Additional provisions prohibited public employees from participating in or public facilities from being used in abortions other than
those necessary to save the life of the mother, banned the use of public funds to counsel a woman to have an abortion, and required physicians to determine the viability of a fetus at twenty or more weeks'
gestation. The Missouri law was challenged by a group of plaintiffs,
including health care professionals employed in public institutions and
two nonprofit abortion service providers, on the grounds that the
extent to which Missouri was regulating abortions amounted to a violation of individual rights as determined in* Roe v. Wade. *The U.S.
Supreme Court upheld the Missouri law. The plurality opinion
included an unusual criticism of a previous decision charging that*
Roe, *in employing a medical model breaking pregnancy into three*

trimesters, reached beyond the framework of the Constitution and rendered the decision unworkable in state laws. Justice Harry Blackmun, who wrote the opinion in Roe, *gave a stinging dissent, accusing the plurality of putting the right to choose abortion at risk.*

Argued April 26, 1989
  Decided July 3, 1989
  CHIEF JUSTICE REHNQUIST announced the judgment of the Court and delivered the opinion of the Court with respect to Parts I, II-A, II-B, and II-C, and an opinion with respect to Parts II-D and III, in which JUSTICE WHITE and JUSTICE KENNEDY join.
  . . . Decision of this case requires us to address four sections of the Missouri Act: (a) the preamble; (b) the prohibition on the use of public facilities or employees to perform abortions; (c) the prohibition on public funding of abortion counseling; and (d) the requirement that physicians conduct viability tests prior to performing abortions. We address these *seriatim.*
  A The Act's preamble, as noted, sets forth "findings" by the Missouri Legislature that "[t]he life of each human being begins at conception," and that "[u]nborn children have protectable interests in life, health, and well-being." Mo. Rev. Stat. §§ 1.205.1(1), (2) (1986). The Act then mandates that state laws be interpreted to provide unborn children with "all the rights, privileges, and immunities available to other persons, citizens, and residents of this state," subject to the Constitution and this Court's precedents. § 1.205.2. n4. In invalidating the preamble, the Court of Appeals relied on this Court's dictum that "'a State may not adopt one theory of when life begins to justify its regulation of abortions.'" 851 F. 2d, at 1075–1076, quoting *Akron v. Akron Center for Reproductive Health, Inc.,* 462 U.S. 416, 444 (1983), in turn citing *Roe v. Wade,* 410 U.S., at 159–162. It rejected Missouri's claim that the preamble was "abortion-neutral," and "merely determine[d] when life begins in a nonabortion context, a traditional state prerogative." 851 F. 2d, at 1076. The court thought that "[t]he only plausible inference" from the fact that "every remaining section of the bill save one regulates the performance of abortions" was that "the state intended its abortion regulations to be understood against the backdrop of its theory of life." *Ibid.* n5. The State contends that the preamble itself is prefatory and imposes no substantive restrictions on abortions, and that appellees therefore do not have standing to challenge it. Brief for Appellants 21–24. Appellees, on the other hand, insist that

the preamble is an operative part of the Act intended to guide the interpretation of other provisions of the Act. Brief for Appellees 19–23. They maintain, for example, that the preamble's definition of life may prevent physicians in public hospitals from dispensing certain forms of contraceptives, such as the intrauterine device. *Id.,* at 22. In our view, the Court of Appeals misconceived the meaning of the *Akron* dictum, which was only that a State could not "justify" an abortion regulation otherwise invalid under *Roe v. Wade* on the ground that it embodied the State's view about when life begins. Certainly the preamble does not by its terms regulate abortion or any other aspect of appellees' medical practice. The Court has emphasized that *Roe v. Wade* "implies no limitation on the authority of a State to make a value judgment favoring childbirth over abortion." *Maher v. Roe,* 432 U.S., at 474. The preamble can be read simply to express that sort of value judgment. We think the extent to which the preamble's language might be used to interpret other state statutes or regulations is something that only the courts of Missouri can definitively decide. State law has offered protections to unborn children in tort and probate law, see *Roe v. Wade, supra,* at 161–162, and § 1.205.2 can be interpreted to do no more than that. . . .

B Section 188.210 provides that "[i]t shall be unlawful for any public employee within the scope of his employment to perform or assist an abortion, not necessary to save the life of the mother," while § 188.215 makes it "unlawful for any public facility to be used for the purpose of performing or assisting an abortion not necessary to save the life of the mother." The Court of Appeals held that these provisions contravened this Court's abortion decisions. 851 F. 2d, at 1082–1083. We take the contrary view. . . . Just as Congress' refusal to fund abortions in *McRae* left "an indigent woman with at least the same range of choice in deciding whether to obtain a medically necessary abortion as she would have had if Congress had chosen to subsidize no health care costs at all," *id.,* at 317, Missouri's refusal to allow public employees to perform abortions in public hospitals leaves a pregnant woman with the same choices as if the State had chosen not to operate any public hospitals at all. The challenged provisions only restrict a woman's ability to obtain an abortion to the extent that she chooses to use a physician affiliated with a public hospital. This circumstance is more easily remedied, and thus considerably less burdensome, than indigency, which "may make it difficult—and in some cases, perhaps, impossible—for some women to have abortions" without public funding. *Maher,* 432 U.S., at 474. Having held that the State's refusal to fund abortions does not violate *Roe v. Wade*, it strains logic to reach a contrary result for the use of public facilities and employees. If the State may "make a value judgment favoring childbirth over abortion and . . . implement that judgment by the allocation of public funds," *Maher, supra*, at 474, surely it may do so through the allocation of other public resources, such as hospitals and medical staff. The Court of Appeals sought to distinguish our cases on the additional ground that "[t]he evidence here showed that all of the public facility's costs in providing abortion services are recouped when the patient pays." 851 F. 2d, at 1083. Absent any expenditure of public funds, the court thought that Missouri was "expressing" more than "its preference for childbirth over abortions," but rather was creating an "obstacle to exercise of the right to choose an abortion [that could not] stand absent a compelling state interest." *Ibid.* We disagree. "Constitutional concerns are greatest," we said in *Maher, supra*, at 476, "when the State attempts to impose its will by the force of law; the State's power to encourage actions deemed to be in the public interest is necessarily far broader." Nothing in the Constitution requires States to enter or remain in the business of performing abortions. Nor, as appellees suggest, do private physicians and their patients have some kind of constitutional right of access to public facilities for the performance of abortions. Brief for Appellees 46–47. Indeed, if the State does recoup all of its costs in performing abortions, and no state subsidy, direct or indirect, is available, it is difficult to see how any procreational choice is burdened by the State's ban on the use of its facilities or employees for performing abortions. . . .

C *[The provision of the Missouri law banning the use of public funds to counsel women to have abortions was rendered moot by the Court.]*

D Section 188.029 of the Missouri Act provides:

"Before a physician performs an abortion on a woman he has reason to believe is carrying an unborn child of twenty or more weeks gestational age, the physician shall first determine if the unborn child is viable by using and exercising that degree of care, skill, and proficiency commonly exercised by the ordinarily skillful, careful, and prudent physician engaged in similar practice under the same or similar conditions. In making this determination of viability, the physician shall perform or cause to be performed such medical examinations and tests as are necessary to make a finding of the gestational age, weight, and lung maturity of the unborn child and shall enter such findings and determination of viability in the medical record of the mother."

As with the preamble, the parties disagree over the meaning of this statutory provision. The State emphasizes the language of the first sentence, which speaks in terms of the physician's determination of viability being made by the standards of ordinary skill in the medical profession. Brief for Appellants 32–35. Appellees stress the language of the second sentence, which prescribes such "tests as are necessary" to make a finding of gestational age, fetal weight, and lung maturity. Brief for Appellees 26–30. . . . The viability-testing provision of the Missouri Act is concerned with promoting the State's interest in potential human life rather than in maternal health. Section 188.029 creates what is essentially a presumption of viability at 20 weeks, which the physician must rebut with tests indicating that the fetus is not viable prior to performing an abortion. It also directs the physician's determination as to viability by specifying consideration, if feasible, of gestational age, fetal weight, and lung capacity. The District Court found that "the medical evidence is uncontradicted that a 20-week fetus is *not* viable," and that "23 1/2 to 24 weeks gestation is the earliest point in pregnancy where a reasonable possibility of viability exists." 662 F. Supp., at 420. But it also found that there may be a 4-week error in estimating gestational age, *id.*, at 421, which supports testing at 20 weeks. In *Roe v. Wade,* the Court recognized that the State has "important and legitimate" interests in protecting maternal health and in the potentiality of human life. 410 U.S., at 162. During the second trimester, the State "may, if it chooses, regulate the abortion procedure in ways that are reasonably related to maternal health." *Id.,* at 164. After viability, when the State's interest in potential human life was held to become compelling, the State "may, if it chooses, regulate, and even proscribe, abortion except where it is necessary, in appropriate medical judgment, for the preservation of the life or health of the mother." *Id.,* at 165. n14. . . . We think that the doubt cast upon the Missouri statute by these cases is not so much a flaw in the statute as it is a reflection of the fact that the rigid trimester analysis of the course of a pregnancy enunciated in *Roe* has resulted in subsequent cases . . . making constitutional law in this area a virtual Procrustean bed. . . .

In the first place, the rigid *Roe* framework is hardly consistent with the notion of a Constitution cast in general terms, as ours is, and usually speaking in general principles, as ours does. The key elements of the *Roe* framework—trimesters and viability—are not found in the text of the Constitution or in any place else one would expect to find a constitutional principle. Since the bounds of the inquiry are essentially indeterminate, the result has been a web of legal rules that have become increasingly intricate, resembling a code of regulations rather than a body of constitutional doctrine. n15. As Justice White has put it, the trimester framework has left this Court to serve as the country's "*ex officio* medical board with powers to approve or disapprove medical and operative practices and standards throughout the United States." *Planned Parenthood of Central Mo. v. Danforth*, 428 U.S., at 99 (opinion concurring in part and dissenting in part). Cf. *Garcia, supra*, at 547. In the second place, we do not see why the State's interest in protecting potential human life should come into existence only at the point of viability, and that there should therefore be a rigid line allowing state regulation after viability but prohibiting it before viability. . . .

The tests that § 188.029 requires the physician to perform are designed to determine viability. The State here has chosen viability as the point at which its interest in potential human life must be safeguarded. See Mo. Rev. Stat. § 188.030 (1986) ("No abortion of a viable unborn child shall be performed unless necessary to preserve the life or health of the woman"). It is true that the tests in question increase the expense of abortion, and regulate the discretion of the physician in determining the viability of the fetus. Since the tests will undoubtedly show in many cases that the fetus is not viable, the tests will have been performed for what were in fact second-trimester abortions. But we are satisfied that the requirement of these tests permissibly furthers the State's interest in protecting potential human life, and we therefore believe § 188.029 to be constitutional. . . .

Because none of the challenged provisions of the Missouri Act properly before us conflict with the Constitution, the judgment of the Court of Appeals is REVERSED.

DISSENT: JUSTICE BLACKMUN, with whom JUSTICE BRENNAN and JUSTICE MARSHALL join, concurring in part and dissenting in part.

Today, *Roe v. Wade*, 410 U.S. 113 (1973), and the fundamental constitutional right of women to decide whether to terminate a pregnancy, survive but are not secure. Although the Court extricates itself from this case without making a single, even incremental, change in the law of abortion, the plurality and Justice Scalia would overrule *Roe* (the first silently, the other explicitly) and would return to the

States virtually unfettered authority to control the quintessentially intimate, personal, and life-directing decision whether to carry a fetus to term. Although today, no less than yesterday, the Constitution and the decisions of this Court prohibit a State from enacting laws that inhibit women from the meaningful exercise of that right, a plurality of this Court implicitly invites every state legislature to enact more and more restrictive abortion regulations in order to provoke more and more test cases, in the hope that sometime down the line the Court will return the law of procreative freedom to the severe limitations that generally prevailed in this country before January 22, 1973. Never in my memory has a plurality announced a judgment of this Court that so foments disregard for the law and for our standing decisions. Nor in my memory has a plurality gone about its business in such a deceptive fashion. At every level of its review, from its effort to read the real meaning out of the Missouri statute, to its intended evisceration of precedents and its deafening silence about the constitutional protections that it would jettison, the plurality obscures the portent of its analysis. With feigned restraint, the plurality announces that its analysis leaves *Roe* "undisturbed," albeit "modif[ied] and narrow[ed]." *Ante,* at 521. But this disclaimer is totally meaningless. The plurality opinion is filled with winks, and nods, and knowing glances to those who would do away with *Roe* explicitly, but turns a stone face to anyone in search of what the plurality conceives as the scope of a woman's right under the Due Process Clause to terminate a pregnancy free from the coercive and brooding influence of the State. The simple truth is that *Roe* would not survive the plurality's analysis, and that the plurality provides no substitute for *Roe's* protective umbrella. I fear for the future. I fear for the liberty and equality of the millions of women who have lived and come of age in the 16 years since *Roe* was decided. I fear for the integrity of, and public esteem for, this Court. I dissent. . . . In the plurality's view, the viability-testing provision imposes a burden on second-trimester abortions as a way of furthering the State's interest in protecting the potential life of the fetus. Since under the *Roe* framework, the State may not fully regulate abortion in the interest of potential life (as opposed to maternal health) until the third trimester, the plurality finds it necessary, in order to save the Missouri testing provision, to throw out *Roe's* trimester framework. *Ante,* at 518–520. In flat contradiction to *Roe,* 410 U.S., at 163, the plurality concludes that the State's interest in potential life is compelling before viability, and upholds the testing provision because it "permissibly furthers" that state interest. . . . No one contests that under the *Roe* framework the State, in order to promote its interest in potential human life, may regulate and even proscribe nontherapeutic abortions once the fetus becomes viable. *Roe,* 410 U.S., at 164–165. If, as the plurality appears to hold, the testing provision simply requires a physician to use appropriate and medically sound tests to determine whether the fetus is actually viable when the estimated gestational age is greater than 20 weeks (and therefore within what the District Court found to be the margin of error for viability, *ante,* at 515–516), then I see little or no conflict with *Roe.* n5. Nothing in *Roe,* or any of its progeny, holds that a State may not effectuate its compelling interest in the potential life of a viable fetus by seeking to ensure that no viable fetus is mistakenly aborted because of the inherent lack of precision in estimates of gestational age. A requirement that a physician make a finding of viability, one way or the other, for every fetus that falls within the range of possible viability does no more than preserve the State's recognized authority. . . . In short, the testing provision, as construed by the plurality, is consistent with the *Roe* framework and could be upheld effortlessly under current doctrine. . . . Having set up the conflict between § 188.029 and the *Roe* trimester framework, the plurality summarily discards *Roe*'s analytic core as "'unsound in principle and unworkable in practice.'" *Ante,* at 518, quoting *Garcia v. San Antonio Metropolitan Transit Authority,* 469 U.S. 528, 546 (1985). This is so, the plurality claims, because the key elements of the framework do not appear in the text of the Constitution, because the framework more closely resembles a regulatory code than a body of constitutional doctrine, and because under the framework the State's interest in potential human life is considered compelling only after viability, when, in fact, that interest is equally compelling throughout pregnancy. *Ante,* at 519–520. The plurality does not bother to explain these alleged flaws in *Roe.* Bald assertion masquerades as reasoning. The object, quite clearly, is not to persuade, but to prevail. . . . The plurality opinion is far more remarkable for the arguments that it does not advance than for those that it does. The plurality does not even mention, much less join, the true jurisprudential debate underlying this case: whether the Constitution includes an "unenumerated" general right to privacy as recognized in many of our decisions, most notably *Griswold v. Connecticut,* 381 U.S. 479 (1965), and *Roe,* and, more specifically, whether, and to what extent, such a right to privacy extends to matters of childbearing and family life, including abortion.

See, *e.g., Eisenstadt v. Baird,* 405 U.S. 438 (1972) (contraception); *Loving v. Virginia,* 388 U.S. 1 (1967) (marriage); *Skinner v. Oklahoma ex rel. Williamson,* 316 U.S. 535 (1942) (procreation); *Pierce v. Society of Sisters,* 268 U.S. 510 (1925) (childrearing). These are questions of unsurpassed significance in this Court's interpretation of the Constitution, and mark the battleground upon which this case was fought, by the parties, by the United States as *amicus* on behalf of petitioners, and by an unprecedented number of *amici.* On these grounds, abandoned by the plurality, the Court should decide this case. But rather than arguing that the text of the Constitution makes no mention of the right to privacy, the plurality complains that the critical elements of the *Roe* framework—trimesters and viability—do not appear in the Constitution and are, therefore, somehow inconsistent with a Constitution cast in general terms. *Ante,* at 518–519. Were this a true concern, we would have to abandon most of our constitutional jurisprudence. As the plurality well knows, or should know, the "critical elements" of countless constitutional doctrines nowhere appear in the Constitution's text. The Constitution makes no mention, for example, of the First Amendment's "actual malice" standard for proving certain libels, see *New York Times Co. v. Sullivan,* 376 U.S. 254 (1964), or of the standard for determining when speech is obscene. See *Miller v. California,* 413 U.S. 15 (1973). Similarly, the Constitution makes no mention of the rational-basis test, or the specific verbal formulations of intermediate and strict scrutiny by which this Court evaluates claims under the Equal Protection Clause. The reason is simple. Like the *Roe* framework, these tests or standards are not, and do not purport to be, rights protected by the Constitution. Rather, they are judge-made methods for evaluating and measuring the strength and scope of constitutional rights or for balancing the constitutional rights of individuals against the competing interests of government. With respect to the *Roe* framework, the general constitutional principle, indeed the fundamental constitutional right, for which it was developed is the right to privacy, see, *e.g., Griswold v. Connecticut,* 381 U.S. 479 (1965), a species of "liberty" protected by the Due Process Clause, which under our past decisions safeguards the right of women to exercise some control over their own role in procreation. As we recently reaffirmed in *Thornburgh v. American College of Obstetricians and Gynecologists,* 476 U.S. 747 (1986), few decisions are "more basic to individual dignity and autonomy" or more appropriate to that "certain private sphere of individual liberty" that the Constitution reserves from the intrusive reach of government than the right to make the uniquely personal, intimate, and self-defining decision whether to end a pregnancy. *Id.,* at 772. It is this general principle, the "'moral fact that a person belongs to himself and not others nor to society as a whole,'" *id.,* at 777, n. 5 (Stevens, J., concurring), quoting Fried, Correspondence, 6 Phil. & Pub. Aff. 288–289 (1977), that is found in the Constitution. See *Roe,* 410 U.S., at 152–153. The trimester framework simply defines and limits that right to privacy in the abortion context to accommodate, not destroy, a State's legitimate interest in protecting the health of pregnant women and in preserving potential human life. *Id.,* at 154–162. Fashioning such accommodations between individual rights and the legitimate interests of government, establishing benchmarks and standards with which to evaluate the competing claims of individuals and government, lies at the very heart of constitutional adjudication. To the extent that the trimester framework is useful in this enterprise, it is not only consistent with constitutional interpretation, but necessary to the wise and just exercise of this Court's paramount authority to define the scope of constitutional rights. . . . That numerous constitutional doctrines result in narrow differentiations between similar circumstances does not mean that this Court has abandoned adjudication in favor of regulation. Rather, these careful distinctions reflect the process of constitutional adjudication itself, which is often highly fact specific, requiring such determinations as whether state laws are "unduly burdensome" or "reasonable" or bear a "rational" or "necessary" relation to asserted state interests. . . .

For my own part, I remain convinced, as six other Members of this Court 16 years ago were convinced, that the *Roe* framework, and the viability standard in particular, fairly, sensibly, and effectively functions to safeguard the constitutional liberties of pregnant women while recognizing and accommodating the State's interest in potential human life. The viability line reflects the biological facts and truths of fetal development; it marks that threshold moment prior to which a fetus cannot survive separate from the woman and cannot reasonably and objectively be regarded as a subject of rights or interests distinct from, or paramount to, those of the pregnant woman. At the same time, the viability standard takes account of the undeniable fact that as the fetus evolves into its postnatal form, and as it loses its dependence on the uterine environment, the State's interest in the fetus' potential human life, and in fostering a regard for human life in general, becomes compelling. As a practical matter, because viability follows "quickening"—the point at which a woman feels movement in her womb—and because viability occurs no earlier than 23 weeks gestational age, it establishes an easily applicable standard for regulating abortion providing a pregnant woman ample time to exercise her fundamental right with her responsible physician to terminate her pregnancy. n9. Although I have stated previously for a majority of this Court that "[c]onstitutional rights do not always have easily ascertainable boundaries," to seek and establish those boundaries remains the special responsibility of this Court. *Thornburgh,* 476 U.S., at 771. In *Roe,* we discharged that responsibility as logic and science compelled. The plurality today advances not one reasonable argument as to why our judgment in that case was wrong and should be abandoned. . . . For today, at least, the law of abortion stands undisturbed. For today, the women of this Nation still retain the liberty to control their destinies. But the signs are evident and very ominous, and a chill wind blows.

Planned Parenthood of Southeastern Pennsylvania, et al. v. Casey (1992)

The Pennsylvania legislature amended its abortion statute to include a number of restrictions on women seeking abortions in the state. These included provisions that a woman be given certain information and that she give her informed consent at least twenty-four hours before the procedure; minors obtain consent from a parent or guardian or exercise a judicial bypass option; married women notify their husbands of their intention to have abortions; facilities adhere to particular reporting requirements; a medical emergency could waive adherence to these requirements, but "medical emergency" was defined by the legislature in a separate statute. Five abortion clinics and one physician brought suit on the basis that each of these requirements was unconstitutional and sought an injunction against their enforcement in the federal court, which granted a permanent injunction. The U.S. Court of Appeals, however, upheld the statute's provisions except for the spousal notification requirement. In a complex ruling, the U.S. Supreme Court affirmed the lower court decision in part, reversed in part, and remanded back to the Pennsylvania Courts. The core issue was whether a woman's decision to have an abortion represented a fundamental right and to what extent states could regulate abortion without violating such a woman's liberty to control her body. In brief, the decision stated that although states may regulate in the area, the restrictions may not pose an "undue burden" on the woman as she exercises her right to choose. The politically charged nature of the subject is reflected in the unusually warm exchanges among the justices in their various opinions.

Argued April 22, 1992
  Decided June 29, 1992
  (As Amended July 2, 1992)
JUSTICE O'CONNOR, JUSTICE KENNEDY, and JUSTICE SOUTER announced the judgment of the Court and delivered the opinion of the Court with respect to Parts I, II, III, V-A, V-C, and VI, an opinion with respect to Part V-E, in which JUSTICE STEVENS joins, and an opinion with respect to Parts IV, V-B, and V-D.

I

Liberty finds no refuge in a jurisprudence of doubt. Yet 19 years after our holding that the Constitution protects a woman's right to terminate her pregnancy in its early stages . . . that definition of liberty is still questioned. Joining the respondents as *amicus curiae,* the United States, as it has done in five other cases in the last decade, again asks us to overrule *Roe.* . . .

After considering the fundamental constitutional questions resolved by *Roe,* principles of institutional integrity, and the rule of *stare decisis,* we are led to conclude this: the essential holding of *Roe v. Wade* should be retained and once again reaffirmed. It must be stated at the outset and with clarity that *Roe's* essential holding, the holding we reaffirm, has three parts. First is a recognition of the right of the woman to choose to have an abortion before viability and to obtain it without undue interference from the State. Before viability, the State's interests are not strong enough to support a prohibition of abortion or the imposition of a substantial obstacle to the woman's effective right to elect the procedure. Second is a confirmation of the State's power to restrict abortions after fetal viability, if the law contains exceptions for pregnancies which endanger the woman's life or health. And third is the principle that the State has legitimate interests from the outset of the pregnancy in protecting the health of the woman and the life of the fetus that may become a child. These principles do not contradict one another; and we adhere to each. Constitutional protection of the woman's decision to terminate her pregnancy derives from the Due

Process Clause of the Fourteenth Amendment. It declares that no State shall "deprive any person of life, liberty, or property, without due process of law." The controlling word in the cases before us is "liberty." Although a literal reading of the Clause might suggest that it governs only the procedures by which a State may deprive persons of liberty, for at least 105 years ... the Clause has been understood to contain a substantive component as well, one "barring certain government actions regardless of the fairness of the procedures used to implement them." ...

Men and women of good conscience can disagree, and we suppose some always shall disagree, about the profound moral and spiritual implications of terminating a pregnancy, even in its earliest stage. Some of us as individuals find abortion offensive to our most basic principles of morality, but that cannot control our decision. Our obligation is to define the liberty of all, not to mandate our own moral code. The underlying constitutional issue is whether the State can resolve these philosophic questions in such a definitive way that a woman lacks all choice in the matter, except perhaps in those rare circumstances in which the pregnancy is itself a danger to her own life or health, or is the result of rape or incest. ... Our law affords constitutional protection to personal decisions relating to marriage, procreation, contraception, family relationships, child rearing, and education. *Carey v. Population Services International,* 431 U.S. at 685. Our cases recognize "the right of the *individual,* married or single, to be free from unwarranted governmental intrusion into matters so fundamentally affecting a person as the decision whether to bear or beget a child." *Eisenstadt v. Baird, supra,* at 453 (emphasis in original). Our precedents "have respected the private realm of family life which the state cannot enter." *Prince v. Massachusetts,* 321 U.S. 158, 166, 88 L. Ed. 645, 64 S. Ct. 438 (1944). These matters, involving the most intimate and personal choices a person may make in a lifetime, choices central to personal dignity and autonomy, are central to the liberty protected by the Fourteenth Amendment. At the heart of liberty is the right to define one's own concept of existence, of meaning, of the universe, and of the mystery of human life. Beliefs about these matters could not define the attributes of personhood were they formed under compulsion of the State. These considerations begin our analysis of the woman's interest in terminating her pregnancy but cannot end it, for this reason: though the abortion decision may originate within the zone of conscience and belief, it is more than a philosophic exercise.

Abortion is a unique act. It is an act fraught with consequences for others: for the woman who must live with the implications of her decision; for the persons who perform and assist in the procedure; for the spouse, family, and society which must confront the knowledge that these procedures exist, procedures some deem nothing short of an act of violence against innocent human life; and, depending on one's beliefs, for the life or potential life that is aborted. Though abortion is conduct, it does not follow that the State is entitled to proscribe it in all instances. That is because the liberty of the woman is at stake in a sense unique to the human condition and so unique to the law. The mother who carries a child to full term is subject to anxieties, to physical constraints, to pain that only she must bear. That these sacrifices have from the beginning of the human race been endured by woman with a pride that ennobles her in the eyes of others and gives to the infant a bond of love cannot alone be grounds for the State to insist she make the sacrifice. Her suffering is too intimate and personal for the State to insist, without more, upon its own vision of the woman's role, however dominant that vision has been in the course of our history and our culture. The destiny of the woman must be shaped to a large extent on her own conception of her spiritual imperatives and her place in society. It should be recognized, moreover, that in some critical respects the abortion decision is of the same character as the decision to use contraception, to which *Griswold v. Connecticut, Eisenstadt v. Baird,* and *Carey v. Population Services International* afford constitutional protection. We have no doubt as to the correctness of those decisions. They support the reasoning in *Roe* relating to the woman's liberty because they involve personal decisions concerning not only the meaning of procreation but also human responsibility and respect for it. As with abortion, reasonable people will have differences of opinion about these matters. One view is based on such reverence for the wonder of creation that any pregnancy ought to be welcomed and carried to full term no matter how difficult it will be to provide for the child and ensure its well-being. Another is that the inability to provide for the nurture and care of the infant is a cruelty to the child and an anguish to the parent. These are intimate views with infinite variations, and their deep, personal character underlay our decisions in *Griswold, Eisenstadt,* and *Carey.* The same concerns are present when the woman confronts the reality that, perhaps despite her attempts to avoid it, she has become pregnant. It was this dimension of personal liberty that *Roe* sought to protect, and its holding invoked the reasoning and the tradition of the precedents we have discussed, granting protection to substantive liberties of the person. *Roe* was, of course, an extension of those cases and, as the decision itself indicated, the separate States could act in some degree to further their own legitimate interests in protecting prenatal life. The extent to which the legislatures of the States might act to outweigh the interests of the woman in choosing to terminate her pregnancy was a subject of debate both in *Roe* itself and in decisions following it. While we appreciate the weight of the arguments made on behalf of the State in the cases before us, arguments which in their ultimate formulation conclude that *Roe* should be overruled, the reservations any of us may have in reaffirming the central holding of *Roe* are outweighed by the explication of individual liberty we have given combined with the force of *stare decisis*. . . .

IV

. . . That brings us, of course, to the point where much criticism has been directed at *Roe,* a criticism that always inheres when the Court draws a specific rule from what in the Constitution is but a general standard. We conclude, however, that the urgent claims of the woman to retain the ultimate control over her destiny and her body, claims implicit in the meaning of liberty, require us to perform that function. Liberty must not be extinguished for want of a line that is clear. And it falls to us to give some real substance to the woman's liberty to determine whether to carry her pregnancy to full term. We conclude the line should be drawn at viability, so that before that time the woman has a right to choose to terminate her pregnancy. We adhere to this principle for two reasons. First, as we have said, is the doctrine of *stare decisis.* Any judicial act of line-drawing may seem somewhat arbitrary, but *Roe* was a reasoned statement, elaborated with great care. We have twice reaffirmed it in the face of great opposition. . . . The second reason is that the concept of viability, as we noted in *Roe,* is the time at which there is a realistic possibility of maintaining and nourishing a life outside the womb, so that the independent existence of the second life can in reason and all fairness be the object of state protection that now overrides the rights of the woman. See *Roe v. Wade,* 410 U.S. at 163. Consistent with other constitutional norms, legislatures may draw lines which appear arbitrary without the necessity of offering a justification. But courts may not. We must justify the lines we draw. And there is no line other than viability which is more workable. To be sure, as we have said, there may be some medical developments that affect the precise point of viability . . . but this is an imprecision within in tolerable limits given that the medical community and all those who must apply its discoveries will continue to explore the matter. The viability line also has, as a practical matter, an element of fairness. In some broad sense it might be said that a woman who fails to act before viability has consented to the State's intervention on behalf of the developing child. The woman's right to terminate her pregnancy before viability is the most central principle of *Roe v. Wade*. It is a rule of law and a component of liberty we cannot renounce. On the other side of the equation is the interest of the State in the protection of potential life. The *Roe* Court recognized the State's "important and legitimate interest in protecting the potentiality of human life." *Roe, supra,* at 162. The weight to be given this state interest, not the strength of the woman's interest, was the difficult question faced in *Roe*. We do not need to say whether each of us, had we been Members of the Court when the valuation of the state interest came before it as an original matter, would have concluded, as the *Roe* Court did, that its weight is insufficient to justify a ban on abortions prior to viability even when it is subject to certain exceptions. The matter is not before us in the first instance, and coming as it does after nearly 20 years of litigation in *Roe's* wake we are satisfied that the immediate question is not the soundness of *Roe's* resolution of the issue, but the precedential force that must be accorded to its holding. And we have concluded that the essential holding of *Roe* should be reaffirmed.

Yet it must be remembered that *Roe v. Wade* speaks with clarity in establishing not only the woman's liberty but also the State's "important and legitimate interest in potential life." *Roe, supra,* at 163. That portion of the decision in *Roe* has been given too little acknowledgment and implementation by the Court in its subsequent cases. Those cases decided that any regulation touching upon the abortion decision must survive strict scrutiny, to be sustained only if drawn in narrow terms to further a compelling state interest. See, *e.g., Akron I, supra,* at 427. Not all of the cases decided under that formulation can be reconciled with the holding in *Roe* itself that the State has legitimate interests in the health of the woman and in protecting the potential life within her. In resolving this tension, we choose to rely upon *Roe,* as against the later cases. *Roe* established a trimester framework to govern abortion regulations. Under this elaborate but rigid construct, almost no regulation at all is permitted during the first trimester of pregnancy; regulations designed to protect the woman's health, but not to further the State's interest in potential life, are permitted during the second trimester; and during the third trimester, when the fetus is viable, prohibitions are permitted provided the life or health of the mother is not at stake. *Roe, supra,* at 163–166. Most of our cases since *Roe* have involved the application of rules derived from the trimester framework. . . . The trimester framework no doubt was erected to ensure that the woman's right to choose not become so subordinate to the State's interest in promoting fetal life that her choice exists in theory but not in fact. We do not agree, however, that the trimester approach is necessary to accomplish this objective. A framework of this rigidity was unnecessary and in its later interpretation sometimes contradicted the State's permissible exercise of its powers. Though the woman has a right to choose to terminate or continue her pregnancy before viability, it does not at all follow that the State is prohibited from taking steps to ensure that this choice is thoughtful and informed. Even in the earliest stages of pregnancy, the State may enact rules and regulations designed to encourage her to know that there are philosophic and social arguments of great weight that can be brought to bear in favor of continuing the pregnancy to full term and that there are procedures and institutions to allow adoption of unwanted children as well as a certain degree of state assistance if the mother chooses to raise the child herself. "'The Constitution does not forbid a State or city, pursuant to democratic processes, from expressing a preference for normal childbirth.'" *Webster v. Reproductive Health Services,* 492 U.S. at 511. . . . It follows that States are free to enact laws to provide a reasonable framework for a woman to make a decision that has such profound and lasting meaning. This, too, we find consistent with *Roe's* central premises, and indeed the inevitable consequence of our holding that the State has an interest in protecting the life of the unborn. We reject the trimester framework, which we do not consider to be part of the essential holding of *Roe.* See *Webster v. Reproductive Health Services,* 492 U.S. at 518 (opinion of REHNQUIST, C. J.); *id.,* at 529 (O'CONNOR, J., concurring in part and concurring in judgment) (describing the trimester framework as "problematic"). Measures aimed at ensuring that a woman's choice contemplates the consequences for the fetus do not necessarily interfere with the right recognized in *Roe,* although those measures have been found to be inconsistent with the rigid trimester framework announced in that case. A logical reading of the central holding in *Roe* itself, and a necessary reconciliation of the liberty of the woman and the interest of the

State in promoting prenatal life, require, in our view, that we abandon the trimester framework as a rigid prohibition on all previability regulation aimed at the protection of fetal life. The trimester framework suffers from these basic flaws: in its formulation it misconceives the nature of the pregnant woman's interest; and in practice it undervalues the State's interest in potential life, as recognized in *Roe.* As our jurisprudence relating to all liberties save perhaps abortion has recognized, not every law which makes a right more difficult to exercise is, *ipso facto,* an infringement of that right. An example clarifies the point. We have held that not every ballot access limitation amounts to an infringement of the right to vote. Rather, the States are granted substantial flexibility in establishing the framework within which voters choose the candidates for whom they wish to vote. . . . The abortion right is similar. Numerous forms of state regulation might have the incidental effect of increasing the cost or decreasing the availability of medical care, whether for abortion or any other medical procedure. The fact that a law which serves a valid purpose, one not designed to strike at the right itself, has the incidental effect of making it more difficult or more expensive to procure an abortion cannot be enough to invalidate it. Only where state regulation imposes an undue burden on a woman's ability to make this decision does the power of the State reach into the heart of the liberty protected by the Due Process Clause. . . .

We give this summary:

(a) To protect the central right recognized by *Roe v. Wade* while at the same time accommodating the State's profound interest in potential life, we will employ the undue burden analysis as explained in this opinion. An undue burden exists, and therefore a provision of law is invalid, if its purpose or effect is to place a substantial obstacle in the path of a woman seeking an abortion before the fetus attains viability.

(b) We reject the rigid trimester framework of *Roe v. Wade.* To promote the State's profound interest in potential life, throughout pregnancy the State may take measures to ensure that the woman's choice is informed, and measures designed to advance this interest will not be invalidated as long as their purpose is to persuade the woman to choose childbirth over abortion. These measures must not be an undue burden on the right.

(c) As with any medical procedure, the State may enact regulations to further the health or safety of a woman seeking an abortion. Unnecessary health regulations that have the purpose or effect of presenting a substantial obstacle to a woman seeking an abortion impose an undue burden on the right.

(d) Our adoption of the undue burden analysis does not disturb the central holding of *Roe v. Wade,* and we reaffirm that holding. Regardless of whether exceptions are made for particular circumstances, a State may not prohibit any woman from making the ultimate decision to terminate her pregnancy before viability.

(e) We also reaffirm *Roe's* holding that "subsequent to viability, the State in promoting its interest in the potentiality of human life may, if it chooses, regulate, and even proscribe, abortion except where it is necessary, in appropriate medical judgment, for the preservation of the life or health of the mother." *Roe v. Wade,* 410 U.S. at 164–165. These principles control our assessment of the Pennsylvania statute, and we now turn to the issue of the validity of its challenged provisions.

V

The Court of Appeals applied what it believed to be the undue burden standard and upheld each of the provisions except for the husband notification requirement. We agree generally with this conclusion, but refine the undue burden analysis in accordance with the principles articulated above. We now consider the separate statutory sections at issue. . . .

A. We . . . conclude that, as construed by the Court of Appeals, the medical emergency definition imposes no undue burden on a woman's abortion right. . . .

In attempting to ensure that a woman apprehend the full consequences of her decision, the State furthers the legitimate purpose of reducing the risk that a woman may elect an abortion, only to discover later, with devastating psychological consequences, that her decision was not fully informed. If the information the State requires to be made available to the woman is truthful and not misleading, the requirement may be permissible. We also see no reason why the State may not require doctors to inform a woman seeking an abortion of the availability of materials relating to the consequences to the fetus, even when those consequences have no direct relation to her health. . . .

On the record before us, and in the context of this facial challenge, we are not convinced that the 24-hour waiting period constitutes an undue burden. We are left with the argument that the various aspects of the informed consent requirement are unconstitutional because they place barriers in the way of abortion on demand. Even the broadest reading of *Roe,* however, has not suggested that there is a constitutional right to abortion on demand. See, *e.g., Doe v. Bolton,* 410 U.S. at 189. Rather, the right protected by *Roe* is a right to decide to terminate a pregnancy free of undue interference by the State. Because the informed consent requirement facilitates the wise exercise of that right, it cannot be classified as an interference with the right *Roe* protects. The informed consent requirement is not an undue burden on that right. . . .

C. The spousal notification requirement is thus likely to prevent a significant number of women from obtaining an abortion. It does not merely make abortions a little more difficult or expensive to obtain; for many women, it will impose a substantial obstacle. We must not blind ourselves to the fact that the significant number of women who fear for their safety and the safety of their children are likely to be deterred from procuring an abortion as surely as if the Commonwealth had outlawed abortion in all cases. . . .

We recognize that a husband has a "deep and proper concern and interest . . . in his wife's pregnancy and in the growth and development of the fetus she is carrying." *Danforth, supra,* at 69. With regard to the children he has fathered and raised, the Court has recognized his "cognizable and substantial" interest in their custody. . . .

If these cases concerned a State's ability to require the mother to notify the father before taking some action with respect to a living child raised by both, therefore, it would be reasonable to conclude as a general matter that the father's interest in the welfare of the child and the mother's interest are equal. . . .

Before birth, however, the issue takes on a very different cast. It is an inescapable biological fact that state regulation with respect to the child a woman is carrying will have a far greater impact on the mother's liberty than on the father's. The effect of state regulation on a woman's protected liberty is doubly deserving of scrutiny in such a case, as the State has touched not only upon the private sphere of the family but upon the very bodily integrity of the pregnant woman. . . .

The husband's interest in the life of the child his wife is carrying does not permit the State to empower him with this troubling degree of authority over his wife. The contrary view leads to consequences reminiscent of the common law. A husband has no enforceable right to require a wife to advise him before she exercises her personal choices. If a husband's interest in the potential life of the child outweighs a wife's liberty, the State could require a married woman to notify her husband before she uses a postfertilization contraceptive. Perhaps next

in line would be a statute requiring pregnant married women to notify their husbands before engaging in conduct causing risks to the
fetus. After all, if the husband's interest in the fetus' safety is a sufficient predicate for state regulation, the State could reasonably conclude that pregnant wives should notify their husbands before drinking alcohol or smoking. Perhaps married women should notify their
husbands before using contraceptives or before undergoing any type
of surgery that may have complications affecting the husband's interest in his wife's reproductive organs. And if a husband's interest justifies notice in any of these cases, one might reasonably argue that it justifies exactly what the *Danforth* Court held it did not justify—a
requirement of the husband's consent as well. A State may not give to
a man the kind of dominion over his wife that parents exercise over
their children. . . .

We next consider the parental consent provision. Except in a medical emergency, an unemancipated young woman under 18 may not
obtain an abortion unless she and one of her parents (or guardian)
provides informed consent as defined above. If neither a parent nor a
guardian provides consent, a court may authorize the performance of
an abortion upon a determination that the young woman is mature
and capable of giving informed consent and has in fact given her
informed consent, or that an abortion would be in her best interests.
We have been over most of this ground before. Our cases establish,
and we reaffirm today, that a State may require a minor seeking an
abortion to obtain the consent of a parent or guardian, provided that
there is an adequate judicial bypass procedure. . . .

E. Under the recordkeeping and reporting requirements of the
statute, every facility which performs abortions is required to file a
report stating its name and address as well as the name and address of
any related entity, such as a controlling or subsidiary organization. In
the case of state-funded institutions, the information becomes public. . . .

In *Danforth*, 428 U.S. at 80, we held that recordkeeping and reporting provisions "that are reasonably directed to the preservation of
maternal health and that properly respect a patient's confidentiality
and privacy are permissible." We think that under this standard, all the
provisions at issue here, except that relating to spousal notice, are constitutional. Although they do not relate to the State's interest in
informing the woman's choice, they do relate to health. The collection
of information with respect to actual patients is a vital element of med-

ical research, and so it cannot be said that the requirements serve no purpose other than to make abortions more difficult. Nor do we find that the requirements impose a substantial obstacle to a woman's choice. At most they might increase the cost of some abortions by a slight amount. While at some point increased cost could become a substantial obstacle, there is no such showing on the record before us.

VI

Our Constitution is a covenant running from the first generation of Americans to us and then to future generations. It is a coherent succession. Each generation must learn anew that the Constitution's written terms embody ideas and aspirations that must survive more ages than one. We accept our responsibility not to retreat from interpreting the full meaning of the covenant in light of all of our precedents. We invoke it once again to define the freedom guaranteed by the Constitution's own promise, the promise of liberty. . . .

DISSENT BY: STEVENS (In Part); BLACKMUN (In Part); REHNQUIST (In Part); SCALIA (In Part) DISSENT: JUSTICE STEVENS, concurring in part and dissenting in part.

. . . My disagreement with the joint opinion begins with its understanding of the trimester framework established in *Roe*. Contrary to the suggestion of the joint opinion, *ante*, 505 U.S. at 876, it is not a "contradiction" to recognize that the State may have a legitimate interest in potential human life and, at the same time, to conclude that that interest does not justify the regulation of abortion before viability (although other interests, such as maternal health, may). The fact that the State's interest is legitimate does not tell us when, if ever, that interest outweighs the pregnant woman's interest in personal liberty. It is appropriate, therefore, to consider more carefully the nature of the interests at stake. First, it is clear that, in order to be legitimate, the State's interest must be secular; consistent with the First Amendment the State may not promote a theological or sectarian interest. . . .

Moreover, as discussed above, the state interest in potential human life is not an interest *in loco parentis*, for the fetus is not a person. Weighing the State's interest in potential life and the woman's liberty interest, I agree with the joint opinion that the State may "express a preference for normal childbirth," that the State may take steps to ensure that a woman's choice "is thoughtful and informed," and that "States are free to enact laws to provide a reasonable framework for a woman to make a decision that has such profound and lasting meaning." ... Serious questions arise, however, when a State attempts to "persuade the woman to choose childbirth over abortion." *Ante,* 505 U.S. at 878. Decisional autonomy must limit the State's power to inject into a woman's most personal deliberations its own views of what is best. The State may promote its preferences by funding childbirth, by creating and maintaining alternatives to abortion, and by espousing the virtues of family; but it must respect the individual's freedom to make such judgments. ... The 24-hour delay requirement fails both parts of this test. The findings of the District Court establish the severity of the burden that the 24-hour delay imposes on many pregnant women. Yet even in those cases in which the delay is not especially onerous, it is, in my opinion, "undue" because there is no evidence that such a delay serves a useful and legitimate purpose. As indicated above, there is no legitimate reason to require a woman who has agonized over her decision to leave the clinic or hospital and return again another day. While a general requirement that a physician notify her patients about the risks of a proposed medical procedure is appropriate, a rigid requirement that all patients wait 24 hours or (what is true in practice) much longer to evaluate the significance of information that is either common knowledge or irrelevant is an irrational and, therefore, "undue" burden. The counseling provisions are similarly infirm. Whenever government commands private citizens to speak or to listen, careful review of the justification for that command is particularly appropriate. In these cases, the Pennsylvania statute directs that counselors provide women seeking abortions with information concerning alternatives to abortion, the availability of medical assistance benefits, and the possibility of child-support payments. §§ 3205(a)(2)(i)-(iii). The statute requires that this information be given to *all* women seeking abortions, including those for whom such information is clearly useless, such as those who are married, those who have undergone the procedure in the past and are fully aware of the options, and those who are fully convinced that abortion is their only reasonable option. Moreover, the statute requires physicians to inform all of their patients of "the probable gestational age of the unborn child." § 3205(a)(1)(ii). This information is of little decisional value in most cases, because 90% of all abortions are performed during the first trimester when fetal age has less relevance than when the fetus nears viability. Nor can the information required by the statute be justified as relevant to any "philosophic" or "social" argument, *ante,* 505 U.S. at 872, either favoring or disfavoring the abortion decision in a particular case. In light of all of these facts, I conclude that the information requirements in [the statute] do not serve a useful purpose and thus constitute an unnecessary—and therefore undue—burden on the woman's constitutional liberty to decide to terminate her pregnancy. Accordingly, while I disagree with Parts IV, V-B, and V-D of the joint opinion, I join the remainder of the Court's opinion.

JUSTICE BLACKMUN, concurring in part, concurring in the judgment in part, and dissenting in part. I join Parts I, II, III, V-A, V-C, and VI of the joint opinion of JUSTICES O'CONNOR, KENNEDY, and SOUTER, *ante*.

. . . I do not underestimate the significance of today's joint opinion. Yet I remain steadfast in my belief that the right to reproductive choice is entitled to the full protection afforded by this Court before *Webster*. And I fear for the darkness as four Justices anxiously await the single vote necessary to extinguish the light. . . . At long last, THE CHIEF JUSTICE and those who have joined him admit it. Gone are the contentions that the issue need not be (or has not been) considered. There, on the first page, for all to see, is what was expected: "We believe that *Roe* was wrongly decided, and that it can and should be overruled consistently with our traditional approach to *stare decisis* in constitutional cases." *Post*, 505 U.S. at 944. If there is much reason to applaud the advances made by the joint opinion today, there is far more to fear from THE CHIEF JUSTICE's opinion. THE CHIEF JUSTICE's criticism of *Roe* follows from his stunted conception of individual liberty. While recognizing that the Due Process Clause protects more than simple physical liberty, he then goes on to construe this Court's personal-liberty cases as establishing only a laundry list of particular rights, rather than a principled account of how these particular rights are grounded in a more general right of privacy. *Post*, 505 U.S. at 951. This constricted view is reinforced by THE CHIEF JUSTICE's exclusive reliance on tradition as a source of fundamental rights. He argues that the record in favor of a right to abortion is no stronger than the record in *Michael H. v. Gerald D.*, 491 U.S. 110, 105 L. Ed. 2d 91, 109 S. Ct. 2333 (1989), where the plurality found no fundamental right to visitation privileges by an adulterous father, or in *Bowers v. Hardwick*, 478 U.S. 186, 92 L. Ed. 2d 140, 106 S. Ct. 2841 (1986), where the Court found no fundamental right to engage in homosexual sodomy, or in a case involving the "'firing [of] a gun . . . into another person's body.'" *Post*, 505 U.S. at 951–952. In THE CHIEF JUSTICE's world, a woman considering whether to terminate a pregnancy is entitled to no more protection than adulterers, murderers, and so-called sexual deviates. Given THE CHIEF JUSTICE's exclusive reliance on tradition, people using contraceptives seem the next likely candidate for his list of outcasts. Even more shocking than THE CHIEF JUSTICE's cramped notion of individual liberty is his complete omission of any discussion of the effects that compelled childbirth and motherhood have on women's lives. The only expression of concern with women's health is purely instrumental—for THE CHIEF JUSTICE, only women's *psychological* health is a concern, and only to the extent that he assumes that every woman who decides to have an abortion does so without serious consideration of the moral implications of her decision. *Post,* 505 U.S. at 967–968. In short, THE CHIEF JUSTICE's view of the State's compelling interest in maternal health has less to do with health than it does with compelling women to be maternal. Nor does THE CHIEF JUSTICE give any serious consideration to the doctrine of *stare decisis.* For THE CHIEF JUSTICE, the facts that gave rise to *Roe* are surprisingly simple: "women become pregnant, there is a point somewhere, depending on medical technology, where a fetus becomes viable, and women give birth to children." *Post,* 505 U.S. at 955. This characterization of the issue thus allows THE CHIEF JUSTICE quickly to discard the joint opinion's reliance argument by asserting that "reproductive planning could take virtually immediate account of" a decision overruling *Roe. Post,* 505 U.S. at 956 (internal quotation marks omitted). THE CHIEF JUSTICE's narrow conception of individual liberty and *stare decisis* leads him to propose the same standard of review proposed by the plurality in *Webster.* "States may regulate abortion procedures in ways rationally related to a legitimate state interest." . . . THE CHIEF JUSTICE then further weakens the test by providing an insurmountable requirement for facial challenges: Petitioners must "'show that no set of circumstances exists under which the [provision] would be valid.'" *Post,* 505 U.S. at 973, quoting *Ohio v. Akron Center for Reproductive Health,* 497 U.S. at 514. In short, in his view, petitioners must prove that the statute cannot constitutionally be applied to *anyone.* Finally, in applying his standard to the spousal-notification provision, THE CHIEF JUSTICE contends that the record lacks any "hard evidence" to support the joint opinion's contention that a "large fraction" of women who prefer not to notify their husbands involve situations of battered women and unreported spousal assault. *Post,* 505 U.S. at 974, n.2. Yet throughout the explication of his standard, THE CHIEF JUSTICE never explains what hard evidence is, how large a fraction is required, or how a battered woman is supposed to pursue an as-applied challenge. Under his standard, States can ban abortion if that ban is rationally related to a legitimate state interest—a standard which the United States calls "deferential, but not toothless." Yet when pressed at oral argument to describe the teeth, the best protection that the Solicitor General could offer to women was that a prohibition, enforced by criminal penalties, *with no exception for the life of the mother,* "could raise very serious questions." Tr. of Oral Arg. 48. Perhaps, the Solicitor General offered, the failure to include an exemption for the life of the mother would be "arbitrary and capricious." *Id.,* at 49. If, as THE CHIEF JUSTICE contends, the undue burden test is made out of whole cloth, the so-called "arbitrary and capricious" limit is the Solicitor General's "new clothes." Even if it is somehow "irrational" for a State to require a woman to risk her life for her child, what protection is offered for women who become pregnant through rape or incest? Is there anything arbitrary or capricious about a State's prohibiting the sins of the father from being visited upon his offspring? But, we are reassured, there is always the protection of the democratic process. While there is much to be praised about our democracy, our country since its founding has recognized that there are certain fundamental liberties that are not to be left to the whims of an election. A woman's right to reproductive choice is one of those fundamental liberties. Accordingly, that liberty need not seek refuge at the ballot box.

In one sense, the Court's approach is worlds apart from that of THE CHIEF JUSTICE and JUSTICE SCALIA. And yet, in another sense, the distance between the two approaches is short—the distance is but a single vote. I am 83 years old. I cannot remain on this Court forever, and when I do step down, the confirmation process for my successor well may focus on the issue before us today. That, I regret, may be exactly where the choice between the two worlds will be made.

CHIEF JUSTICE REHNQUIST, with whom JUSTICE WHITE, JUSTICE SCALIA, and JUSTICE THOMAS join, concurring in the judgment in part and dissenting in part.

. . . In arguing that this Court should invalidate each of the provisions at issue, petitioners insist that we reaffirm our decision in *Roe v. Wade, supra,* in which we held unconstitutional a Texas statute making it a crime to procure an abortion except to save the life of the mother. We agree with the Court of Appeals that our decision in *Roe* is not

directly implicated by the Pennsylvania statute, which does not prohibit, but simply regulates, abortion. But, as the Court of Appeals
found, the state of our post-*Roe* decisional law dealing with the regulation of abortion is confusing and uncertain, indicating that a reexamination of that line of cases is in order. Unfortunately for those who
must apply this Court's decisions, the reexamination undertaken
today leaves the Court no less divided than beforehand. Although
they reject the trimester framework that formed the underpinning of
Roe, JUSTICES O'CONNOR, KENNEDY, and SOUTER adopt a
revised undue burden standard to analyze the challenged regulations.
We conclude, however, that such an outcome is an unjustified constitutional compromise, one which leaves the Court in a position to
closely scrutinize all types of abortion regulations despite the fact that
it lacks the power to do so under the Constitution. . . . In *Roe v. Wade,*
the Court recognized a "guarantee of personal privacy" which "is
broad enough to encompass a woman's decision whether or not to terminate her pregnancy." 410 U.S. at 152–153. We are now of the view
that, in terming this right fundamental, the Court in *Roe* read the earlier opinions upon which it based its decision much too broadly.
Unlike marriage, procreation, and contraception, abortion "involves
the purposeful termination of a potential life." *Harris v. McRae,* 448
U.S. 297, 325, 65 L. Ed. 2d 784, 100 S. Ct. 2671 (1980). The abortion
decision must therefore "be recognized as *sui generis,* different in kind
from the others that the Court has protected under the rubric of personal or family privacy and autonomy." *Thornburgh v. American College of Obstetricians and Gynecologists, supra,* at 792 (WHITE, J., dissenting). One cannot ignore the fact that a woman is not isolated in
her pregnancy, and that the decision to abort necessarily involves the
destruction of a fetus. See *Michael H. v. Gerald D., supra,* at 124, n.4.
(To look "at the act which is assertedly the subject of a liberty interest
in isolation from its effect upon other people [is] like inquiring
whether there is a liberty interest in firing a gun where the case at hand
happens to involve its discharge into another person's body"). Nor do
the historical traditions of the American people support the view that
the right to terminate one's pregnancy is "fundamental." The common
law which we inherited from England made abortion after "quickening" an offense. At the time of the adoption of the Fourteenth Amendment, statutory prohibitions or restrictions on abortion were commonplace; in 1868, at least 28 of the then 37 States and 8 Territories
had statutes banning or limiting abortion. J. Mohr, *Abortion in Amer-*

ica 200 (1978). By the turn of the century virtually every State had a law prohibiting or restricting abortion on its books. By the middle of the present century, a liberalization trend had set in. But 21 of the restrictive abortion laws in effect in 1868 were still in effect in 1973 when *Roe* was decided, and an overwhelming majority of the States prohibited abortion unless necessary to preserve the life or health of the mother. *Roe v. Wade,* 410 U.S. at 139–140; *id.,* at 176–177, n.2 (REHNQUIST, J., dissenting). On this record, it can scarcely be said that any deeply rooted tradition of relatively unrestricted abortion in our history supported the classification of the right to abortion as "fundamental" under the Due Process Clause of the Fourteenth Amendment. We think, therefore, both in view of this history and of our decided cases dealing with substantive liberty under the Due Process Clause, that the Court was mistaken in *Roe* when it classified a woman's decision to terminate her pregnancy as a "fundamental right" that could be abridged only in a manner which withstood "strict scrutiny." In so concluding, we repeat the observation made in *Bowers v. Hardwick,* 478 U.S. 186, 92 L. Ed. 2d 140, 106 S. Ct. 2841 (1986):

"Nor are we inclined to take a more expansive view of our authority to discover new fundamental rights imbedded in the Due Process Clause. The Court is most vulnerable and comes nearest to illegitimacy when it deals with judge-made constitutional law having little or no cognizable roots in the language or design of the Constitution." *Id.,* at 194.

We believe that the sort of constitutionally imposed abortion code of the type illustrated by our decisions following *Roe* is inconsistent "with the notion of a Constitution cast in general terms, as ours is, and usually speaking in general principles, as ours does." *Webster v. Reproductive Health Services,* 492 U.S. at 518 (plurality opinion). The Court in *Roe* reached too far when it analogized the right to abort a fetus to the rights involved in *Pierce, Meyer, Loving,* and *Griswold,* and thereby deemed the right to abortion fundamental. . . .

The joint opinion thus turns to what can only be described as an unconventional—and unconvincing—notion of reliance, a view based on the surmise that the availability of abortion since *Roe* has led to "two decades of economic and social developments" that would be undercut if the error of *Roe* were recognized. *Ante,* 505 U.S. at 856. The joint opinion's assertion of this fact is undeveloped and totally conclusory. In fact, one cannot be sure to what economic and social developments the opinion is referring. Surely it is dubious to suggest that women have reached their "places in society" in reliance upon *Roe,* rather than as a result of their determination to obtain higher education and compete with men in the job market, and of society's increasing recognition of their ability to fill positions that were previously thought to be reserved only for men. *Ante,* 505 U.S. at 856. In the end, having failed to put forth any evidence to prove any true reliance, the joint opinion's argument is based solely on generalized assertions about the national psyche, on a belief that the people of this country have grown accustomed to the *Roe* decision over the last 19 years and have "ordered their thinking and living around" it. *Ante,* 505 U.S. at 856. As an initial matter, one might inquire how the joint opinion can view the "central holding" of *Roe* as so deeply rooted in our constitutional culture, when it so casually uproots and disposes of that same decision's trimester framework. Furthermore, at various points in the past, the same could have been said about this Court's erroneous decisions that the Constitution allowed "separate but equal" treatment of minorities, see *Plessy v. Ferguson,* 163 U.S. 537, 41 L. Ed. 256, 16 S. Ct. 1138 (1896), or that "liberty" under the Due Process Clause protected "freedom of contract," see *Adkins v. Children's Hospital of District of Columbia,* 261 U.S. 525, 67 L. Ed. 785, 43 S. Ct. 394 (1923); *Lochner v. New York,* 198 U.S. 45, 49 L. Ed. 937, 25 S. Ct. 539 (1905). The "separate but equal" doctrine lasted 58 years after *Plessy,* and *Lochner's* protection of contractual freedom lasted 32 years. However, the simple fact that a generation or more had grown used to these major decisions did not prevent the Court from correcting its errors in those cases, nor should it prevent us from correctly interpreting the Constitution here. . . .

Cruzan v. Director, Missouri Department of Public Health (1990)

Like Karen Quinlan's tragic story, Nancy Cruzan's case captured the nation's attention and raised a public discussion of the "right to die." Front-page coverage in the New York Times *provided details of oral arguments made before the Supreme Court in* Cruzan v. Director, Missouri Department of Public Health.

"Right-to-Die Case Gets First Hearing in Supreme Court"
By Linda Greenhouse, Special to the *New York Times*

WASHINGTON, Dec. 6—Both sides of a right-to-die case received a skeptical hearing today at the Supreme Court, where the Justices spent much of an hourlong argument probing for a narrow basis on which to resolve a question as profound as ever reaches them.

This was the first time the Court had ever confronted an issue that dozens of lower courts have addressed in the last decade: whether there is a constitutional right to discontinue unwanted life-sustaining medical treatment. The courtroom was filled to capacity, reflecting the national interest generated by the case, involving a comatose Missouri woman who has been kept alive for six years through artificial feeding against her family's wishes.

Justices Press Lawyers

With intense questioning, the Justices pushed the lawyers into the farthest rhetorical corners of their arguments, and then appeared unpersuaded by the answers. They heard the state of Missouri assert that it could constitutionally require a patient, even a conscious and rational one, to continue to receive food and water against the patient's will. And they heard an argument on behalf of the comatose woman that the Constitution requires a state to defer to a family's judgment when a patient's own wishes about continuing life-sustaining treatment are not clear.

But where a middle ground might be in this constitutional dispute was not immediately apparent.

The case is an appeal by the family of the Missouri woman, Nancy Cruzan, from the Missouri Supreme Court's refusal to permit removal of the tube that has supplied her with food and water for more than six years. Ms. Cruzan, now 32 years old, suffered devastating brain injuries in an automobile accident and will never regain consciousness, although the tube can maintain her in what neurologists call a "persistent vegetative state" for 30 years or more.

A year before the accident, Ms. Cruzan told a friend that she would never want to live as a "vegetable." But she never gave specific instructions on the subject, and the Missouri Supreme Court found that her comments did not provide "clear and convincing evidence" of her wishes that the court said was required to overcome the state's "unqualified interest in life."

Justice Anthony M. Kennedy asked William H. Colby, the Cruzan family's lawyer, whether the case could be resolved by a ruling that "we need a clear determination" of the patient's wishes, "and if it can't be made, the state simply opts for life."

"Interest in Protecting Life"

"Certainly the state has an interest in protecting life," Mr. Colby replied. But he said the state could not simply declare that "we have an unqualified interest in all situations."

Justice Kennedy interrupted: "Not in all situations, just where the wishes of the person can't be determined with accuracy."

"All that does," Mr. Colby said, "is get you in the next stage," at which "the Court must decide whether to resolve the ambiguity from the perspective of the state or the patient's family."

"The question is: Who decides?" Mr. Colby continued. "This Court has always deferred to the special competency of families to know what values are important to family members."

At this point, Justice Antonin Scalia sprung a trap that he had set for Mr. Colby earlier in the argument. Earlier, Justice Scalia had asked: "What if a person says, 'I am of sound mind but it is my desire to die. I'm in pain and my quality of life is nil.' Must a state allow that person to refuse food and water?"

Medical Treatment Issue

Mr. Colby replied that the 14th Amendment's guarantee of liberty "protects that person's right to be free from state intrusion." But he had said a refusal to accept medical treatment need not be honored if it was "irrational" as in the case of a Jehovah's Witness who wanted to prevent life-saving treatment for a child. Such refusals were motivated not by the child's best interest but by the parents' religion, he said.

So when Mr. Colby said that the Court should defer to the family's wishes about ending treatment for Ms. Cruzan, Justice Scalia said: "But that's not what you said about the Jehovah's Witness. You said that was a religious belief." Decisions about whether life is worth living, Justice Scalia said, are based on "philosophical beliefs."

"It's a philosophical debate," Justice Scalia continued. "I can read the ancient philosophers and find it there. Why can't the state say, 'We don't deal with philosophy, we deal with physics, and life must be preserved'?"

Robert L. Presson, an assistant attorney general of Missouri, said there was no constitutionally required role for the family in deciding whether an unconscious person should be permitted to die. He said that in any event, a state can never be required to participate in "state-assisted suicide."

Did that mean that even a "competent person" would be unable to refuse food and water? Justice John Paul Stevens asked.

"The state could constitutionally override even a competent individual's choice to refuse food and water," Mr. Presson replied.

Justice Kennedy observed that "if that's true, there is not need to inquire" about whether an unconscious person has such a right.

Justice Harry A. Blackmun, who had been largely silent through the argument, appeared exasperated with the Missouri lawyer. "Have you ever seen a person in a persistent vegetative state?" he asked.

"I have seen Nancy Cruzan herself," Mr. Presson replied. This was evidently not the answer that Justice Blackmun expected.

"You have seen Nancy? Have you seen any others?" he asked.

Mr. Presson replied that he had seen Ms. Cruzan and others in the state rehabilitation hospital that cares for patients in that condition.

Solicitor General's Argument

The Federal Government had not been involved in the Cruzan case or in other right-to-die cases. But Kenneth W. Starr, the Solicitor General, sought and received the Court's permission to argue on behalf of Missouri. He told the Court that the 14th Amendment "should not be interpreted to force the states or the Federal Government to embrace a particular procedure or approach" in the care of incompetent patients.

Mr. Starr asked the Court to rule that any policy is acceptable as long as it is "reasonably designed to serve a legitimate state interest."

Justice Byron R. White asked Mr. Starr whether a state could decide that it would never permit the withdrawal of a feeding tube, no matter how clear the evidence of the patient's wishes.

"That raises a very difficult question that I'm not prepared to answer authoritatively," the Solicitor General said.

Because of her brain damage, Ms. Cruzan does not experience pain. Justice Stevens asked Mr. Starr whether in the case of a patient suffering "continuous pain," the Constitution would permit a state to insist that life-support measures continue.

"I think not," Mr. Starr said, adding that such a policy would amount to oppression by the state.

A Constitutional Matter

"So you agree that the Federal Constitution is implicated," Justice Stevens said.

"If there is a condition of suffering," Mr. Starr replied.

Justice Stevens pressed him further, asking, What if the patient felt no pain but had given "unequivocal evidence of intent" not to remain alive?

The Constitution would be "clearly implicated" in that case, Mr. Starr agreed. He described the constitutional right at issue as a "significant liberty interest in being free of unwanted intrusions."

In the language of constitutional analysis that is familiar to the Court, the phrase "liberty interest" has a particular meaning, representing the lowest level of constitutional protection. . . .

Reprinted by permission from the *New York Times*, December 7, 1989, p. 1.

The decision, written by Chief Justice William Rehnquist, preserved a competent, terminally ill patient's liberty to refuse life-supporting medical technologies. But the Court also allowed Missouri's requirement that, in the case of an incompetent patient, family members must provide clear and compelling evidence that termination of life support represents the wishes of the patient, on the grounds that the state also has a compelling interest in protecting life. Despite this 1990 decision, the boundaries between individual bodily autonomy and the state's authority to regulate the human body continue to be challenged in the courts today.

Argued December 6, 1989

Decided June 25, 1990

CHIEF JUSTICE REHNQUIST delivered the opinion of the Court.

We granted certiorari to consider the question of whether Cruzan has a right under the United States Constitution which would require the hospital to withdraw life-sustaining treatment from her under these circumstances. At common law, even the touching of one person by another without consent and without legal justification was a battery. . . . This notion of bodily integrity has been embodied in the requirement that informed consent is generally required for medical treatment. . . .

The logical corollary of the doctrine of informed consent is that the patient generally possesses the right not to consent, that is, to refuse treatment. Until about 15 years ago and the seminal decision in *In re Quinlan*, 70 N.J. 10, 355 A.2d 647, cert. denied sub nom. *Garger v. New Jersey*, 429 U.S. 922 (1976), the number of right-to-refuse-treatment decisions were relatively few. Most of the earlier cases involved patients who refused medical treatment forbidden by their religious beliefs, thus implicating First Amendment rights as well as common law rights of self-determination. More recently, however, with the advance of medical technology capable of sustaining life well past the point where natural forces would have brought certain death in earlier times, cases involving the right to refuse life-sustaining treatment have burgeoned. . . .

After Quinlan, however, most courts have based a right to refuse treatment either solely on the common law right to informed consent or on both the common law right and a constitutional privacy right. . . .

Reasoning that the right of self-determination should not be lost merely because an individual is unable to sense a violation of it, the court held that incompetent individuals retain a right to refuse treatment. It also held that such a right could be exercised by a surrogate decisionmaker using a "subjective" standard when there was clear evidence that the incompetent person would have exercised it. Where such evidence was lacking, the court held that an individual's right could still be invoked in certain circumstances under objective "best interest" standards. Thus, if some trustworthy evidence existed that the individual would have wanted to terminate treatment, but not enough to clearly establish a person's wishes for purposes of the subjective standard, and the burden of a prolonged life from the experience of pain and suffering markedly outweighed its satisfactions, treatment could be terminated under a "limited-objective" standard. Where no trustworthy evidence existed, and a person's suffering would make the administration of life-sustaining treatment inhumane, a "pure-objective" standard could be used to terminate treatment. If none of these conditions obtained, the court held it was best to err in favor of preserving life.

The court also rejected certain categorical distinctions that had been drawn in prior refusal-of-treatment cases as lacking substance for decision purposes: the distinction between actively hastening death by terminating treatment and passively allowing a person to die of a disease; between treating individuals as an initial matter versus withdrawing treatment afterwards; between ordinary versus extraordinary treatment; and between treatment by artificial feeding versus other forms of life-sustaining medical procedures. . . .

[T]he common law doctrine of informed consent is viewed as generally encompassing the right of a competent individual to refuse medical treatment. Beyond that, these decisions demonstrate both similarity and diversity in their approach to a decision on what all agree is a perplexing question with unusually strong moral and ethical overtones.

State courts have available to them for decision a number of sources—state constitutions, statutes, and common law—which are not available to us. In this Court, the question is simply and starkly whether the United States Constitution prohibits Missouri from choosing the rule of decision which it did. This is the first case in which we have been squarely presented with the issue of whether the United States Constitution grants what is in common parlance referred to as a "right to die." . . .

The Fourteenth Amendment provides that no State shall "deprive any person of life, liberty, or property, without due process of law." The principle that a competent person has a constitutionally protected liberty interest in refusing unwanted medical treatment may be inferred from our prior decisions. In *Jacobson v. Massachusetts*, for instance, the Court balanced an individual's liberty interest in declining an unwanted smallpox vaccine against the State's interest in preventing disease. Decisions prior to the incorporation of the Fourth Amendment into the Fourteenth Amendment analyzed searches and seizures involving the body under the Due Process Clause and were thought to implicate substantial liberty interests. . . .

[F]or purposes of this case, we assume that the United States Constitution would grant a competent person a constitutionally protected right to refuse lifesaving hydration and nutrition. Petitioners go on to assert that an incompetent person should possess the same right in this respect as is possessed by a competent person. . . .

The difficulty with petitioners' claim is that, in a sense, it begs the question: an incompetent person is not able to make an informed and voluntary choice to exercise a hypothetical right to refuse treatment or any other right. Such a "right" must be exercised for her, if at all, by some sort of surrogate. Here, Missouri has in effect recognized that, under certain circumstances, a surrogate may act for the patient in electing to have hydration and nutrition withdrawn in such a way as to cause death, but it has established a procedural safeguard to assure that the action of the surrogate conforms as best it may to the wishes expressed by the patient while competent. Missouri requires that evidence of the incompetent's wishes as to the withdrawal of treatment be proved by clear and convincing evidence. The question, then, is whether the United States Constitution forbids the establishment of this procedural requirement by the State. We hold that it does not.

Whether or not Missouri's clear and convincing evidence requirement comports with the United States Constitution depends in part on what interests the State may properly seek to protect in this situation. Missouri relies on its interest in the protection and preservation of human life, and there can be no gainsaying this interest. As a general matter, the States—indeed, all civilized nations—demonstrate their commitment to life by treating homicide as serious crime. Moreover, the majority of States in this country have laws imposing criminal penalties on one who assists another to commit suicide. We do not think a State is required to remain neutral in the face of an informed and voluntary decision by a physically able adult to starve to death.

But in the context presented here, a State has more particular interests at stake. The choice between life and death is a deeply personal decision of obvious and overwhelming finality. We believe Missouri may legitimately seek to safeguard the personal element of this choice through the imposition of heightened evidentiary requirements. It cannot be disputed that the Due Process Clause protects an interest in life as well as an interest in refusing life-sustaining medical treatment. Not all incompetent patients will have loved ones available to serve as surrogate decisionmakers. And even where family members are present, "[t]here will, of course, be some unfortunate situations in which family members will not act to protect a patient." A State is entitled to guard against potential abuses in such situations. Similarly, a State is entitled to consider that a judicial proceeding to make a determination regarding an incompetent's wishes may very well not be an adversarial one, with the added guarantee of accurate factfinding that the adversary process brings with it. Finally, we think a State may properly decline to make judgments about the "quality" of life that a particular individual may enjoy, and simply assert an unqualified interest in the preservation of human life to be weighed against the constitutionally protected interests of the individual.

In our view, Missouri has permissibly sought to advance these interests through the adoption of a "clear and convincing" standard of proof to govern such proceedings. . . .

The more stringent the burden of proof a party must bear, the more that party bears the risk of an erroneous decision. We believe that Missouri may permissibly place an increased risk of an erroneous decision on those seeking to terminate an incompetent individual's life-sustaining treatment. An erroneous decision not to terminate results in a maintenance of the status quo; the possibility of subsequent developments such as advancements in medical science, the discovery of new evidence regarding the patient's intent, changes in the law, or simply the unexpected death of the patient despite the administration of life-sustaining treatment, at least create the potential that a wrong decision will eventually be corrected or its impact mitigated. An erroneous decision to withdraw life-sustaining treatment, however, is not susceptible of correction. . . .

[W]e conclude that a State may apply a clear and convincing evidence standard in proceedings where a guardian seeks to discontinue nutrition and hydration of a person diagnosed to be in a persistent vegetative state. We note that many courts which have adopted some sort of substituted judgment procedure in situations like this, whether they limit consideration of evidence to the prior expressed wishes of the incompetent individual, or whether they allow more general proof of what the individual's decision would have been, require a clear and convincing standard of proof for such evidence.

The Supreme Court of Missouri held that, in this case, the testimony adduced at trial did not amount to clear and convincing proof of the patient's desire to have hydration and nutrition withdrawn. In so doing, it reversed a decision of the Missouri trial court, which had found that the evidence "suggest[ed]" Nancy Cruzan would not have desired to continue such measures, but which had not adopted the standard of "clear and convincing evidence" enunciated by the Supreme Court. The testimony adduced at trial consisted primarily of Nancy Cruzan's statements, made to a housemate about a year before her accident, that she would not want to live should she face life as a "vegetable," and other observations to the same effect. The observations did not deal in terms with withdrawal of medical treatment or of hydration and nutrition. We cannot say that the Supreme Court of Missouri committed constitutional error in reaching the conclusion that it did.

Petitioners alternatively contend that Missouri must accept the "substituted judgment" of close family members even in the absence of substantial proof that their views reflect the views of the patient. . . . Here again, petitioners would seek to turn a decision which allowed a State to rely on family decisionmaking into a constitutional requirement that the State recognize such decisionmaking. But constitutional law does not work that way.

No doubt is engendered by anything in this record but that Nancy Cruzan's mother and father are loving and caring parents. If the State were required by the United States Constitution to repose a right of "substituted judgment" with anyone, the Cruzans would surely qualify. But we do not think the Due Process Clause requires the State to repose judgment on these matters with anyone but the patient herself. Close family members may have a strong feeling—a feeling not at all ignoble or unworthy, but not entirely disinterested, either—that they do not wish to witness the continuation of the life of a loved one which they regard as hopeless, meaningless, and even degrading. But there is no automatic assurance that the view of close family members will necessarily be the same as the patient's would have been had she been confronted with the prospect of her situation while competent. All of the reasons previously discussed for allowing Missouri to require clear and convincing evidence of the patient's wishes lead us to conclude that the State may choose to defer only to those wishes, rather than confide the decision to close family members.

The judgment of the Supreme Court of Missouri is AFFIRMED.

Washington, et al., Petitioners v. Harold Glucksberg, et al. (1997)

In 1997 the U.S. Supreme Court heard two companion cases on the question of whether the Constitution protects an individual's right to commit suicide with the aid of a physician. Legislatures in New York and Washington outlawed the practice, and the laws' opponents in each state challenged the statutes. Writing for the plurality in Washington v. Glucksberg, *Chief Justice William Rehnquist, who also wrote the Cruzan opinion, denied that the Constitution's guarantee of individual liberty denied states the power to prohibit the practice; states' compelling interests in protecting life, Rehnquist argued, must be upheld. Concurring opinions by Justices O'Connor and Stevens, however, gave differing interpretations of the issue of individual versus state interests, opening the door for future right to die cases to be brought before the Court.*

Argued January 8, 1997
Decided June 26, 1997
CHIEF JUSTICE REHNQUIST delivered the opinion of the Court:

The question presented in this case is whether Washington's prohibition against "causing" or "aiding" a suicide offends the Fourteenth Amendment to the United States Constitution. We hold that it does not. . . .

The plaintiffs asserted "the existence of a liberty interest protected by the Fourteenth Amendment which extends to a personal choice by a mentally competent, terminally ill adult to commit physician-assisted suicide." Relying primarily on *Planned Parenthood v. Casey,* 505 U.S. 833 (1992), and *Cruzan v. Director, Missouri Department of Public Health,* 497 U.S. 261 (1990), the District Court agreed and concluded that Washington's assisted-suicide ban is unconstitutional because it "places an undue burden on the exercise of [that] constitutionally protected liberty interest." . . . A panel of the Court of Appeals for the Ninth Circuit reversed, emphasizing that "in the two hundred and five years of our existence no constitutional right to aid in killing oneself has ever been upheld by a court of final jurisdiction." *Compassion in Dying v. Washington,* 49 F.3d 586, 591 (1995). . . . The Ninth Circuit heard the case en banc, reversed the panel's decision, and affirmed the District Court. . . . We granted certiorari, and now reverse.

Though deeply rooted, the States' assisted-suicide bans have in recent years been reexamined and, generally, affirmed. Because of advances in medicine and technology, Americans today are increasingly likely to die in institutions, from chronic illnesses. . . . Public concern and democratic action are therefore sharply focused on how best to protect dignity and independence at the end of life, with the result that there have been many significant changes in state laws and in attitudes those laws reflect. Many States, for example, now permit "living wills," surrogate health-care decisionmaking, and the withdrawal or refusal of life-sustaining medical treatment. At the same time, however, voters and legislators continue for the most part to reaffirm their States' prohibitions on assisting suicide.

The Washington statute at issue in this case . . . was enacted in 1975 as part of a revision of that State's criminal code. Four years later, Washington passed its Natural Death Act, which specifically stated that the "withholding or withdrawal of life-sustaining treatment . . . shall not, for any purpose, constitute a suicide" and that "nothing in this chapter shall be construed to condone, authorize, or approve mercy killing. . . ." In 1991, Washington voters rejected a ballot initiative which, had it passed, would have permitted a form of physician-assisted suicide. Washington then added a provision to the Natural Death Act expressly excluding physician-assisted suicide. . . .

[T]he states are currently engaged in serious, thoughtful examinations of physician-assisted suicide and other similar issues. . . . Despite changes in medical technology and notwithstanding an increased emphasis on the importance of end-of-life decisionmaking, we have not retreated from this prohibition. Against this backdrop of history, tradition, and practice, we now turn to respondents' constitutional claim.

The Due Process Clause guarantees more than fair process, and the "liberty" it protects includes more than the absence of physical restraint. . . . The Clause also provides heightened protection against government interference with certain fundamental rights and liberty interests. In a long line of cases, we have held that, in addition to the specific freedoms protected by the Bill of Rights, the "liberty" specially protected by the Due Process Clause includes the rights to marry, *Loving v. Virginia*, 388 U.S. 1 (1967); to have children, *Skinner v. Oklahoma ex. Rel. Williamson*, 316 U.S. 535 (1942); to direct the education and upbringing of one's children, *Meyer v. Nebraska*, 262 U.S. 390 (1923); *Pierce v. Society of Sisters*, 268 U.S. 510 (1925); to marital privacy, *Griswold v. Connecticut*, 381 U.S. 479 (1965); to use contraception, *ibid; Eisenstadt v. Baird*, 405 U.S. 438 (1972); to bodily integrity, *Rochin v. California*, 342 U.S. 165 (1952); and to abortion, *Casey*. . . . We have also assumed, and strongly suggested, that the Due Process Clause protects the traditional right to refuse unwanted life-saving medical treatment. *Cruzan*, 497 U.S. at 278–279. . . .

By extending constitutional protection to an asserted right or liberty interest we, to a great extent, place the matter outside the arena of public debate and legislative action. We must therefore "exercise the utmost care whenever we are asked to break new ground in this field" lest the liberty protected by the Due Process Clause be subtly transformed into the policy preferences of the members of this Court, *Moore*, 431 U.S. at 502 (plurality opinion). . . .

In our view, however, the development of this Court's substantive-due-process jurisprudence . . . has been a process whereby the outlines of the "liberty" specially protected by the Fourteenth Amendment— never fully clarified, to be sure, and perhaps not capable of being fully clarified—have at least been carefully refined by concrete examples involving fundamental rights found to be deeply rooted in our legal tradition. This approach tends to rein in the subjective elements that are necessarily present in due-process judicial review. In addition, by establishing a threshold requirement—that a challenged state action implicate a fundamental right—before requiring more than a reasonable relation to a legitimate state interest to justify the action, it avoids the need for complex balancing of competing interests in every case.

Turning to the claim at issue here, the Court of Appeals stated that "properly analyzed, the first issue to be resolved is whether there is a liberty interest in determining the time and manner of one's death," 79 F. 3d, at 801, or in other words, "is there a right to die?," *id.*, at 799. Similarly, respondents assert a "liberty to choose how to die" and a right to "control of one's final days," Brief for Respondents 7, and describe the asserted liberty as "the right to choose a humane, dignified death," *id.*, at 15, and "the liberty to shape death," *id.*, at 18. As noted above, we have a tradition of carefully formulating the interest at stake in substantive-due-process cases. For example, although *Cruzan* is often described as a "right to die" case . . . we were, in fact, more precise: we assumed that the Constitution granted competent persons a "constitutionally protected right to refuse lifesaving hydration and nutrition." . . . The Washington statute at issue in this case prohibits "aiding another person to attempt suicide" . . . and, thus, the question before us is whether the "liberty" specially protected by the Due Process Clause includes a right to commit suicide which itself includes a right to assistance in doing so. . . .

To hold for respondents, we would have to reverse centuries of legal doctrine and practice, and strike down the considered policy of almost every State. . . .

Respondents contend, however, that the liberty interest they assert *is* consistent with this Court's substantive-due-process line of cases, if not with this Nation's history and practice. Pointing to *Casey* and *Cruzan,* respondents read our jurisprudence in this area as reflecting a general tradition of "self-sovereignty" . . . and as teaching that the "liberty" protected by the Due Process Clause includes the "basic and intimate exercises of personal autonomy. . . . According to respondents, our liberty jurisprudence, and the broad, individualistic principles it reflects, protects the "liberty of competent, terminally ill adults to make end-of-life decisions free of undue government interference. Brief for Respondents 10. The question presented in this case, however, is whether the protections of the Due Process Clause include a right to commit suicide with another's assistance. . . .

The right assumed in *Cruzan,* however, was not simply deduced from abstract concepts of personal autonomy. Given the common-law rule that forced medication was a battery, and the long legal tradition protecting the decision to refuse unwanted medical treatment, our assumption was entirely consistent with this Nation's history and constitutional traditions. The decision to commit suicide with the assistance of another may be just as personal and profound as the decision to refuse unwanted medical treatment, but it has never enjoyed similar legal protection. Indeed, the two acts are widely and reasonably regarded as quite distinct. . . .

Respondents also rely on *Casey.* . . . That many of the rights and liberties protected by the Due Process Clause sound in personal autonomy does not warrant the sweeping conclusion that any and all important, intimate, and personal decisions are so protected . . . and *Casey* did not suggest otherwise.

The history of the law's treatment of assisted suicide in this country has been and continues to be one of the rejection of nearly all efforts to permit it. That being the case, our decisions lead us to conclude that the asserted "right" to assistance in committing suicide is not a fundamental liberty interest protected by the Due Process Clause. The Constitution also requires, however, that Washington's assisted-suicide ban be rationally related to legitimate government interests. . . . This requirement is unquestionably met here. . . .

First, Washington has an "unqualified interest in the preservation of human life." *Cruzan,* 497 U.S. at 282. The State's prohibition on assisted suicide, like all homicide laws, both reflects and advances its commitment to this interest. . . .

Relatedly, all admit that suicide is a serious public-health problem, especially among individuals in otherwise vulnerable groups. . . . Those who attempt suicide—terminally ill or not—often suffer from depression or other mental disorders. . . .

The State also has an interest in protecting the integrity and ethics of the medical profession. . . .

Next, the State has an interest in protecting vulnerable groups— including the poor, the elderly, and disabled persons—from abuse, neglect, and mistakes. . . .

The State's interest here goes beyond protecting the vulnerable from coercion; it extends to protecting disabled and terminally ill people from prejudice, negative and inaccurate stereotypes, and "societal indifference." *Compassion in Dying,* 49 F. 3d, at 592. The State's assisted-suicide ban reflects and reinforces its policy that the lives of terminally ill, disabled, and elderly people must be no less valued than the lives of the young and healthy, and that a seriously disabled person's suicidal impulses should be interpreted and treated the same way as anyone else's. . . .

Finally, the State may fear that permitting assisted suicide will start it down the path to voluntary and perhaps even involuntary euthanasia. . . .

JUSTICE O'CONNOR, concurring:

Death will be different for each of us. For many, the last days will be spent in physical pain and perhaps the despair that accompanies physical deterioration and a loss of control of basic bodily and mental functions. Some will seek medication to alleviate that pain and other symptoms.

The Court frames the issue in this case as whether the Due Process Clause of the Constitution protects a "right to commit suicide which itself includes a right to assistance in doing so," *ante,* at 18, and concludes that our Nation's history, legal traditions, and practices do not support the existence of such a right. I join the Court's opinions because I agree that there is no generalized right to "commit suicide." But respondents urge us to address the narrower question whether a mentally competent person who is experiencing great suffering has a constitutionally cognizable interest in controlling the circumstances of his or her imminent death. I see no need to reach that question in the context of the facial challenges to the New York and Washington laws at issue here. . . . The parties and *amici* agree that in these States a patient who is suffering from a terminal illness and who is experiencing great pain has no legal barriers to obtaining medication, from qualified physicians, to alleviate that suffering, even to the point of causing unconsciousness and hastening death. . . . In this light, even assuming that we would recognize such an interest, I agree that the State's interests in protecting those who are not truly competent or facing imminent death, or those whose decisions to hasten death would not be truly voluntary, are sufficiently weighty to justify a prohibition against physician-assisted suicide. . . .

Every one of us at some point may be affected by our own or a family member's terminal illness. There is no reason to think that the democratic process will not strike the proper balance between the interests of terminally ill, mentally competent individuals who seek to end their suffering and the State's interests in protecting those who might seek to end life mistakenly or under pressure. As the Court recognizes, States are presently undertaking extensive and serious evaluation of physician-assisted suicide and other related issues. . . .

JUSTICE STEVENS, concurring in the judgments.
. . . In *Cruzan v. Director, Missouri Department of Public Health,* 497 U.S. 261 (1990), the Court assumed that the interest in liberty protected by the Fourteenth Amendment encompassed the right of a terminally ill patient to direct the withdrawal of life-sustaining treatment. . . .

Cruzan, however, was not the normal case. Given the irreversible nature of her illness and the progressive character of her suffering, Nancy Cruzan's interest in refusing medical care was incidental to her more basic interest in controlling the manner and timing of her death. In finding that her best interests would be served by cutting off the nourishment that kept her alive, the trial court did more than simply vindicate Cruzan's interest in refusing medical treatment; the court, in essence, authorized affirmative conduct that would hasten her death. When this Court reviewed this case and upheld Missouri's requirement that there be clear and convincing evidence establishing Nancy Cruzan's intent to have life-sustaining nourishment withdrawn, it made two important assumptions: (1) that there was a "liberty interest" in refusing unwanted treatment protected by the Due Process Clause; and (2) that this liberty interest did not "end the inquiry" because it might be outweighed by the relevant state interests. I agree with both of these assumptions, but I insist that the source of Nancy Cruzan's right to refuse treatment was not just a common-law rule. Rather, this right is an aspect of a far broader and more basic concept of freedom that is even older than the common law. This freedom embraces, not merely a person's right to refuse a particular kind of unwanted treatment, but also her interest in dignity, and in determining the character of the memories that will survive long after her death. In recognizing that the State's interests did not outweigh Nancy Cruzan's liberty interest in refusing medical treatment, *Cruzan* rested not simply on the common-law right to refuse medical treatment, but—at least implicitly—on the even more fundamental right to make this "deeply personal decision." . . .

Cruzan did give recognition, not just to vague, unbridled notions of autonomy, but to the more specific interest in making decisions about how to confront an imminent death. Although there is no absolute right to physician-assisted suicide, *Cruzan* makes it clear that some individuals who no longer have the option of deciding whether to live or die because they are already on the threshold of death have a constitutionally protected interest that may outweigh the State's interest in preserving life at all costs. The liberty interest at stake in a case like this differs from, and is stronger than, both the common-law right to refuse medical treatment and the unbridled interest in deciding whether to live or die. It is an interest in deciding how, rather than whether, a critical threshold shall be crossed. . . .

There may be little distinction between the intent of a terminally-ill patient who decides to remove her life-support and one who seeks the assistance of a doctor in ending her life; in both situations, the patient is seeking to hasten a certain, impending death. The doctor's intent might also be the same in prescribing lethal medication as it is in terminating life support. A doctor who fails to administer medical treatment to one who is dying from a disease could be doing so with an intent to harm or kill that patient. Conversely, a doctor who prescribes lethal medication does not necessarily intend the patient's death—rather the doctor may seek simply to ease the patient's suffering and to comply with her wishes. The illusory character of any differences in intent of causation is confirmed by the fact that the American Medical Association unequivocally endorses the practice of terminal sedation—the administration of sufficient doses of pain-killing medication to terminally ill patients to protect them from excruciating pain even when it is clear that the time of death will be advanced. The purpose of terminal sedation is to ease the suffering of the patient and comply with her wishes, and the actual cause of death is the administration of heavy doses of lethal sedatives. This same intent and causation may exist when a doctor complies with a patient's request for lethal medication to hasten her death.

Thus, although the differences the majority notes in causation and intent between terminating life-support and assisting in suicide support the Court's rejection of the respondents' facial challenge, these distinctions may be applicable to particularly terminally ill patients and their doctors. Our holding today in *Vacco v. Quill* that the Equal Protection Clause is not violated by New York's classification, just like our holding in *Washington v. Glucksberg* that the Washington statute is not invalid on its face, does not foreclose the possibility that some applications of the New York statute may impose an intolerable intrusion on the patient's freedom.

There remains room for a vigorous debate about the outcome of particular cases that are not necessarily resolved by the opinions announced today. How such cases may be decided will depend on their specific facts. In my judgment, however, it is clear that the so-called "unqualified interest in the preservation of human life," *Cruzan,* 497 U.S. at 282, *Glucksberg, ante,* at 24, is not itself sufficient to outweigh the interest in liberty that may justify the only possible means of preserving a dying patient's dignity and alleviating her intolerable suffering.

Oregon's Death with Dignity Act

In 2001 the U.S. attorney general issued a directive that the State of Oregon's Death with Dignity Act violated a federal law regulating drugs. The Controlled Substances Act, John Ashcroft asserted, prohibited physicians from dispensing medication to patients for the purpose of assisting them to end their own lives. The state of Oregon requested a summary judgment from the U.S. District Court, or an opinion as to the attorney general's authority to issue such a directive. Joining the plaintiffs were several terminally ill patients who submitted declarations supporting the Oregon law. The following statement from "Jane Doe #1" illustrates the profound and intensely personal nature of the issue before the Oregon court.

Jane Doe #1 hereby declares as follows:

14. My illness has dramatically impaired my ability to maintain social contacts, depriving me of a principal source of meaning and joy in my life. I have derived my greatest joy in life from being with and working with others and simply being with family and friends.

15. I understand that I will have more frequent and severe pain as my illness progresses. I will attempt to manage this with medication, but there is a point at which the adverse side effects of the pain medication may become intolerable to me. One side effect is sedation to the point of surrendering a conscious state. Being forced into that state is abhorrent to me. I understand that if I am unwilling to be sedated into an unconscious state, my pain may not be relieved. I am comforted to know that I can control the time of my death and act to have a humane and peaceful death under the Oregon Act if and when my dying pro-

cess becomes intolerable to me. If this option is denied to me I will lose this comfort, I will feel trapped in a terrible situation.

16. I understand that the federal government lawyers have told the court that "life is good" and that any patient who may want to pursue options under Oregon's Death with Dignity Act must be experiencing depression that, if treated, would eliminate my interest in controlling the timing and manner of my death under the Oregon law. I disagree with the federal government lawyers.

First, with regard to the statement that "life is good" ... I too believe, in general, that life is good. I have lived a good life. However, in the advanced state of a terminal illness, with my body ravaged by disease, with pain and distressing symptoms a part of my daily life, with loss of bodily function and integrity, loss of mobility and independence, loss of ability to get out and participate in a meaningful way, life ceases to be good. This is especially true where all of these problems are cumulative, they all overlap and together are becoming intolerable to me. All of this is progressing, with only one possible outcome, my death. The question is not whether I want to live a "good life," I have done that. I cannot choose to return to a "good life": that is no longer an option. The question is whether I can die a "good death," with dignity and in a humane manner before the final ravages of my illness kill me slowly and painfully.

Second, with regard to my mental state: I am not, nor have I ever been, depressed. My physicians have advised that in their professional opinions I am not suffering from depression or any other form of mental impairment, and that I am mentally competent to make the decision to hasten my death under Oregon's law. My decision to control the timing and manner of my death is consistent with my most deeply held values and beliefs. Doing so will enable me to preserve and honor my remaining self. To be forced to endure a lingering and protracted dying process, after the point that the process has become intolerable to me, would contradict my values and beliefs.

17. My husband died from a burst aneurysm more than 14 years ago. He was kept alive for 28 days before the physicians finally accepted his final wishes to withdraw the life support system. I have no intention of going through such a protracted and lingering dying process.

18. I do not have any financial concerns, but I must be frugal because I do not have a great deal of income.

19. I am a Christian and believe God understands and accepts my decision to proceed with the option to pursue the use of Oregon's Death with Dignity Act.

20. I have not been coerced internally or externally into pursuing my options under Oregon's Death with Dignity Act. . . .

A number of physicians' groups joined in the Oregon case as amici curiae, or friends of the court. This excerpt from their brief criticizes the Ashcroft directive as an obstacle to physicians' ability to act in the best interests of their patients. Doctors challenged the notion that non-medically trained officers of the federal Drug Enforcement Agency have the professional competence to make decisions such as what amount of medicine would constitute a lethal dose for a particular patient. The changing nature of medicine, they argued, renders such decisions to be the sole province of medical practitioners.

Brief of Amici Curiae American Academy of Pain Management, California Medical Association, American Geriatrics Society, San Francisco Medical Society, the Society of General Internal Medicine and a Coalition of Distinguished Pain and Palliative Care Professionals in Support of Plaintiff

I. Introduction

. . . The Directive, and agency statement issued with no public comment, erases established public policy by permitting the United States Drug Enforcement Administration ("DEA") to investigate and prosecute physicians who prescribe medications to terminally ill patients to hasten their deaths. The Attorney General's unprecedented and unilateral determination will have significant effects: it upsets a longstanding tradition of deference to state regulation of medical practice and in doing so interferes both with the state of Oregon's Death with Dignity Act and with physicians' ability to care for terminally ill patients throughout the country. Implementation of the Directive will also cut off a robust political debate explicitly sanctioned by the Supreme Court. Finally the Government's amorphous justification for the Directive will, by its very breadth and vagueness, cast a pall over physicians' decision making nationwide. Confronted with the formidable possibility of medically untrained law enforcement shadowing their decisionmaking, many health care professionals will retreat from their obligations to their terminally ill patients. . . .

Physicians across the country have responded with alarm to the Attorney General's recent announcement that actions in compliance with the ODWDA will henceforth be considered a violation of the CSA. This alarm stems from the edict-like nature of the Ashcroft Directive (the "Directive"), purporting to determine what is and what is not acceptable medical practice, as well as the vague public interest justification the Government proffers in its support. The Directive's bald usurpation of the states' *and* the medical community's roles as arbiters of appropriate medical care, an issue heretofore fully free of DEA intermeddling, suggests to the medical community that any physician in any state who "fulfill[s] his [or her] moral and professional obligation to relieve suffering" could soon be treated as a potential criminal by law enforcement agents interpreting the Directive.

The threatened investigation and prosecution of Oregon physicians complying with the ODWDA will therefore exert a *nationwide* chilling effect on the treatment of pain. Under the Directive, a physician's delicate decisionmaking process, already difficult, particularly when treating terminally ill patients enduring pain, will now be subject to DEA second-guessing. The Government's edict ignores the complex reality that confronts physicians. . . .

If medical experts cannot draw a line between strictly palliative care and the hastening of death there is no reason to think that federal drug enforcement agents are more likely to accurately or rationally construct a proper division between appropriate pain relief and the Directive's proscriptions. . . . Because it is impossible to determine where the Government might choose to construct its line, physicians faced with the threat of criminal investigation, revocation of their prescription licenses, and even possible imprisonment will likely err on the side of undertreating those patients with the most severe pain. . . .

The Directive's broad sweep—and the possibility of further, even more invasive Directives—must necessarily counsel physicians to be prudent, for under the Government's view, a single prescription, dispensed in accord with the relevant standard of care, could trigger an investigation and prosecution. This is not a trivial concern for physicians, for the mere fact of an investigation can have extremely serious consequences. Investigations, even where no disciplinary action results, may result in the loss of reputation and privileges that could have the same effect as the loss of a license. In this new regime, where DEA agents untrained in medicine determine the appropriateness of a prescription, the highest costs imposed by the Ashcroft Directive will ultimately be borne by patients with intractable pain.

Even if the Government does not avail itself of its newly-decided power to invade vast swaths of medical practice, the Directive will inevitably have a chilling effect upon all physicians who deal with the terminally ill. Physicians who are not familiar with the nuances of the law may simply avoid prescribing pain medication altogether so as to avoid what they may perceive, rightly or wrongly, as the shadow of the law. More significantly, research suggests that physician attitudes remain strongly biased toward risk reduction away from pain alleviation. . . .

[T]he Directive also glosses over the significant medical issues involved in palliative care. For example, the Directive purports to create a distinction between the "proper' distribution of pain medication and the "improper" use of medicine to hasten death. Unfortunately, the Directive's distinction is truly a distinction without difference, for it is a well-accepted fact that the practice of medicine sometimes entails the application of the doctrine of "double effect," which acknowledges the value of treating the severe pain of the terminally ill even when it is known that a consequence of that treatment may be the hastening of death. Ignoring this difficulty, the Directive purports to have DEA agents second-guess a physician in an area where pain relief and death are inextricably joined. This widely embraced doctrine is too complex to be adequately figured into the enforcement of the CSA. . . .

In *Glucksberg*, Justice Stevens noted that "the American Medical Association unequivocally endorses the practice of terminal sedation . . ." *Glucksberg*, 521 U.S. at 751. The Ashcroft Directive does nothing more than pay lip service to these very real concerns and makes no effort to parse among the myriad ways pain medications may be used. . . .

On April 17, 2002, Judge Robert E. Jones of the U.S. Court for the District of Oregon issued his ruling in State of Oregon and Peter A. Rasmussen, et al., v. John Ashcroft. *As this excerpt demonstrates, Judge Jones relied in part on the precedent set in the* Glucksberg *case, particularly the "door" that Justices Stevens and O'Connor had left open in that opinion.*

Opinion and Order

 . . . In *Glucksberg,* the Supreme Court was called upon to decide whether the state of Washington's statutory ban on assisted suicide violated the Due Process Clause. In a thoughtful opinion, the Court acknowledged that "[t]hroughout the Nation, Americans are engaged in an earnest and profound debate about the morality, legality, and practicality of physician-assisted suicide." The Court recounted the various states' "serious, thoughtful examinations" of the issues in this difficult debate, including Oregon's 1994 enactment of the Oregon Act. *See* 521 U.S. at 716–19. The court declined to "strike down the considered policy choice of the State of Washington," deferring instead to that state's resolution of the debate. 521 U.S. at 719, 724, 735.

In her concurring opinion in *Glucksberg,* Justice O'Connor further elaborated that

> [t]here is no reason to think the democratic process will not strike the proper balance between the interests of terminally ill, mentally competent individuals who would seek to end their suffering and the State's interests in protecting those who might seek to end life mistakenly or under pressure. . . . States are presently undertaking extensive and serious evaluation of physician-assisted suicide and other related issues. . . . In such circumstances, "the . . . challenging task of crafting appropriate procedures for safeguarding . . . liberty interests is entrusted to the 'laboratory of the States' . . . in the first instance." *Glucksberg,* 521 U.S. at 737

As the Court acknowledged in *Glucksberg,* the citizens of Oregon, through their democratic initiative process, have chosen to resolve the moral, legal, and ethical debate on physician-assisted suicide for themselves by voting—not once, but twice—in favor of the Oregon Act. The Oregon Act attempts to resolve this "earnest and profound debate" by "strik[ing] the proper balance between the interests of terminally ill, mentally competent individuals who would seek to end their suffering and the State's interests in protecting those who might seek to end life mistakenly or under pressure." *Glucksberg,* 521 U.S. at 737.

With publication of the Ashcroft directive, Ashcroft essentially nullified the Oregon Act and four years of Oregon experience in implementing it. In response to what it perceived as an unwarranted and unauthorized intrusion into the sovereign interests of Oregon, the medical practices of Oregon physicians, and the end-of-life decisions made by terminally-ill Oregonians, plaintiff state of Oregon ("plaintiff") immediately commenced this lawsuit to, among other things, enjoin Ashcroft and the other defendants from giving the Ashcroft directive any legal effect. A temporary restraining order, issued on November 8, 2001, remains in effect.

Despite the enormity of the debate over physician-assisted suicide, the issues in this case are legal ones and, as pertain to my disposition, are fairly narrowly drawn. My resolution of the legal issues does not require any delving into the complex religious, moral, ethical, medical, emotional or psychological controversies that surround physician-assisted suicide or "hastened death" (as the parties sometimes describe it), because in Oregon, those controversies have been—for now—put to rest. . . .

The determination of what constitutes a legitimate medical practice or purpose traditionally has been left to the individual states. State statutes, state medical boards, and state regulations control the practice of medicine. The CSA was never intended, and the USDOJ and DEA were never authorized, to establish a national medical practice or act as a national medical board. To allow an attorney general—an appointed executive whose tenure depends entirely on whatever administration occupies the White House—to determine the legitimacy of a particular medical practice without a specific congressional grant of such authority would be unprecedented and extraordinary. As stated, the practice of medicine is based on state standards, recognizing, of course, national enactments that, within constitutional limits, specifically and clearly define what is lawful and what is not. Without doubt there is tremendous disagreement among highly respected medical practitioners as to whether assisted suicide or hastened death is a legitimate medical practice, but opponents have been heard and, absent a specific prohibitive federal statute, the Oregon voters have made the legal, albeit controversial, decision that such a practice is legitimate in this sovereign state. . . .

I again emphasize that I resolve this case as a matter of statutory interpretation, and my interpretation of the statutory text and meaning is that the CSA does not prohibit practitioners from prescribing and dispensing controlled substances in compliance with a carefully-worded state legislative act. Thus, the Ashcroft directive is not entitled to deference under any standard and is invalid. I also emphasize that my task is not to criticize those who oppose the concept of assisted suicide for any reason. Many of our citizens, including the highest respected leaders of this country, oppose assisted suicide. But the fact that opposition to assisted suicide may be fully justified, morally, ethically, religiously or otherwise, does not permit a federal statute to be manipulated from its true meaning to satisfy even a worthy goal. . . .

Key People, Laws, and Concepts

American Medical Association

The largest national organization of U.S. physicians. It was founded in 1847 to raise the professional standards and training and licensing of physicians in the United States in an era when "regular" practitioners competed with other medical sects in the field of health care. In the 1920s, it became a powerful lobbying organization for physicians' political interests.

Ashcroft, John

Attorney general of the United States under the presidential administration of George W. Bush, 2001 to the present. In 2001 he directed the state of Oregon to cease enforcing its Death with Dignity Act, a law that permits physicians to prescribe lethal medication to terminally ill but mentally competent patients.

Blackmun, Harry A.

Justice of the U.S. Supreme Court, 1970–1994. In 1973 he wrote the majority opinion in *Roe v. Wade* establishing a woman's right to abortion.

Blackstone, William

An English legal scholar who wrote *Commentaries on the Laws of England* in the eighteenth century, which became the authoritative source on common law in the American colonies and the United States well into the nineteenth century.

Bowers v. Hardwick

A 1986 U.S. Supreme Court case in which the majority decided that the concept of a constitutional "right to privacy" established in *Griswold v. Connecticut* (1965) did not forbid states from outlawing the sexual act of sodomy, even among consenting adults.

Brandeis, Louis D.

Justice of the U.S. Supreme Court, 1916–1939. In *Zucht v. King* (1922), he determined that states' compulsory vaccination laws for public schoolchildren did not violate the constitutional rights of children or their parents.

Buck v. Bell

The 1927 U.S. Supreme Court decision that upheld Virginia's compulsory sterilization law as a constitutional use of the state's responsibility to protect the public welfare.

Compassion in Dying Federation

National organization that in 2001 brought suit against Attorney General Ashcroft's directive to stop enforcement of the Oregon Death with Dignity Act.

Comstock Laws

Named after the antivice crusader Anthony Comstock, this term refers to a law passed by Congress in 1873, making it a crime to import, transport, or mail articles of "indecent or immoral nature" or any "article of medicine . . . for causing abortion," as well as to a host of similar state laws passed in its wake. The Comstock laws were used to prevent the dissemination of contraceptives or information about birth control.

Coverture

An Anglo-American doctrine in common law in which married women had no independent legal status. Under the laws of coverture, married women did not possess many of the rights of citizenship, including voting and owning property; they also were entitled to certain protections, such as the financial support of their husbands.

Cruzan v. Director, Missouri Department of Public Health

The 1990 U.S. Supreme Court decision establishing that a competent individual has a right to refuse life-supporting medical treatment but that states also have a compelling interest in regulating the area, such as requiring family members acting on behalf of the patient to present clear and compelling evidence of the patient's wishes.

Douglas, William O.

Justice of the U.S. Supreme Court, 1939–1975. He wrote the majority opinions in *Skinner v. Oklahoma* (1942), establishing that individuals have a fundamental right to reproduce and *Griswold v. Connecticut*, establishing a right to privacy.

Due Process Clause

Found in the Fourteenth Amendment to the Constitution, this clause prohibits states from enacting measures that will infringe upon the individual's rights to life, liberty, and property without due process of law. It has served as a basis for many challenges to statutes restricting individual bodily autonomy. The Fifth Amendment's due process clause prohibits infringements on these individual rights by the federal government.

Eisenstadt v. Baird

A 1972 decision by the U.S. Supreme Court that found unconstitutional a Massachusetts statute making it a crime to "sell, lend, or give away any contraceptive drug, medicine, instrument, or article," unless it was provided to married persons by physicians and pharmacists. The Court found that the state did not have a compelling interest in regulating these matters and thus the privacy rights of individuals must be respected.

Equal Protection Clause

Found in the Fourteenth Amendment, this clause commands states to guarantee citizens the equal protection of the laws. It has served as the basis for many challenges to statutes restricting bodily autonomy.

Eugenics

A branch of the social sciences that gained currency in the United States during the period from approximately 1850 to 1940, this broad movement promoted both the encouragement of breeding among "fit" individuals ("positive eugenics") and the regulation or prohibition of breeding among the "unfit" ("negative eugenics").

Germ Theory of Contagion

A medical theory that gained acceptance in the United States in the last quarter of the nineteenth century. Because it attributed the spread of disease to microscopic bacteria and viruses transmitted through human contact, the germ theory had a profound effect on public health practices, policies, and laws.

Griswold v. Connecticut

In this landmark 1965 decision, the U.S. Supreme Court established that a right to individual privacy may be derived from other constitutional protections enumerated in the Constitution.

Harlan, John Marshall

Justice of the U.S. Supreme Court, 1877–1911. He wrote the majority opinion in *Jacobson v. Massachusetts* (1905) upholding a state's use of police powers to enact compulsory vaccination measures during an epidemic of contagious disease. This opinion has served as the founding precedent for many public health laws and policies.

Holmes, Oliver Wendell, Jr.

Justice of the U.S. Supreme Court, 1902–1932. He wrote the majority opinion in *Buck v. Bell* (1927) upholding states' authority to enact compulsory sterilization measures in the interest of protecting public health and safety.

In re Quinlan

A 1975 opinion by the New Jersey Supreme Court finding that the parents of a woman in a persistent vegetative state had the authority to act in accordance with their daughters' previously stated wishes that she be removed from a respirator that was sustaining her life. The Court ruled that, although Karen Ann Quinlan was no longer an autonomous person, her previous directives must be protected by the constitutional right to privacy asserted ten years earlier in *Griswold v. Connecticut*.

Jacobson v. Massachusetts

The 1905 decision by the U.S. Supreme Court that upheld a Massachusetts' statute empowering local health authorities to compel citizens to be vaccinated or else be punished by fine or imprisonment.

Lochner v. New York

A decision by the U.S. Supreme Court in 1905 determining that a New York law regulating the maximum hours bakers could work was not a legitimate public health measure and thus violated individual liberty.

Locke, John

Seventeenth-century English legal theorist whose treatise on individual liberty and personal autonomy served as the foundation of bodily autonomy doctrines in American legal thought.

Muller v. Oregon

In this 1908 opinion, the U.S. Supreme Court ruled that an Oregon statute regulating the maximum hours laundresses could work did not violate individual liberty because it was a valid measure for the protection of the public health and safety. The Court said that the state had a compelling interest in protecting the reproductive health of women as the mothers of future citizens.

Ohio v. Akron Center for Reproductive Health

A 1990 U.S. Supreme Court decision in which the justices allowed an Ohio statute placing certain restrictions on unmarried minors receiving abortions. The justices ruled that the statute did not infringe on a woman's constitutional right to abortion.

Planned Parenthood v. Casey

In this complex 1992 decision, the U.S. Supreme Court upheld some parts and overruled other parts of a Pennsylvania abortion law placing various restrictions on women's access to abortions. The Court established that, although according to *Roe v. Wade*, states may regulate abortion, any such restrictions must not place an "undue burden" upon a woman seeking to exercise her right to abortion because such burdens amounted to violations of the due process clause of the Fourteenth Amendment. Subsequently, the "undue burden" doctrine has been applied in the area of "right to die" statutes.

Pure Food and Drug Act

An act of Congress in 1906 that used the national legislature's power over interstate commerce to authorize federal regulation of the purity and safety of the nation's food supply.

Quarantine

Named for the medieval practice of requiring passengers on ships to remain in port for forty days before entering a city, quarantine is the public health practice of prohibiting individuals to freely move in or out of a designated area when infectious disease is present. Legal tradition has long recognized the power of quarantine as a legitimate use of governmental authority, even though such restrictions curtail individual liberty.

Quill v. Vacco

A 1997 U.S. Supreme Court decision in which the plurality ruled that a New York statute making physician-assisted suicide illegal did not violate the Fourteenth Amendment's equal protection clause. It is the companion case to *Washington v. Glucksberg*.

Rehnquist, William

Chief Justice of the U.S. Supreme Court, 1972 to the present. He wrote the majority opinion in *Cruzan v. Director, Missouri Department of Public Health* (1990), as well as the subsequent "right to die" decisions *Washington v. Glucksberg* (1997) and *Quill v. Vacco* (1997).

Roe v. Wade

The landmark 1973 decision by the U.S. Supreme Court that determined a woman's right to receive an abortion was grounded in her liberty interest in making a decision about whether to carry a pregnancy to full term. At the same time, the Court said that a state may demonstrate a compelling interest in regulating or even prohibiting abortion once a fetus was "viable," or able to live independently of the mother's body.

Sanger, Margaret

Twentieth-century advocate of birth control who challenged the Comstock laws that prohibited the distribution of contraception and birth control advice. She went on to become the first president of the International Planned Parenthood Association and was instrumental in supporting research leading to the development of the birth control pill.

Sectarian Medicine

A term describing the various medical theories and practices that challenged what we know today as "regular" medicine in the period from approximately 1820 to 1880. Among these medical "sects" were hydropathy, homeopathy, and Thomsonianism.

Skinner v. Oklahoma

A 1942 U.S. Supreme Court opinion that asserted procreation as a fundamental right. It overturned an Oklahoma law mandating sterilization for three-time offenders of certain specified crimes on the grounds that the law was unequal in its application and thus a violation of the Fourteenth Amendment's equal protection clause.

Slaughterhouse Cases

An 1873 U.S. Supreme Court decision that upheld a Louisiana law regulating commercial butchering by granting monopoly rights to one slaughterhouse in New Orleans. The Court ruled that the Louisiana statute did not violate individual rights under the Fourteenth Amendment.

Washington v. Glucksberg

A 1997 U.S. Supreme Court decision ruling that a Washington law prohibiting physician-assisted suicide did not violate the Fourteenth Amendment's due process clause. It is the companion case to *Quill v. Vacco.*

Webster v. Reproductive Services

A 1989 opinion in which the U.S. Supreme Court determined that a Missouri statute regulating abortion did not violate women's constitutional rights. The law prohibited public employees from participating in and public facilities from being used in abortions unless the operation was necessary to save the mother's life and required physicians to ascertain whether a fetus of twenty or more weeks gestational age was viable before performing an abortion.

Chronology

1868   Fourteenth Amendment to the Constitution ratified. The due process clause and the equal protection clause of this amendment will provide the basis for many challenges concerning the right to bodily autonomy in the twentieth century.

1873   U.S. Supreme Court interpretation of the Fourteenth Amendment for the first time in the *Slaughterhouse Cases,* supporting a state's authority to infringe on individual liberty in the name of protecting the public's welfare.

1905   U.S. Supreme Court decision in *Jacobson v. Massachusetts,* upholding that state's compulsory vaccination laws as a valid exercise of police powers in the face of an epidemic of infectious disease.

1907   Indiana became the first state to mandate sterilization of people convicted of certain crimes.

1922   U.S. Supreme Court decision in *Zucht v. King,* upholding a Texas statute requiring public schoolchildren to be vaccinated against smallpox, even though no epidemic was present.

1927   U.S. Supreme Court decision in *Buck v. Bell* that ruled that a Virginia law mandating sterilization for institutionalized persons deemed "feebleminded" by a special commission was a valid exercise of police powers to protect the general welfare.

1942   U.S. Supreme Court decision in *Skinner v. Oklahoma* that determined that an Oklahoma compulsory sterilization law for three-time offenders of certain specified crimes violated the equal protection clause of the Fourteenth Amendment. Although the opinion asserted that reproduction constituted a fundamental right, the Court also said that this right may be infringed upon to protect public health and safety if the law were applied so as not to violate individuals' rights to due process and equal protection.

1965   U.S. Supreme Court decision in *Griswold v. Connecticut* that invalidated a Connecticut statute outlawing the distribution of contraceptives or birth control information to married couples. The Court ruled that many enumerated rights in the Constitution create a "zone of privacy" around the individual and thus privacy itself is a constitutional right.

1972   U.S. Supreme Court opinion in *Eisenstadt v. Baird* that overturned a Massachusetts law prohibiting the distribution of contraceptives to unmarried persons on the grounds that it violated the fundamental right to privacy established in *Griswold v. Connecticut.*

1973   U.S. Supreme Court decision in *Roe v. Wade* that determined a woman's liberty interest was broad enough to include a right to abortion. The opinion also recognized that states may have a compelling interest in regulating or even prohibiting abortion once the fetus becomes "viable," or able to live independently of the mother's body.

1975   New Jersey Supreme Court ruling *In re Quinlan,* allowing the parents of a patient in a persistent vegetative state to remove her from a life-sustaining respirator. The Court ruled that, although Karen Ann Quinlan was no longer an autonomous person, her previous directives must be protected by the constitutional right to privacy asserted ten years earlier in *Griswold v. Connecticut.*

1986   U.S. Supreme Court decision in *Bowers v. Hardwick,* in which the Court determined that a Georgia law outlawing sodomy did not represent a violation of the individual's privacy rights because engaging in sodomy is not recognized as a fundamental right.

1989   U.S. Supreme Court decision in *Webster v. Reproductive Services,* ruling that a Missouri statute prohibiting public employees from participating in and public facilities from being used in abortions did not violate women's constitutional rights.

1990   U.S. Supreme Court opinion in *Cruzan v. Director, Missouri Department of Public Health,* ruling that competent individuals may refuse to be sustained by life-supporting technologies. Family members may act for incompetent patients, provided there is clear and compelling evidence of the patient's wishes. States, however, may also regulate in the area in the interest of protecting life.

1992   U.S. Supreme Court decision in *Planned Parenthood v. Casey* that state regulations on abortion may not place an "undue burden" on women seeking an abortion because doing so constituted a violation of the due process clause of the Fourteenth Amendment.

1997   Two companion decisions rendered by the U.S. Supreme Court. In *Quill v. Vacco,* the Court ruled that New York's statute prohibiting physician-assisted suicide did not violate the equal protection clause of the Fourteenth Amendment. In *Washington v. Glucksberg,* the Court ruled that Washington's prohibition on physician-assisted suicide did not violate the due process clause of the Fourteenth Amendment. Although the plurality opinion made a distinction between "letting" a patient die and "making" a patient die, concurring opinions differed over the extent to which an individual's liberty to make end-of-life decisions must be protected, leaving the door open to future challenges.

2002   A U.S. District Court ruled in *State of Oregon and Peter Rasmussen, et al. v. John Ashcroft* that the federal Controlled Substances Act did not authorize the attorney general to prevent Oregon from implementing its Death with Dignity Act, which allows physicians to dispense medications to patients for the purpose of committing suicide.

Table of Cases

Annotated Bibliography

Benedict, Michael Les. 1996. *The Blessings of Liberty: A Concise History of the Constitution of the United States.* Lexington, MA: D. C. Heath.

A concise but thorough narrative of the development of the constitution in the broader context of U.S. history.

Curry, Lynne. 1999. *Modern Mothers in the Heartland: Gender, Health, and Progress in Illinois, 1900–1930.* Columbus: Ohio State University Press.

An examination of changes in public health law and policy brought to Illinois by the popularization of the germ theory.

Dudziak, Mary L. 1986. **"Oliver Wendell Holmes as a Eugenic Reformer: Rhetoric in the Writing of Constitutional Law."** *Iowa Law Review* 71, no. 3 (March): 833–867.

Although there are many excellent biographies of the Supreme Court justice, this article focuses specifically on Holmes's ideas about eugenics and how they are reflected in the language of the *Buck v. Bell* opinion.

Duffy, John. 1993. *From Humors to Medical Science: A History of American Medicine.* Urbana: University of Illinois Press.

A general overview of the history of American medicine, focusing on physicians, medical education, and the emergence of specialized practice fields.

Dworkin, Ronald. 1994. *Life's Dominion: An Argument about Abortion, Euthanasia, and Individual Freedom.* New York: Vintage Books.

A leading U.S. legal scholar carefully examines the philosophical, moral, and legal conceptualizations of the "right to life" and the "right to die."

Filene, Peter G. 1998. *In the Arms of Others: A Cultural History of the Right to Die in America.* Chicago: Ivan R. Dee.

A thoughtful examination of how the "right to die" emerged as a concept in law and popular thought, including in-depth analyses of *In re Quinlan* and *Cruzan v. Director, Missouri Department of Public Health.*

Foucault, Michel. 1975. *Discipline and Punish: The Birth of the Prison.* Translated by Alan Sheridan. New York: Vintage Books.

One of several seminal works by the French philosopher whose writings on the relationships between the body and social control served as the intellectual foundations for many subsequent works on law, medicine, and social policy.

Garrow, David J. 1994. *Liberty and Sexuality: The Right to Privacy and the Making of* Roe v. Wade. New York: Maxwell Macmillan International.

Important study of the constitutional right to privacy and its application to abortion rights.

Gillman, Howard. 1993. *The Constitution Besieged: The Rise and Demise of Lochner Era Police Powers Jurisprudence.* Durham: Duke University Press.

In-depth analysis of legal doctrine concerning the powers and limits of the state, formed within the context of a rapidly industrializing nation.

Gordon, Linda. 1990. *Woman's Body, Woman's Right: Birth Control in America.* Rev. ed. New York: Penguin Books.

Comprehensive social history of birth control in the United States.

Gould, Stephen J. 1985. **"Carrie Buck's Daughter."** *Constitutional Commentary* 2, no. 2: 331–339.

The late eminent paleontologist discusses the scientific flaws underpinning *Buck v. Bell.*

Hall, Kermit. 1989. *The Magic Mirror: Law in American History.* New York: Oxford University Press.

An engaging narrative of major ideas in the history of U.S. law.

Haller, John S., Jr. 1981. *American Medicine in Transition, 1840–1910.* Urbana: University of Illinois Press.

Discusses the period in which "regular" physicians worked to organize and professionalize their practices in the face of competition from the "irregulars."

Hoy, Suellen. 1995. *Chasing Dirt: The American Pursuit of Cleanliness.* New York: Oxford University Press.

An overview of theories and practices regarding sanitation, public health, and hygiene in the United States.

Hyde, Alan. 1997. *Bodies of Law.* Princeton: Princeton University Press.

A challenging collection of essays exploring legal concepts of bodily autonomy, including an insightful analysis of *Jacobson v. Massachusetts.*

Irons, Peter. 1999. *A People's History of the Supreme Court.* New York: Penguin Books.

Examines constitutional development from the perspective of the individuals whose cases shaped this history.

Kens, Paul. 1998. **Lochner v. New York:** *Economic Regulation on Trial.* Lawrence: University of Kansas Press.

Provides interesting information on the circumstances behind the "bakeshop case," with attention to the public health dimensions of economic regulation in the early twentieth century.

Kevles, Daniel J. 1985. *In the Name of Eugenics: Genetics and the Uses of Human Heredity.* New York: Alfred A. Knopf.

Essential history of the eugenics movement in U.S. history.

Kline, Wendy. 2001. *Building a Better Race: Gender, Sexuality, and Eugenics from the Turn of the Century to the Baby Boom.* Berkeley: University of California Press.

Analysis of the U.S. eugenics movement with special attention to issues of gender and sexuality.

Kraut, Alan M. 1994. *Silent Travelers: Germs, Genes, and the "Immigrant Menace."* Baltimore: Johns Hopkins University Press.

Fascinating analysis of how nativist fears about immigrants have shaped public health law and policy in the United States.

Leavitt, Judith Walzer. 1996. *Typhoid Mary: Captive to the Public's Health.* Boston: Beacon Press.

Excellent, focused study on the intersections of law and medicine in the case of the notorious Mary Mallon, the first identified healthy carrier of the typhoid bacillus.

Lombardo, Paul A. 1982. **"Eugenic Sterilization in Virginia: Aubrey Strode and the Case of *Buck v. Bell.*"** Ph.D. diss., University of Virginia.

The authoritative study of Carrie Buck's case.

Mohr, James C. 1978. *Abortion in America: The Origins and Evolution of National Policy, 1880–1900.* New York: Oxford University Press.

Focuses on the critical period of changes in abortion law and policy at the end of the nineteenth century.

———. 1993. *Doctors and the Law: Medical Jurisprudence in the Nineteenth Century.* New York: Oxford University Press.

A study of the intersections of law and medicine in the nineteenth century that provides a foundation for understanding developments in the twentieth century.

Mohr, Richard D. 1987. **"AIDS, Gays, and State Coercion."** *Bioethics* 1, no. 1: 36–50.

Extremely critical account of early public policy responses to the discovery of HIV/AIDS as a serious public health threat in the United States.

Novak, William J. 1996. *The People's Welfare.* Chapel Hill: University of North Carolina Press.

Important work analyzing the development of police powers in the nineteenth century and emphasizing the tradition of popular support for public health and safety measures.

Parmet, Wendy. 1996. **"From *Slaughterhouse* to *Lochner:* The Rise and Fall of the Constitutionalization of Public Health."** *American Journal of Legal History* 40: 476–505.

Carefully focused analysis of the incorporation of public health laws into constitutional jurisprudence in the late nineteenth and early twentieth centuries.

Przybyszweski, Linda. 1999. *The Republic According to John Marshall Harlan.* Chapel Hill: University of North Carolina Press.
A biography of the Supreme Court justice whose tenure (1877–1911) spanned an important period of change in constitutional history.

Rao, Radhika. 2000. **"Property, Privacy, and the Human Body."** *Boston University Law Review* 80: 360–460.
Useful discussion of the two major concepts in bodily autonomy jurisprudence, the body as property and the right of privacy.

Reagan, Leslie J. 1997. *When Abortion Was a Crime: Women, Medicine, and Law in the United States, 1867–1973.* Berkeley: University of California Press.
Fascinating examination of the intersections of law and medicine in the history of abortion in the United States.

Ross, Michael A. 1998. **"Justice Miller's Reconstruction: The *Slaughterhouse Cases*, Health Codes, and Civil Rights in New Orleans, 1861–1873."** *Journal of Southern History* 44: 649–676.
Helpful overview of the case that "constitutionalized" public health laws.

Schwartz, Bernard. 1993. *A History of the Supreme Court.* Oxford: Oxford University Press.
Useful one-volume overview of Supreme Court history.

Starr, Paul. 1982. *The Social Transformation of American Medicine.* New York: Basic Books.
Authoritative study on the history of American medicine, with special attention to the tensions between public health and private medical practice in the nineteenth and early twentieth centuries.

Toby, James A. 1947. *Public Health Law.* New York: Commonwealth Fund.
Essential primer on basic public health law in the United States.

Tomes, Nancy. 1998. *The Gospel of Germs.* Cambridge: Harvard University Press.
Excellent study of the impact of the germ theory on U.S. health policies and practices.

Tucker, Jonathan B. 2001. *Scourge: The Once and Future Threat of Smallpox.* New York: Atlantic Monthly Press.
Discusses smallpox epidemics in the past as well as the possibility of future outbreaks caused by bioterrorism.

Urofsky, Melvin I., and Paul Finkelman, eds. 2002. *A March of Liberty,* vols. 1 and 2. New York: Oxford University Press.

Two-volume survey of U.S. legal and constitutional history that provides more depth than other texts.

Weddington, Sarah. 1992. *A Question of Choice.* New York: Penguin Books.

A rare look inside a landmark case from the perspective of one of its key players, the attorney who argued for "Roe" before the Supreme Court.

Woloch, Nancy. 1996. *Muller v. Oregon.* New York: Bedford Books.

Provides fascinating detail on a critical case in the history of public health jurisprudence.

Zola, Irving Kenneth. 1972. **"Medicine as an Institution of Social Control."** *Sociological Review* 20: 487–504.

A classic analysis of power relations between physicians and patients.

Index

About the Author

Lynne Curry is an assistant professor of history at Eastern Illinois University.